Hope and Honor

Hope and Honor

Jewish Resistance during the Holocaust

RACHEL L. EINWOHNER

OXFORD
UNIVERSITY PRESS

OXFORD
UNIVERSITY PRESS

Oxford University Press is a department of the University of Oxford. It furthers
the University's objective of excellence in research, scholarship, and education
by publishing worldwide. Oxford is a registered trade mark of Oxford University
Press in the UK and certain other countries.

Published in the United States of America by Oxford University Press
198 Madison Avenue, New York, NY 10016, United States of America.

Library of Congress Cataloging-in-Publication Data
Names: Einwohner, Rachel L., author.
Title: Hope and honor : Jewish resistance during the Holocaust / Rachel L. Einwohner.
Description: New York : Oxford University Press, [2022] |
Includes bibliographical references and index.
Identifiers: LCCN 2021037360 (print) | LCCN 2021037361 (ebook) |
ISBN 9780190079444 (paperback) | ISBN 9780190079437 (hardback) |
ISBN 9780190079468 (epub)
Subjects: LCSH: World War, 1939–1945—Jewish resistance. |
World War, 1939–1945—Participation, Jewish. |
Holocaust, Jewish (1939–1945)—Poland—Warsaw. |
Holocaust, Jewish (1939–1945)—Lithuania—Vilnius. |
Holocaust, Jewish (1939–1945)—Poland—Łódź.
Classification: LCC D810.J4 E34 2022 (print) | LCC D810.J4 (ebook) |
DDC 940.53/47089924—dc23
LC record available at https://lccn.loc.gov/2021037360
LC ebook record available at https://lccn.loc.gov/2021037361

DOI: 10.1093/oso/9780190079437.001.0001

For Those Who Went Before Me

Contents

List of Illustrations

FIGURES

TABLES

Timeline of Important Events

Interwar period	Vilna is part of Poland			
September 1, 1939	Germany invades Poland			
September 28, 1939	Vilna is occupied by Soviet Union; Warsaw and Łódź are occupied by Germany			
February 8, 1940				Łódź Ghetto is announced
October 12, 1940		Warsaw Ghetto is announced		
June 22, 1941	Germany invades Soviet Union			
June 24, 1941			German forces arrive in Vilna	
June–September 1941			40,000 Jews killed in Ponar	
September 6, 1941			Vilna Ghetto is announced	
December 31, 1941			FPO forms	
January 16, 1942				Deportations begin in Łódź Ghetto
July 22, 1942		Great Deportation begins in Warsaw Ghetto		
July 22, 1942		Warsaw Judenrat Head Adam Czerniakow commits suicide		

July 28, 1942	ŻOB forms	
September 4, 1942		Łódź "Eldest" Chaim Rumkowski gives his "Give me your children!" speech
April 19, 1943	Warsaw Ghetto Uprising begins	
July 16, 1943		FPO leader Itzik Wittenberg turns himself in to Gestapo
September 1–24, 1943		Vilna Ghetto is liquidated
September 1, 1943		FPO members begin leaving for the forests
September 14, 1943		Vilna Ghetto Chief Jacob Gens is killed by Gestapo
July 13, 1944		Vilna is liberated by the Red Army
August 1, 1944	Warsaw Uprising begins	
August 30, 1944		Chaim Rumkowski is sent to Auschwitz on last train from Łódź
August–December 1944	Warsaw is destroyed	
January 19, 1945		Łódź is liberated by the Red Army
May 7, 1945	Germany formally surrenders to Allied forces	

Preface

The ability to pinpoint the origins of one's interests in a particular topic may or may not be an important quality for a scholar to have. Nonetheless, I can remember exactly when I first became interested in the topic of Jewish resistance. In April 1993 I was visiting my parents at my childhood home in California. My parents subscribed to the *New York Times*, a luxury too rich for my then-grad student self. During my visit I happened to notice the front section for April 19, 1993—the 50th anniversary of the Warsaw Ghetto Uprising. On that date, the newspaper ran an article titled, "Memories Live of the Warsaw Ghetto Battle." It told the story of a 16-year-old Jewish teen, Lillian Lazar, who was part of an uprising in the Warsaw Ghetto in 1943. Armed with only scissors and rocks, she and others fought against Nazi soldiers attempting to deport them to the death camps and destroy the Jewish ghetto.

I distinctly remember reading that article while sitting on my parents' bed in their sunny, pleasant bedroom. I also remember thinking, quite incredulously, "*They fought back?!!*" I had no idea that Jewish victims of the Holocaust had ever resisted against their oppressors. This lack of awareness of an important part of Jewish history was quite surprising, given my background: I was raised in an observant Jewish home by my parents, two individuals with very strong Jewish identities and fierce commitments to Jewish culture, history, and religion. I was also extremely close to my maternal grandmother, a Polish Jew who fled her native Warsaw in 1939 after the German invasion. Along with my grandfather, she survived World War II in a series of Soviet labor camps before eventually immigrating to Israel and later the United States. My parents and grandmother were easily the most influential adults in my life when I was growing up, and while I certainly rebelled against many of the things they would have liked me to do, I often listened to them in matters of Jewish culture and heritage. That is, through my family, I learned—or thought I learned—about my history. I knew that my mother's parents fled the Nazis in Poland but that, sadly, many others did not make it. In Hebrew school, I learned more about the Holocaust, as well as other periods of persecution of the Jewish people throughout history. For some reason, though,

I was never taught that some Jews resisted during the Holocaust. Before April 1993, I, like many people, shared a sense that European Jews were largely passive victims of the Nazi genocide and did little to resist their oppression.

Learning about Jewish resistance has both increased my pride in my own Jewish heritage and provided the impetus for this book. Before learning about the Warsaw Ghetto Uprising I never questioned why Jews did not (apparently) fight back; I took it for granted that the Nazi genocidal regime was too powerful and its methods of destruction too efficient for anything or anyone to stop it. Once I learned that Jewish resistance occurred, however, this Jewish sociologist wanted to know why. The answers to that question are in the pages that follow.

I am humbled by all the assistance and support I received in the process of researching and writing this book. I am indebted to Jo Reger, for her friendship as well as her ongoing support of this project. Jo read many drafts of the book proposal and its chapters, and was instrumental in introducing me to the process of book publishing. She was also my personal cheerleader as I worked on the book. She is a boss in every sense (every good sense!). I am equally grateful to Nancy Whittier, whose scholarly talent is surpassed only by her kindness; she too encouraged me at every step along the way. One of the many gifts that Nancy and Jo gave me was an introduction to their, and now my, editor at Oxford, James Cook. His insights and guidance have shaped this entire book, and he has helped me turn an academic interest into a story with broader appeal. Thank you, James. Thanks go as well to Holly McCammon, a gracious and prolific scholar whose work has inspired me for decades. I was thrilled to host Holly, Jo, and Nancy for a virtual book workshop in May 2020 that helped me fine-tune this manuscript. Joining us were my friends and colleagues Tom Maher and Robin Stryker, who added their support and keen insights.

I also thank my family, the Einwohner/Korc/Vinetz/Gildengers/Ronen/ Golbert *mishpoche*. I especially thank my mother, Alisa Korc Einwohner, whose support as well as translation skills and cultural knowledge of Eastern European Jewry were enormously helpful in this research. In addition, my sisters Rina and Rebecca and my brother Ethan showed great interest in my work and as well as confidence in my ability to complete it, which helped me more than they'll ever know. I also thank Ethan for helping me with translations from Hebrew. Thanks go as well to my father, Theodore Einwohner (z"l), and my grandmother, Hadassah Korc (z"l). Sadly, their deaths precluded our ever having any detailed discussions about this book, but they have an imprint on every page nonetheless. My father's deep love for books, religion, and Jewish history was brought to mind constantly as I did this research, and whenever I read a name or word in Polish, I heard my grandmother's gentle voice saying it.

This research was supported by grants from the National Science Foundation, #SES-0817659, and the National Endowment for the Humanities, #FT-54703-06. In addition, I received a tremendous amount of institutional support from Purdue University for this research. A PRF Summer Faculty Grant, Dean's Incentive Grant, and Library Scholar's Grant, along with a research leave in the Spring of 2000, supported my initial re-search on the Warsaw Ghetto Uprising, and a fellowship from the Center for Behavioral and Social Sciences in the Spring of 2007 allowed me to do much of the groundwork for the broader comparison of the Vilna and Łódź cases. Another fellowship from the Center for Social Sciences in the Spring of 2016 and a sabbatical leave in 2018 gave me the uninterrupted time necessary to complete the manuscript, and an ENGAGE grant from the College of Liberal Arts supported the aforementioned book workshop. I thank my Department Head Linda Renzulli and my Jewish Studies colleagues Dan Frank, Rebekah Klein-Pejšová, Gordon Mork (z"l), Bob Melson, Gordon Young (z"l), and Joe (z"l), Rose, and Nina Haberer, for their support as well as opportuni-ties to present my research. Bob Melson and Gordon Mork deserve special accolades. I first mentioned my interests in Jewish resistance to Gordon, an historian whom I met on my interview at Purdue in February 1998, and he encouraged me in this project for the rest of his life. Soon after joining the faculty at Purdue, I also met Bob, an eminent genocide scholar with a re-markable story of his own survival during the Holocaust. He quickly became a personal hero of mine, and the fact that he supported me and my work was nothing short of thrilling. Both honored me by allowing me to present aspects of this research in their popular and important course on Holocaust and Genocide.

My students will also find their imprints on this book. I relied heavily on my fierce graduate students Elle Rochford and Baylee Hudgens for their research assistance and feedback during the final push to complete this book. Elle lent her considerable artistic talents to creating the maps in this book, and she and Baylee were both instrumental to the afore-mentioned workshop and to finding images for the book. Thank you both. I was also especially lucky to work with a number of talented undergraduates at Purdue, all of whom are long gone from campus. Thank you all: Michelle Carreon, Meghan Darling,

Emily Fairchild, Justin Glon, Alex Hanna, Allegra Lukac, Tom Lenz, Sarah MacLeod, and Anne Schwichtenberg. Many friends and colleagues also read and commented on various drafts of the components of this book. I'm especially grateful to Jennifer Earl, Tom Maher (again), Robin Stryker (again), Tom Shriver, Heidi Reynolds-Stenson, Suzanne Staggenborg, Kathleen Blee, Verta Taylor, Leila Rupp, David Meyer, Jean Beaman, Danielle Kane, Michelle Gawerc, Kevin Stainback, and Margaret Tillman. I am also thankful for opportunities to present my work at Purdue as well as at the University of Arizona, the University of Cincinnati, the University of Pittsburgh, University of Illinois—Chicago, UC Santa Barbara, UC Irvine, Oklahoma State University, and the Illinois Holocaust Museum and Education Center; another talk was scheduled for the University of Dayton in April 2020 was canceled due to the COVID-19 pandemic. I have also had numerous conversations about this work with different students, both graduates and undergraduates; these include Soon Seok Park, Andrew Raridon, Jared Wright, Becka Alper, Stephanie Wilson, and Ariel Moon. Many other friends and neighbors, both in West Lafayette and Chicago, deserve mention for keeping me happy, well fed, and in decent cardiovascular shape; special thanks go to Felicia Roberts, Danny Weiss, Lisa Goffman, Bill Saxton, Loren Olson, Melissa Remis, Bertin Mbongo, Beth Strickland, Mia Lewis, Noam Shpancer, Ann Clark, Jay McCann, Barb Brown, Dave Kiser, Rebecca Sullivan, Sharon Williams, Quinnel Gutwein, Bridget Walsh, Martin Curd, Patricia Curd, Patti Thomas, Angelica Duran, Jessica Huber, Ryan LeCount, Jackie Ziven-LeCount, Yvette DeBois, Marvin Jackson, Katie Watson, Scott McIntosh, Annie Pursel, Mary Ann McMorrow, Doug Winzelberg, Elise Auerbach, and the late and dearly missed O. Michael Watson (z"l). Special shout-outs go to: Jennifer Leventhal, for her interest in this book as well as her assistance with the arrangements for our trip to Warsaw in April 2019; Rena Aiken at Camera Outfitters in Lafayette, IN, for her expertise and assistance with some of the images and maps in this book; Nandhini Thanga Alagu at Newgen Knowledge Works for going beyond the extra mile with the book's production; and Emily Benitez at Oxford University Press for patiently guiding me through the manuscript process and answering my endless questions. I also owe a special debt of thanks to Jocelyn Hollander and Toska Olson, my dear friends from graduate school, and Judy Howard and Diane Lye, our teachers, mentors, and friends. Although it has been a long time since we lived and worked near each other, each of these women contributed to this project in numerous ways; equally importantly, they gave me love, support, and friendship when I needed it the most, and I will be grateful to them always. I am similarly eternally grateful for the love and companionship of my beloved beagle Niehaus, whose long life overlapped with my early work on this book and whose memory still makes me smile (and cry). Thanks go as well to my childhood friends who have heard me speak about bits and pieces of this book for many years. You are a wonderful and much beloved mob, too large to mention everyone by name; however, you all know who you are. Last but certainly not least, I thank my *bashert*, my wonderful husband Chuck Golbert, for his adventurous spirit (which was tested with some airline challenges on our trip to Warsaw in April 2019), his tremendous, unfailing love and encouragement, and his keen editorial eye and artistic talents (the latter of which are illustrated throughout this book).

A large portion of the data for this book comes from the Shoah Foundation. I owe a huge debt of gratitude to Doug Ballman, the archivist (and, it turns out, a Purdue grad). Thanks go as well to Dave "Superman" Carter and Nerea Llamas at the University of Michigan, who allowed me access to the data in electronic form. Kathy (Sarah Chava) Wood was both a talented and patient transcriptionist, and Becka Alper was simply the best research assistant ever.

I cannot end these acknowledgments without honoring the memory of all the victims of the Holocaust, including members of my own family. The latter include my maternal great grandparents, my maternal great uncle, and my maternal great aunts. My great grandfather Moshe was beaten to death by Nazi soldiers in the streets of Warsaw. While the details regarding the other family members listed above are largely unknown, all are believed to have died in, or soon after deportation from, the Warsaw Ghetto. Although I never met any of these individuals, neither they nor their deaths will ever be forgotten.

Chicago, IL
April 2021

1

Studying Jewish Resistance

The residential parts of Warsaw's Muranów District are comprised mostly of apartment buildings rather than single-family homes. Strolling past these buildings on a sunny day, a visitor finds the neighborhood to be a quiet, pleasant place. Residents walk their dogs and chat with their neighbors, and children ride skateboards and scooters, sometimes with ice cream in hand. Yet while peaceful today, this neighborhood had a very different feel eighty years ago, during World War II. The Muranów District was once the walled-in Warsaw Ghetto, home to nearly half a million Jews under Nazi occupation. In fact, the district literally rests atop the ruins of the Ghetto, which was destroyed by Nazi forces in the spring of 1943.

A number of public memorials in Muranów commemorate the Ghetto and the Jewish community that once lived there. Many are found on an official memorial trail, a semi-circular route following Stawki and Dubois streets (*ulica Stawki* and *ulica Dubois* in Polish) in a small section of the neighborhood. This trail blends in easily with the neighborhood, as most of its markers are nearly the same gray color as the sidewalks. Among them, sixteen granite blocks commemorate some of the Ghetto's most famous residents and places. The trail begins near still-used train tracks at the corner of Stawki and Dzika streets, the former site of the *Umschlagplatz*, the open square from which Warsaw Jews were loaded onto transport trains and sent away to camps. There, a white marble memorial, horizontal in orientation, evokes the shape of a freight car. Engraved with the first names of Polish Jewish victims—men's names on one side, women's on the other—this monument symbolizes the experiences of hundreds of thousands of European Jews, in Warsaw and elsewhere, as they were taken to their deaths.

The granite blocks that mark the continuation of the memorial trail begin across the street from the *Umschlagplatz*. Each is labeled clearly, one on side in Polish (*Trakt Pamięci Męczeństwa I Walki Żydów*, or Memorial Route of the

Hope and Honor. Rachel L. Einwohner, Oxford University Press. © Oxford University Press 2022.
DOI: 10.1093/oso/9780190079437.003.0001

Martyrdom and Struggle of the Jews) and the other in Hebrew (*Nativ HaZikaron L'Shoah ve L'Giborat HaYehudim*, the Jewish Holocaust and Heroism Memorial Trail). The trail continues along Stawki and then DuBois streets and ends at a prominent, powerful sculpture. Created by Warsaw-born Israeli artist Natan Rapoport in 1948, this piece now faces the POLIN Museum of the History of Polish Jews, a 43,000 square foot glass and sand-colored stone structure that opened in April 2013. Yet in contrast to the modern, gleaming museum, the Rapoport sculpture is smaller, darker, and denser. As shown in Figure 1.1, it

Figure 1.1 Natan Rapaport's "Monument to the Ghetto Fighters," April 2019.
Credit: Charles P. Golbert

depicts a number of individuals, including an elderly adult as well as a babe in arms; many are wearing rags and showing bare, lean flesh. Some of these individuals are anguished, while others stand proudly.

The figures in the Rapoport sculpture are framed by a wall of gray stone blocks, symbolic of the brick walls that once surrounded the Warsaw Ghetto.[1] Incredibly, some sections of the actual Ghetto wall remain in the district, having survived both the destruction of Warsaw and its postwar reconstruction. Some parts of the original wall are well marked—physically, with signage, and virtually, with Google maps—while others are unmarked but easy to spot in parking lots and construction sites. Yet even where the Ghetto wall is missing, its boundaries remain: sidewalks throughout the district are embedded with decorative tiles that indicate the former location of the wall. The remaining parts of the wall, the memorials, and the POLIN museum itself all ask the visitor to remember the Jews who once lived in Warsaw.

One of these memorials is arguably more meaningful than the rest, but it can also be the easiest to miss—especially in the spring and summer, when the surrounding trees are in full leaf. Located near the corner of Dubois and Miła streets, this memorial consists of a small grassy mound set far back from the street. Atop the mound, and accessed by two flights of shallow steps, sits a large, engraved boulder; another, triangle-shaped stone is set on the ground, near the foot of the steps, toward the street entrance. Shown in Figure 1.2, this site marks the location of a building whose address was once 18 Miła Street.[2] There, on May 8, 1943, young Jewish activists in their teens and twenties—members of an organization called the Jewish Fighting Organization (*Żydowska Organizacja Bojowa*, or ŻOB)—perished in an armed uprising against Nazi forces. Because all the buildings on Miła Street—and everywhere else in the Ghetto—were destroyed during the uprising, the fighters' bodies were never exhumed. This small grassy mound is therefore both a memorial and a burial site. An inscription on the triangular shaped stone there reads in part:

> Grave of the fighters of the Warsaw Ghetto Uprising built from the rubble of Miła Street, one of the liveliest streets of pre-war Jewish Warsaw . . . It is the place of rest of over one hundred fighters, only some of whom are known by name. Here they rest, buried where they fell, to remind us that the whole world is their grave.

Figure 1.2 Memorial at Miła 18, April 2019.
Credit: Charles P. Golbert

The Myth of Jewish Passivity

The monument at Miła 18 does not simply memorialize victims of the Holocaust, those who lost their lives as a direct result of the orchestrated efforts to isolate, brutalize, and, ultimately, murder European Jews and other ethnic groups. Importantly, it memorializes *resisters*, who opposed the Nazis' genocidal plans. Resistance is also central to the meaning of the Rapoport sculpture, whose title is "Monument to the Ghetto Heroes." In fact, a close look at the sculpture shows that some of its subjects are armed: the central figure in that piece, a man brandishing a hand grenade, is meant to depict Mordechai Anielewicz,[3] the famed leader of the ŻOB who died at Miła 18, while the individuals standing behind him clutch a dagger and machine gun, respectively.

The thought of a monument to armed Jewish resistance during the Holocaust may be surprising to some. Holocaust memorials themselves are not unusual, of course. Sociologist Arlene Stein (2014: 3) writes that the U.S. has witnessed "the rise of a Holocaust memorial culture that has broad resonance." Memorials to individuals and groups who perished during the Holocaust are found throughout the U.S. and in other parts of the world, in large cities and small towns alike. Many countries are also committed to Holocaust education and remembrance. The International Holocaust Remembrance Alliance includes thirty-four member countries, one "liasion" country, and an additional eight "observer countries" (the latter nine of which are in the process of applying for full membership); all forty-three countries are required to commit to the Stockholm Declaration of the International Forum on the Holocaust, which includes a "pledge to strengthen our efforts to promote education, remembrance, and research about the Holocaust."[4] As a member country of the IHRA, the United States offers Holocaust-related educational material in both public and private schools.[5]

In the United States and elsewhere, therefore, people are not *uneducated* about the Holocaust. Yet, Jewish *resistance* is not generally stressed in dominant narratives about this tragic period. On the contrary, popular accounts of the Holocaust—especially in the United States—typically cast Jews as woeful victims, powerless against a genocidal regime. This trend is especially true of Hollywood films dealing with Holocaust themes. For instance, award-winning Holocaust movies such as *Schindler's List* are colored prominently by themes of tragedy and victimhood; they depict Jews who survive, yet do so either out of sheer luck or because of benevolent interventions from others, typically Gentiles.[6] Thus, despite broad and well-intentioned exposure to Holocaust educational materials, the haunting Holocaust images with which many people are familiar tend to center on starving, hollow-eyed victims behind barbed wire or packed into cattle cars, seemingly resigned to their fate—or, following the oft-used phrase, going "like sheep to the slaughter."[7] Even those broadly recognized acts of agency—such as the well-known decision made by the family of Anne Frank to go into hiding in their "secret annex" in Amsterdam in an attempt to avoid deportation—do little to offset overall beliefs about Jewish passivity during the Holocaust. In fact, Anne Frank is often seen as a powerless (albeit optimistic) victim rather than as a member of a group of individuals who took action to protect themselves.[8]

Given such well-accepted portrayals, it is a common assumption that European Jews were largely passive in the face of Nazi atrocities. This assumption naturally lends itself to questions about resistance. Why were the Jews such passive victims? *Why didn't they resist?*

Questions about the apparent lack of Jewish resistance are not posed by the lay public alone. In fact, some influential scholarly writings on the Holocaust echo this theme. Historian Raul Hilberg's *The Destruction of European Jews*, the first in-depth scholarly exploration of the Holocaust, did little to acknowledge Jewish resistance; in fact, Hilberg writes that the Jewish reaction to the Holocaust was "characterized by almost complete lack of resistance" (1979: 662). Hannah Arendt's reporting on the post-war trial of S.S. Chief Adolf Eichmann, who orchestrated mass deportations of European Jews to the death camps, provides what is perhaps the most infamous example of an influential piece of writing that perpetuated the myth of Jewish passivity. First published in installments in the *New Yorker* and later as her book *Eichmann in Jerusalem* (1963) Arendt's account briefly yet notably decried the "cooperation" between Jewish community leaders and Nazi officials that facilitated the deliverance of Jews to their deaths. Thus, not only did she claim that Jews failed to resist meaningfully against the Nazis, but she insinuated that they were at least partly culpable in their own murders. Heated debates about this position ensued in the aftermath of the book's publication,[9] and while Arendt was discredited by many, her argument still received some support. One supporter was Bruno Bettelheim, himself a Holocaust survivor. Bettelheim's own writings also illustrate his position on Jews' culpability and passivity during the Holocaust. In his essay "The Ignored Lessons of Anne Frank," published in *Harper's Magazine* in November 1960, he argues that the Frank family's decision to go into hiding, during which they attempted to live as normally as possible (to the extent that living in hiding is "normal"), led to their own destruction: by carrying on as normal they were not prepared to resist when they were finally discovered. Instead, Bettelheim argues that they could have—and should have—fought back:

> There is little doubt that the Franks, who were able to provide themselves with so much, could have provided themselves with a gun or two had they wished. They could have shot down at least one or two of the "green police"

who came for them. There was no surplus of such police. The loss of an SS with every Jew arrested would have noticeably hindered the functioning of the police state. The fate of the Franks wouldn't have been very different, because they all died anyway except for Anne's father. But they could have sold their lives dearly instead of walking to their death. (1960: 46)

Other, more sympathetic voices have condemned such views, including Justice Michael Musmanno, an American judge who presided over Nazi war crimes trials and was a witness for the prosecution at the Eichmann trial. In the September 1963 issue of the *National Jewish Monthly*, Musmanno asked, "What kind of mentality is it that will argue that these naked men, woman and children could in some way have overcome their killers bristling with firearms?"[10] Yet, while such voices decry the victim-blaming of Bettelheim and Arendt, they still reinforce assumptions of Jewish passivity, even if inadvertently. Even survivor and Nobel Laureate Elie Wiesel, whose writing has done so much to keep the memory of the Holocaust and its victims alive, questioned his own lack of resistance:

I attended the Eichmann trial, I heard the prosecutor try to get the witnesses to talk by forcing them to expose themselves and to probe the innermost recesses of their being: Why didn't you resist? Why didn't you attack your assassins when you still outnumbered them? Pale, embarrassed, ill at ease, the survivors all responded in the same way: "You cannot understand. Anyone who was not there cannot imagine it." Well, I was there. And I still do not understand . . . I still do not understand why I did not throw myself on the Kapo who was beating my father before my very eyes. (1995: 263)

Debates notwithstanding, the myth of Jewish passivity during the Holocaust is just that: a myth. Survivors, as well as historians and other scholars, have worked painstakingly to set the record straight. Their work documents uprisings in the ghettos and camps as well as partisan activity in the forests.[11] Ongoing research at Yad Vashem, Israel's national Holocaust museum and archive, and the United States Holocaust Memorial Museum's Miles Lerman Center for the Study of Jewish Resistance is continually uncovering and documenting instances of Jewish resistance. Yet despite these efforts, assumptions about Jewish passivity remain, especially in the West. Indeed, as Middleton-Kaplan notes (2014: 3), they have a "tenacious persistence."

Asking the Right Question

The myth of Jewish passivity is so widespread partly because it rests on a narrow conceptualization of resistance, one that equates resistance with armed, physical struggle. As a corrective, sociologist and Holocaust survivor Nechama Tec defines resistance as acts that are "motivated by the intention to thwart, limit, or end the exercise of power of the oppressor over the oppressed" (2014: 44). This broader view demonstrates the breadth of Jewish resistance activities, including what Tec calls "unarmed humane resistance," or efforts at self-help that "contributed to the perpetuation of Jewish life while challenging the validity of Nazi policies of annihilation" (2014: 66). In her 2013 book, *Resistance: Jews and Christians who Defied the Nazi Terror*, Tec documents Jewish resistance in its many forms, ranging from collective armed resistance to individual acts such as smuggling food into the ghettos, preserving documents as a form of witnessing the atrocities, and delivering fatal morphine shots to hospital patients to prevent their deaths at the hands of Nazi soldiers.[12] Philosopher Berel Lang (2014) takes another approach to debunking the myth of Jewish passivity, arguing that Jews did not resist any less frequently than other groups brutalized by the Nazis during World War II, such as Soviet prisoners of war. Still, the apparent inaction of Jewish victims is all that is questioned, and the myth endures.

I suggest that it is time to ask a different question about Jewish resistance during the Holocaust. But with this book, my goal is not to dispel the myth of Jewish passivity. Instead, I argue that the fact of Jewish resistance itself deserves explanation. Rather than asking why Jews didn't resist, I ask the opposite: Why *did* they resist?

This question might be answered easily if it is treated as a question of Jews' motivation for resistance. Understandably, Jewish resisters may have wanted to fight back to seek revenge for the murders of their families and communities, and potentially to save their own lives. However, my question is not one of motivation (although, as I emphasize throughout this book, Jews' perceptions of what they could do to save their lives were crucial to their decisions about resistance). Instead, my focus is limited to collective, organized efforts at resistance, in the form of sustained armed uprisings in Jewish ghettos in Nazi-occupied Europe. It is these resistance efforts, I argue, that need explaining. European Jews were deprived of all rights under Nazi occupation, including their rights to home and property; ultimately, they were deprived of their right to life. Subject to a powerful occupying military, they were systematically and forcibly removed from their homes and places of business, in some cases sent directly to killing fields and extermination camps and in other cases interned in ghettos where they endured isolation, starvation, and disease before being deported to the camps. Under these conditions, how *did* they fight back?

I pose this particular question about Jewish resistance in order to learn something new about the dynamics of protest and resistance. In fact, from the perspective of social scientific theory and research on social movements and collective action, Jewish resistance is much more problematic than a lack of resistance would have been. Sociologists and other social scientists have developed a large body of research showing that collective protest occurs when protesters both recognize a window of opportunity for action and have the material resources and belief in themselves to get their protest off the ground.[13] But as I show in this book, members of Jewish resistance movements in Nazi-occupied Europe acted in the absence of these factors. How did European Jews manage to overcome these apparent barriers to collective action? And what can collective acts of Jewish resistance teach us about social movements and protest more generally?

Goals of This Book

This book has three main goals. First and foremost, accounts of Jewish resistance during the Holocaust make for an important story, one I wish to share with readers. This book draws on a variety of data, including oral testimonies, published and unpublished diaries and memoirs, and underground newspapers and other writings produced both by survivors and those who perished to show how Jews living under Nazi occupation reached decisions about whether or not to stage armed resistance. These poignant, sobering materials give voice to survivors and victims of a tragedy that simply must never be forgotten. Powerfully, they illustrate struggles for survival and the inherent dangers in attempting resistance under severely repressive conditions. Moreover, they show how remarkable it is that the armed uprisings that are the focus of this book happened at all. With this presentation, I hope to bring a nuanced perspective to discussions of Jewish reactions to the Holocaust, one that moves beyond victim-blaming and highlights the difficulties of decisions about resistance.

A second goal is to demonstrate the relevance of sociology to the study of the Holocaust. Scholarship on the Holocaust usually comes from the humanities: historians have provided a vast literature on the Holocaust, as have scholars of literature, art, and film. As a sociologist, I approach this topic somewhat differently, using the methods of my discipline. One key way that sociologists analyze the world around them is by employing theory; as noted above, I draw on theories from the field of social movements to both problematize and explain Jewish resistance. I argue that extant theories, which claim that mass resistance happens when potential resisters have both the means and the opportunity for collective action, fall short in their ability to account for armed Jewish resistance during the Holocaust. I discuss those theories, and how I use them, in more detail in Chapter 2. That chapter also presents my main argument, which is that armed Jewish resistance happened when and where Jews in the Nazi-created ghettos correctly assessed the dangers facing them—not an easy task, given the vast system of propaganda designed to obscure the truth about deportations and death camps—and believed that armed resistance was the proper course of action. Thus, I argue that *conclusions* about threat, and how best to *respond* to that threat, explain resistance.

In addition to my use of sociological theory, I employ the basic insight of social science methodology that variation is central to arriving at causal explanations. The idea here is simple: to understand why Jews resisted, it is helpful to compare instances in which armed resistance did happen with instances where it did not. Specifically, my analysis centers on a comparison of three Jewish ghettos under Nazi occupation—Warsaw (where sustained armed resistance against the Nazis took place), Vilna (where Jewish activists planned for such resistance in the ghetto but could not achieve those goals), and Łódź (where efforts at armed resistance did not emerge)—with an aim toward understanding when, where, and why Jews resisted.

Lastly, my goal is to contribute to the body of research on social movements. Scholars are increasingly recognizing the limitations of extant theories in this field, which are based largely on studies of protest in Western democracies. The U.S. civil rights movement stands apart as the single most influential case in the development of our ideas about movements and why they happen, while studies of the cycle of protest in the 1960s in both North America and Western Europe contributed greatly to the current state of academic knowledge about protest and collective action as well (see Bell 2016; Tarrow 1983). We therefore know a tremendous amount about protest in democracies. We also know a great deal about left-wing/progressive/liberal movements. This knowledge is not problematic in and of itself, but the danger lies in assuming that movements operate similarly, across all contexts. In particular, we lack a clear understanding of the dynamics of protest and resistance under conditions of extreme repression. By offering a study of armed resistance staged by seemingly powerless victims against a fascist regime equipped with one of the strongest armies in the world, I hope to help correct that oversight. In doing so, I join other scholars who have worked toward addressing this substantive bias in social movement research by studying, for instance, U.S. social movements on the extreme right[14] as well as movements worldwide operating under repressive conditions,[15] including a small but growing number of social scientists interested in resistance and rescue during the Holocaust and other genocides.[16] Therefore, while this book focuses empirically on events of the past, its "newness" is achieved by examining collective action in an authoritarian setting that is different from the other cases that have comprised the bulk of social movement research. I study what scholars refer to as a "deviant case," one that seems to operate differently than the research literature in this field would suggest. By doing so, I hope to contribute to the social movement literature. As I explain in more detail in the conclusion of this book, this analysis also has implications for other cases of protest and resistance under conditions of extreme repression and constraints, such as enslaved peoples' rebellions and prison riots.

A Sociological Approach

Methodologically, sociologists use a variety of tools, both qualitative and quantitative, to collect and analyze data. In this book I employ several modes of social scientific analysis to answer my central question about Jewish resistance.

Typically, sociologists conduct research by selecting a sample of data from a larger population of interest and then using some systematic method to search for and identify patterns in those data. Researchers may have different goals in selecting their samples. For instance, a researcher may wish to select a random sample of cases from a larger population and use tools of statistical inference to make claims about the population, based on analyses of the sample. Instead, I use an approach favored by many comparative-historical sociologists, who select small samples of cases not randomly, but purposely, because their chosen cases have particular characteristics that make them useful for comparison.[17] I model my inquiry on what is known as Mill's (1986 [1874]) Method of Difference, a form of causal logic put forth by the 19th century philosopher John Stuart Mill. Following Mill, a systematic comparison of cases that share certain similarities yet differ on an outcome of interest can identify the mechanisms that produce those different outcomes. Thus, I select a similar group of cases—three large Jewish ghettos under Nazi occupation—in which residents reached very different decisions about resistance. I then compare those cases to learn something about why resistance happens.

Case Selection and Analytic Strategy

The Nazi-created Jewish ghettos that existed during World War II were fenced-off areas within certain cities and towns, to which European Jews were forcibly relocated and in which they were confined (Corni 2002; Duneier 2016). The ghettos were distinct from the concentration and death camps that are familiar to many people. While the ghettos themselves were not created for the purpose of on-site, mass murder, residents were usually deported to the death camps from the ghettos (Corni 2002; Hilberg 1979). The process of ghettoization was therefore part of the overall system designed to destroy European Jewry. According to the United States Holocaust Memorial Museum, there were at least 1,143 such ghettos during the war.[18]

Though they varied in size and structure, most Jewish ghettos under Nazi occupation were located in relatively small districts or sections of an established city, and usually in older, more run-down neighborhoods. Not surprisingly, population densities in these ghettos were extreme. Hilberg (1979: 151) describes the Nazi-created Jewish ghetto as "a tightly packed slum area, without parks, empty lots, or open spaces." Seeing the Jewish population as a source of cheap labor, Nazi officials created factories in some ghettos, where Jews worked creating products for the German war effort. Thus, ghettos served the dual purpose of concentrating the Jewish population in such a way that facilitated the eventual deportations to the death camps, and of creating a labor force that could be exploited before being exterminated (Corni 2002; Hilberg 1979). Further, when confined to the ghettos, Jews could no longer buy food on the open market, and the lack of available space in the ghettos made it difficult to produce food by growing crops or tending livestock. Food shortages were therefore a prominent feature of ghetto life as well. Hunger, crowding, and subsequent disease all took their toll on the ghetto communities, creating causalities even before Jews were sent to the death camps. In fact, the Nazi-created ghettos in Poland accounted for the deaths of one-fifth of all Polish Jews.[19]

My study focuses on three Jewish ghettos during World War II: the ghettos of Warsaw, Vilna,[20] and Łódź. Although these ghettos were located in what are two different states today (Warsaw and Łódź in Poland, and Vilna, or Vilnius, in Lithuania), they have important similarities that make them useful for comparison. Notably, they were among the largest, in terms of population, of the Jewish ghettos in Nazi-occupied Eastern Europe. The cities that housed these three ghettos each had a sizable Jewish presence before World War II, with Jews comprising roughly 30 percent of each city's population, and each was a prominent center of Jewish cultural, political, and religious life. Warsaw was the capital of Poland and had a population of over 350,000 Jews in 1931, before the onset of World War II.[21] Vilna, known as "the Jerusalem of Lithuania," was the birthplace of important religious and political movements and home to the renowned rabbi and 18th century Talmudic scholar known as the Gaon of Vilna.[22] Jews were also well represented in Łódź, a city with a vibrant textile industry (hence its nickname as the "Manchester of Poland"), and played vital roles as factory owners, managers, and workers.[23]

Though similar in many ways, the ghettos in these three cities were also distinct from one another, which means that by comparing them we can learn something more than we learn from studying one alone. Notably, each ghetto was located in a different region of Nazi influence. After Germany's invasion of Poland in September 1939, Poland was divided into three regions (see Figure 1.3): the northern and western parts of the country (including Łódź) were incorporated into Germany and became part of the Reich; the central and southern sections (including Warsaw) were occupied by Germany and became known as the General Government; and the eastern regions (including Vilna) were deeded to the Soviet Union as part of Hitler's pre-war pact with Stalin but then fell to German hands after the invasion of the Soviet Union in the summer of 1941.[24] Although Jews living in each region ultimately suffered the same tragedy, the trajectory of the German conquest of Eastern Europe, as well as differences in the German administration of the Reich, General Government, and occupied Soviet territories, meant

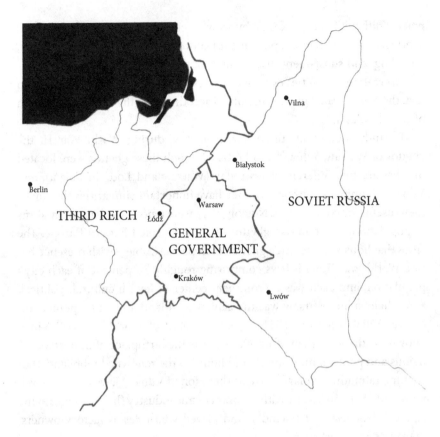

Figure 1.3 Map of Poland at the start of World War II.
Credit: Elle Rochford

that Jews in each ghetto understood their situation in distinct ways, seeing different opportunities for their protection and survival.

The most important difference between these three ghettos, from the perspective of this book, centers on the emergence of resistance in each. While Tec (2013) and others rightly emphasize that Jews resisted in many ways, my focus is on sustained, armed collective resistance in the ghettos. My cases illustrate three outcomes. As noted earlier, there was an armed uprising against the Nazis in the Warsaw Ghetto. A similar uprising was planned in the Vilna Ghetto, but activists were not able to bring those plans to fruition. In contrast, Jews in Łódź did not plan for armed resistance at all. That is not to say that Jews in Warsaw used armed tactics exclusively, or that Jews in Vilna and Łódź did not resist at all; on the contrary, as I demonstrate in the chapters that follow, Jews in all three ghettos fought back against the repressive and oppressive conditions they faced, in many ways. My unit of analysis is not the individual; I am not attempting to explain why some individuals participated in resistance while others did not. Instead, I focus on the ghettos. The main variation across these three ghettos—a sustained ghetto uprising in one ghetto, but not the other two—provides a basis for a study of the emergence of resistance. By comparing these ghettos, it is possible to identify some of the reasons why collective, armed resistance happens in extremely repressive settings.

Time and Place

Beyond my case selection and study design, I employ comparative-historical methods by taking the role of time and place seriously. Both are central to comparative-historical analysis. Typically, researchers study some phenomenon or process over time, and leverage their analysis through the use of comparison (i.e., examining how the process operates similarly or differently in different spaces) (Mahoney 2004; Tilly 1989). Yet, scholars argue that "time" and "place" are more than a backdrop for comparative-historical analysis. As Stryker (1996) notes, while some researchers treat time as a contextual variable, others argue for a more "eventful" analysis of time, one that focuses on the contingent sequencing of events and outcomes (Sewell 1996). The same is true of space. While a classic comparative-historical study inquiry might ask why some outcome happened in one country but not another, variation across countries or other spaces reflects more than differences in geographical location. In this regard, the distinction between space and place is useful. Sociologist Thomas Gieryn (2000) writes that "place" is more than simply a point in space. A place has physicality: it is created of some material and has an architectural form. Beyond that, a place has meaning to those who reside in or interact with it, although those meanings can be varied, fluid, and subject to change over time. "Space" is the area, defined by geometry and volume, in which "place" is found.[25] As Gieryn puts it, "place is space filled up by people, practices, objects, and representations" (2000: 465).

My examination of the ghettos of Warsaw, Vilna, and Łódź draws on both time and place to construct a narrative of each ghetto. As I show later, meaningful events in the histories of the Warsaw and Vilna ghettos served as important turning points that provided cues to ghetto residents about the likely outcomes of their actions and guided their decision-making about resistance. Further, I point out the properties of place—the built environment, and its consequences for the people living in that space—that shaped each community's understanding of their circumstances. Notably, while all three ghettos were segregated spaces in which Jews were concentrated and literally walled off from the rest of the city, the Łódź Ghetto— described as "hermetically sealed" by some scholars—was more isolated than the others. The relative isolation of each ghetto, itself a function of place, meant that Jews in the different ghettos had different access to information from beyond the ghetto walls, which also affected their decisions about resistance. Place played another role in the stories of these three ghettos. As I explain in more detail in Chapter 4, which focuses on the Vilna Ghetto, that ghetto's proximity to surrounding forests where partisan units carried out acts of sabotage and other anti-Nazi resistance gave Jews living in that ghetto more options for resistance than in other places. Thus, time and place affected ghetto residents' abilities to assess the dangers facing them, as well as their decisions about the appropriateness of armed resistance as a response.

Data Sources

I use both primary and secondary sources to compare my three cases. I use these data to construct narratives of each ghetto, with the goal of understanding how and why sustained armed resistance happened in one ghetto but not the other two. Secondary sources come largely from published historical research and are cited throughout this book. My primary sources are varied; they include underground newspapers, letters, and other documents preserved from the ghettos, and published and unpublished diaries and memoirs written by the residents of Warsaw, Vilna, and Łódź. Another key source of primary data is the University of Southern California's Shoah Foundation Institute's Visual History Archive.[26] The size and searchability of the archive, along with the relatively standardized nature of the individual testimonies themselves, allowed me to sample the testimonies systematically, thereby using social science methodology in another way. In this book I draw on 120 randomly sampled testimonies from among all the archive's English-language testimonies from Jewish survivors who spent time during the war in at least one of the ghettos of Warsaw, Vilna, or Łódź. I describe all my data, along with their advantages and disadvantages, in more detail in the Appendix.

The Experience and Ethics of Holocaust Research

I found this work both meaningful and challenging. I had many emotional and physical reactions when reading these materials, especially the diaries and testimonies. I cried frequently. At times, the witnesses' accounts of the ghetto conditions and the brutalities they experienced literally turned my stomach. Survivors' descriptions of dangerous flights from their homes and hiding places also made my heart race. While I never had nightmares, I sometimes had trouble sleeping, either falling asleep or staying asleep.

I do not think my reactions are surprising, given the subject matter; many people reading these materials would have similar responses. However, I also had some unexpected reactions to my work with these data. For example, I experienced discomfort when performing the seemingly mundane tasks of data management. With 120 oral testimonies and volumes of other materials, I needed a way to organize and keep track of all my sources. Data management was especially important while working with the testimony transcripts, which were in electronic form. To aid in this task, my research assistant created a series of spreadsheets to record information about each of the testimonies (e.g., demographic information about each survivor and whether the interview had been transcribed yet). Further, following standard social science research practices when using personally identifying information, we organized each testimony by means of an ID number (provided by the archive itself, which of course needed its own way to manage 52,000 testimonies). Yet in a profoundly disturbing moment, one day when I sat down to read some testimonies, I realized what the spreadsheets entailed—a list of Jewish individuals selected from a larger population, with age, gender, and ID number, neatly typed into an Excel sheet. These ostensibly innocent worksheets unwittingly bore a resemblance to the meticulous records kept by the very perpetrators of the genocide I was studying.

That unsettling realization led to another. I had used the standard methods of my discipline to select a sample of individuals for study, yet "selection" has a different, much more ominous connotation when used in reference to victims of the Holocaust. The whole notion of "selecting a sample" therefore felt eerie when applied to oral testimony data from Holocaust survivors, many of whom owed their own lives to their abilities—or luck—in surviving much more dangerous selections during the Holocaust. While my collection and management of a small subset of archived testimonies is not the same thing as selecting individuals for murder, I found the use of the term "selection" with respect to my data troubling. I should note that the use of random sampling strategies did not bother me when I first began this research; nor did it bother my research assistant (like me, a Jewish woman), who performed the actual task of selecting our sample. Instead, this awareness unfolded over time.

Reactions like mine are what sociologist Janet Jacobs (2004) refers to as "double vision," or an ethical dilemma that stems from the tension between having sympathy for the subjects of one's research and maintaining the objectiveness necessary to conduct the research. These experiences gave me new insights into the ethics of social science research and compelled me to revise the protocol that had been approved by my university's Institutional Review Board (IRB), the agency that oversees human subjects research. Although I had initially planned to use pseudonyms when quoting individual survivors—another standard practice in social science research, typically used to protect individuals' identity—my horror at the dehumanizing nature of my record-keeping Excel sheet invigorated my desire to restore the dignity to those who were victimized by the Holocaust. Therefore, in this book I use the survivors' real names (a practice allowed by the Shoah Foundation archive).[27] Still, I felt pangs of conscience when referring to my "analysis" and "sample" and other such terminology to describe my analytic approach. Those feelings persist to this day.[28]

This discussion is my attempt to both reflect upon and pay proper respect to my cases and data. Although I am trained as a sociologist, and am committed to the systematic analysis of data, doing this work taught me the importance of recognizing that research subjects are people first. Similarly, while cases can and should be selected for analytically important reasons, my cases are also places, sites imbued with history and meaning, where real people lived (and died). The traumatic stories and events described in this book necessarily center the human experience, but all social science can and should strive to put the "people" back into our analyses, no matter our subject matter, data, or method.

Despite these reflections, some readers might still find my social scientific approach inappropriate or even offensive. This point goes beyond the troubling use of terms like "selection" and speaks to the broader enterprise of comparative studies of genocide. I understand this perspective; these individuals argue that the Holocaust was an episode of such unimaginable horror and suffering as to be unique and, therefore, incomparable. Some commentators suggest that comparing the Holocaust to other cases (e.g., other cases of genocide) robs the Holocaust of its meaning and lends credence to those who deny that the Holocaust happened at all. Any study of the Holocaust must therefore recognize the debates about its uniqueness.[29]

Although my analysis does not involve the direct comparison of cases of Jewish resistance during the Holocaust with other cases of collective action, because my overall theoretical objective is to draw implications for social movement research, I do argue implicitly that collective Jewish resistance during the Holocaust may be meaningfully compared to collective resistance in other contexts. In fact, in the Conclusion of this book I make that argument more explicit, by discussing the implications of this study for protest and resistance in a variety of settings. However, by doing so I do not intend to diminish the tragedy of the Holocaust in any way. I argue simply that the fact that Jewish resistance happened during the Holocaust, under conditions that would seem to render it impossible, is of importance to the study of collective action and may help enhance our understanding of protest and resistance in other settings. More broadly, I follow Owens, Su, and Snow's (2013: 71) argument about social science approaches to the study of genocide. They write,

> Although all episodes of genocide and mass killing are inevitably unique in many ways, they also incorporate more general social processes that are inherently comparable. Comparative analysis of how unique and contingent historical circumstances interact with more general social processes and mechanisms holds the promise of advancing general knowledge about why and how genocides occur.[30]

In the rest of this book, I attempt to understand collective, armed Jewish resistance during the Holocaust by examining resistance efforts in the ghettos of Warsaw, Vilna, and Łódź. I have tried my best to give this topic its due.

Chapters to Follow

Because one of my goals is to contribute to theoretical discussions about the emergence of social movements, Chapter 2 presents a more detailed presentation of those theories. There, I explain the core theoretical concepts with which I engage—the concepts of opportunity, threat, and framing—and outline my argument about Jewish resistance during the Holocaust. My argument stresses the importance of what I call *critical conclusions* (i.e., Jews' assessment of the opportunities and threats facing them in the ghettos) and *resonant responses*, or responses to the opportunities and threats that made sense, given the way Jews in the ghettos understood their situation. However, readers who are less interested in these theoretical underpinnings may wish to skip ahead to Chapter 3. Chapters 3–5 each present case studies of the ghettos of Warsaw, Vilna, and Łódź. Together, these chapters flesh out the theoretical argument I present in Chapter 2. They demonstrate how critical conclusions and resonant responses help explain why Jews were able to stage a sustained armed uprising in Warsaw, but not in Vilna or Łódź.

Chapter 3 begins with a description of the Warsaw Ghetto Uprising. It then reintroduces the book's overall question: why did Jews resist, given the apparent barriers to their collective action? I show that while Warsaw Jews lacked opportunity, this deficit did not preclude action; Jews in the Warsaw Ghetto actually mobilized *precisely because* they had no opportunity, calling for resistance only once they realized the true aims of the Nazi genocidal regime and concluded that there was no real chance for Jews to survive. I argue that this realization was a critical conclusion, one that reflected an assessment of threat. Interpretive processes (what social movement scholars call "framing") were important to the emergence of collective resistance as well: members of the resistance organizations framed the idea of resistance not as something that would thwart the Nazis and save Jews, but as a way to die with honor and dignity. Thus, collective action emerged not in response to opportunity, but in response to threat, which made the idea of resistance possible and resonant with Jews' understanding of their situation in the ghetto. However, this critical conclusion and resonant response was not arrived at easily. This chapter illustrates that resistance fighters had an immense task; namely, to convince the ghetto masses to accept an unimaginable, unacceptable conclusion (i.e., the inevitability of their deaths at the hands of the Nazis). Yet, important events in the ghetto, such as the onset of mass deportations to the death camp Treblinka, made the resistance frame resonant and facilitated collective action.

Chapter 4 focuses on the Vilna Ghetto. In Vilna, resistance fighters planned for armed resistance but were not able to win the support of the rest of the community and ended up escaping to nearby forests and joining with partisan units carrying out acts of sabotage against the Nazis. This chapter asks: why were resistance fighters in Warsaw able to bring their plans for a ghetto uprising to fruition, whereas resistance fighters in Vilna were not? I turn to a narrative of the Vilna Ghetto, describing the events that led to the formation of resistance organizations, as well as the activists' decision to call off plans for an armed revolt in the ghetto. I show that there were two different sets of critical conclusions and resonant responses in the ghetto: one proffered by members of the FPO (*Fareynikte Partizaner Organizatsye*, or United Partisans Organization) that was very similar to the arguments made by the ŻOB and another fighting organization, the *Żydowski Związek Wojskowy* (ŻZW) or Jewish Military Union, in Warsaw, and the other by Jacob Gens, the Nazi-appointed head of the ghetto *Judenrat* (Jewish Council). Gens, who opposed resistance, presented a "work to live" frame, arguing that Jews in the ghetto could survive by following the Nazis' rules and working as laborers in the ghetto factories. Despite a brief period of armed resistance, the infamous "Witenberg incident," during which the ghetto community joined Gens in clamoring for FPO leader Itzhak Witenberg, a Communist, to turn himself in to the Nazis, showed the FPO that it did not have the support of the ghetto masses. Competing assessments of threat, and different resonant responses, ultimately hampered resistance efforts in Vilna.

Chapter 5 presents an analysis of the Łódź Ghetto, the only ghetto of the three in which plans for armed resistance against the Nazis never emerged. It was also the longest-lasting of the ghettos, and it was never completely liquidated or destroyed. This chapter provides a narrative of the events in the ghetto, from the Nazi invasion and creation of the ghetto through the liberation of its small surviving Jewish population by the Red Army in 1945. Whereas time and place matter to the stories of all three ghettos, the Łódź Ghetto best illustrates the importance of place. I show that structural and geographical features of the Łódź Ghetto contributed to the critical conclusions and resonant responses that can explain the lack of armed resistance in the ghetto. The severe isolation of the Łódź Ghetto, whose residents were essentially cut off from all contact with other ghettos, prevented Jews in Łódź from hearing about events in other places and made the smuggling of weapons and other materials for armed resistance virtually impossible. In contrast, Jews in the Warsaw and Vilna ghettos were able to receive, albeit with difficulty, communications and supplies from beyond their ghetto walls, facilitating armed resistance. Łódź's isolation prevented the development of a critical conclusion of genocide and hopelessness in two ways. First, without knowledge of mass killings of Jews elsewhere in Europe, Jews in Łódź had fewer sources of information on which to base a conclusion of genocide. Second, Łódź was such an isolated place that even by ghetto standards, the food supply was restricted, as Jews were unable to smuggle food in to supplement their starvation rations. In this place, hunger became a greater threat to people's lives than deportation, and the resonant response to that greater threat was to try to find food—i.e., by putting all their efforts into working in the ghetto factories instead of organizing for resistance. Despite their suffering, Łódź Jews remained hopeful that they could survive long enough for the war (and the Nazi occupation) to end. Interestingly, the primary and secondary data give hints that youth activist groups did exist in the Łódź ghetto and met occasionally, but the prevalent hunger and all-consuming focus on food left little energy for planning armed resistance (much less carrying it out). Place therefore shaped decisions about resistance by affecting the conclusions that people reached and how best to respond to them. The predominant response, one promoted by controversial Ghetto leader Chaim Rumkowski, was to work rather than resist.

I conclude with Chapter 6, which begins by revisiting debates about Jewish resistance during the Holocaust: while some argue that much more resistance should have happened, I suggest that the fact that any resistance happened at all is impressive. I then show what the story of resistance in Warsaw, Vilna, and Łódź teaches us about social movements, rebellions, and other forms of collective action, both past and present. I end with a discussion of the relevance of my argument to contemporary hate, as well as a broader message of hope.

2

Understanding Resistance

Theoretical Underpinnings

When the uprising began in the Warsaw Ghetto in April 1943, Ghetto fighter
Chaim Frimer was stationed on a balcony. From his position, he could watch
German soldiers from above as they entered the Ghetto. He later described
what he saw:

> From the balcony I could see all their helplessness and loss of discipline.
> The air was full of outcry and shouting. Many made for the nearest walls
> in search of shelter, but everything was blocked and barricaded, and death
> pursued them on all sides. Amid the noise, the confusion, and the cries
> of the wounded, I heard a sort of accompaniment from one German who
> seemed to be smitten with astonishment: "*Die Juden haben Waffen! Die
> Juden haben Waffen!* [The Jews have weapons!]." (quoted in Schoenberner
> 2004: 205)

The first shots fired by Jews in the Warsaw Ghetto Uprising caught Nazi
soldiers off guard. In a way, this case catches social movement theorists by
surprise as well: sustained, collective resistance happened in the Warsaw
Ghetto when, according to the theories, it never should have.

One of my goals in this book is to use the story of Jewish resistance in
the ghettos of Warsaw, Vilna, and Łódź to contribute to theories about social movements, and especially theories that explain when and why social
movements happen. Jewish resistance during the Holocaust presents a challenge to these theories, and it can be useful for refining and even rethinking
them. In this chapter, I discuss some of the key concepts and developments
in theories of social movement emergence and show how my inquiry can
help move those discussions forward. I then outline my own theoretical argument, based on what I call *critical conclusions* and *resonant responses*.

Hope and Honor. Rachel L. Einwohner, Oxford University Press. © Oxford University Press 2022.
DOI: 10.1093/oso/9780190079437.003.0002

Using Social Movement Theory to Study Jewish Resistance

Admittedly, theories of social movement emergence were not originally intended to account for armed resistance against authoritarian regimes. Yet, these theories are not merely a set of "strawperson" arguments for my analysis. The fact that these theories are ill-equipped to account for Jewish resistance is central to my inquiry. What can we learn about protest by studying Jewish resistance during the Holocaust?

While the armed resistance that I focus on in this book is different in many ways from the protests that usually draw the interest of social movement scholars, social movement theory may still be used as a lens through which to view and understand it. There is no single definition of a social movement, but most researchers agree that movements are organized, sustained, collective attempts to further the goals of some group, typically in opposition to some government or authoritative structure (Tarrow 1998; see also Jasper 1997; McAdam 1982). Based on this description, armed Jewish resistance in the ghettos of Nazi-occupied Eastern Europe shares many attributes with other social movements. First, such resistance was planned and organized, with clear leadership and an organizational structure (Arad 1982; Gutman 1994; Kurzman 1993; Lubetkin 1981; Zuckerman 1993). In addition, like many other cases in social movement research, many participants in the resistance movements in the ghettos were active in other political organizations and movements before their involvement in armed resistance and were recruited through these pre-existing activist networks (Arad 1982; Cochavi 1995; Cohen 2000; Lubetkin 1981; Zuckerman 1993). These activists did not use tactics traditionally associated with contemporary protest, such as marches and demonstrations; nor did they engage with authorities to achieve policy or social change goals. The setting in which they worked made such tactics useless: because Jews living under the Nazi regime lacked citizenship rights as well as broad public support, mass marches and similar actions would not have been effective and, indeed, would likely have led to increased repression. Instead, these activists turned to armed resistance, a type of resistance that many social movement scholars have studied.[1] Finally, and perhaps most importantly, cases of collective Jewish resistance are similar to other social movements because they were socially and politically motivated. As I demonstrate in more detail later, and as others have found (Arad 1982; Cohen 2000; Gutman 1982, 1994), resistance leaders planned and staged collective resistance not primarily to preserve their own lives, but to preserve the dignity and honor of the Jewish people as a whole. In the context of a genocidal regime intent on cleansing Europe of its Jews, whom the regime regarded as "subhuman," such action was a political statement.

Yet while there are similarities between Jewish resistance during the Holocaust and other social movements, I am more interested in the *differences* than in the similarities. In this book, I follow other scholars (Goldstone and Useem 1999; Meyer 2002) who posit that we must expand our conceptualization of social movements, as well as our repertoire of empirical cases, to gain a firmer understanding of the dynamics of protest and resistance as a whole. In fact, I argue that an examination of Jewish resistance makes an important contribution to the field of social movements *precisely because* it is so different from other, more traditional sites of inquiry. These differences allow us to use these ghetto uprisings to push our understanding of what social movements are and, especially, why they happen. In particular, I argue that armed Jewish resistance during the Holocaust occurred in settings characterized by levels of resources, opportunity, and threat—three central theoretical concepts in the study of social movements—that actually would appear to make such resistance impossible. By solving the puzzle of Jewish resistance, we can enhance our understanding of protest and why it happens.

Theories of Social Movement Emergence

I ground my inquiry in a rich scholarly literature, developed largely by sociologists and political scientists, that offers different theoretical explanations for why social movements happen. Two dominant theories of movement emergence, which have formed the bedrock for much of the social scientific research on social movements for the past several decades, are resource mobilization theory and political opportunity theory. Resource mobilization theory (Jenkins 1983; McCarthy and Zald 1977) was itself a reaction to earlier, more psychological theories of movement emergence that posited that protest was largely grievance-based, the product of either a mass alienation from society or some suddenly imposed stressor that caused spontaneous outbursts of collective action (Gurr 1970; Kornhauser 1959; Turner and Killian 1957). Those earlier theories, collectively referred to as the "classical model" of movement emergence (McAdam 1982; Morris 1981), portrayed the act of protest—and, by extension, the individuals who participated in such acts—as irrational and impulsive. However, the widespread protest movements of the 1960s in the United States and elsewhere ushered in new ways of thinking about the origins and nature of collective protest.

In response both to the 1960s movements and the limitations of the classical model's ability to account for them, resource mobilization theorists argued that protest was explained not by anger or grievances, but by the amount of resources available to be mobilized by an aggrieved yet rational population (Jenkins 1983; McCarthy and Zald 1977; Tilly 1978). Resources were not usually defined, but were understood to be the "stuff" of protest needed to get collective action off the ground; McCarthy and Zald's partial illustrative list included "legitimacy, money, facilities, and labor" (1977: 1220). Following this theory, research flourished with work that focused on the organizational aspects of protest, showing how protest activity was planned and staged by organized, rational actors drawing on available resources (financial, organizational, and so on) and mobilizing in pursuit of political goals (Cress and Snow 1996; Jenkins and Perrow 1977; Staggenborg 1991).

Soon after the development of resource mobilization theory, another influential theory was born from scholarship focused on the U.S. civil rights movement. Political process theory (McAdam 1982) shared resource mobilization theory's portrayal of social movements as rational and organized, yet emphasized indigenous organization and the ability of movement participants to generate their own resources (Morris 1981, 1984). This theory also introduced the concept of political opportunity as a central factor in the emergence of collective action. Theorists working in this tradition, which has now come to be known as political opportunity theory, pointed to the importance of understanding changes in the broader political environment—e.g., in the structure of elections and political parties, elite cleavages, and state crises—that would render the environment either "open" or "closed" to protest; "openings" would afford nascent movements the political space and support needed to mobilize (Eisinger 1973; Kitschelt 1986; Meyer 2004; Reger 2018; Tarrow 1989; for similar arguments about revolutions, see Goldstone 1991; Skocpol 1979; Tilly 1978). McAdam's (1982) version of the theory also stressed the importance of actors' interpretations of opportunity. In an oft-quoted phrase, he notes (1982: 48), "Mediating between opportunity and action are people and the subjective meanings they attach to their situations." As a result, he introduced the concept of "cognitive liberation" to his model, arguing that protest would not emerge unless resources and opportunity coincided with protesters' awareness of their chances for action and a belief in their abilities to succeed.

Following the insight that opportunities need to be perceived as such in order to pave the way for protest, subsequent research has examined perceptions of opportunity and how activists assess their political environment and make strategic and tactical choices based on those assessments (Gamson and Meyer 1996; Kurzman 1996). For instance, McCammon's (2012) study of the U.S. women's jury movement focuses on how activists in different states interpreted the signals present in their political environment and then made (or failed to make) decisions about collective action. Similarly, Taylor's (1989) study of the U.S. women's movement between 1945 and 1966, a time of social retrenchment against the gains women had made during World War II, shows how feminist activists in the National Women's Party remained in "abeyance," maintaining their organization and commitment to feminism during a time characterized by a lack of political opportunity (see also Rupp and Taylor 1987).

Together, resource mobilization theory and political opportunity theory argue that mass protest occurs when aggrieved individuals are organized, have access to the resources necessary for protest, and operate in an environment that they see as conducive to successful collective action. Although the past several decades of social movement scholarship has witnessed critiques of these theories—e.g., that the theories are overly structural, pay insufficient attention to emotion and cultural processes, and fail to theorize race despite being based largely on the U.S. civil rights movement[2]—they have been quite influential and have received empirical support when applied to the study of protest in democratic settings[3] as well as some authoritarian settings.[4]

My inquiry takes these theories as a starting point. The problem, though, is that they do not get me very far. That is because if resource mobilization theory and political opportunity theory are correct, sustained armed Jewish resistance should never have happened. European Jews under Nazi occupation were a besieged and stateless people, confined to certain areas and forced to give up their property and livelihoods; they lacked all rights of citizenship and were in no position to benefit from any shifts in the political system, even if such shifts had occurred. Nor did they have any hope that collective resistance would succeed in changing their political situation. In short, the factors stressed by foundational theories of social movement emergence were absent: Jews in the Nazi-created ghettos had precious few resources (and, certainly, not enough weapons and training needed to stage armed resistance against a powerful occupying military force). Nor did they experience any of the "openings" argued by many theorists to pave the way for the emergence of collective action. So how can we explain their resistance?[5]

The Mobilizing Power of Threat

Understanding armed Jewish resistance during the Holocaust requires a different way of thinking about the factors that give rise to collective action. In this book, I engage with a growing theoretical literature focused on the mobilizing power of *threat*. This concept, which has been used to explain protest in a variety of settings, is especially fruitful for understanding collective action in non-democratic, authoritarian contexts, where political opportunities are severely restricted (Alimi 2007a; Almeida 2003; Einwohner 2003; Einwohner and Maher 2011; Loveman 1998; Maher 2010; Shriver, Adams, and Longo 2015).

What do social movement scholars mean when they talk about threat? Whereas opportunity refers to openings in the political and economic system that facilitate collective action, threat is the disadvantages in the broader social environment that are harmful (or potentially so, if unaddressed). Tarrow (1998: 86) defines threat as dangers to groups' "interests, values, and, at times, survival," and Martin (2013: 10) treats it as "anticipated losses of economic or personal security." Yet while opportunity and threat can both facilitate collective action, they operate differently. Opportunity is the "pull," an opening in the political system that beckons collective action by giving potential actors the sense that they can succeed, while threat is the "push" that compels collective action to prevent a bad situation from getting worse.

Repression, typically from the state, can be a threat that affects collective action. Dissent is often of sufficient concern to authorities that they act to prevent, punish, or otherwise counteract it (Barkan 1984; Davenport 2014; Earl 2003; Fernandez 2008; Khawaja 1993; Moss 2014; Reynolds-Stenson 2022; Snyder 1976). State repression can therefore constitute a threat to challengers' interests (Almeida 2003; Loveman 1998; Reese et al. 2005). Such threats can be conceptualized in terms of costs: repression makes collective action costly (Barkan 1984), and the anticipation of violence, jailing, or other costs associated with action may make potential actors rethink their plans to resist. Yet while my focus is on a case of collective action in an extremely repressive setting, in which the state was the main agent of repression, my treatment of threat is not limited to expectations of state repression. More broadly,

I follow Goldstone and Tilly's (2001) conceptualization, and especially their emphasis on action. For them, threat includes the cost of inaction: it is "the costs that a social group will incur from protest, or that it expects to suffer *if it does not take action*" (2001: 183; emphasis added). Similarly, Almeida (2003: 347) writes, "threat denotes the probability that existing benefits will be taken away or new harms inflicted if challenging groups fail to act collectively." Following these scholars, I treat threat not as reactive (see Khajawa 1993), but proactive. Although the question "How will the authorities punish us if we act collectively?" is certainly relevant to decisions about resistance, I focus on the costs of inaction rather than the cost of action. In my use, threat is forward thinking; the relevant question here is, "What will happen to us if we fail to act?" Threat is therefore also distinct from grievances, or those subjectively experienced disadvantages that compel collective action (McKane and McCammon 2018; Simmons 2016). Threat is the expectation of something bad to come, while grievances are those bad things that are already happening (see Almeida 2018).

Seen this way, political threats are not limited to authoritarian contexts, and exist in a wide variety of settings (see Almeida 2018 for a review). For instance, the 2017 Women's March, the largest single-day protest in U.S. history, mobilized in response to the threats posed by the Trump presidency. Plans for the March began almost immediately after Donald Trump's election in November 2016 (Fisher 2019; McKane and McCammon 2018). Similarly, the Black Lives Matter movement, which mobilized widespread street protests in the summer of 2020 following the murder of George Floyd by a Minneapolis police officer, began years earlier as a response to the ongoing police killings of Black people in the United States (Bell 2016; Kahn-Cullors and bandele 2018). Threats also lie in new policies that take away benefits for members of a movement or otherwise work against their interests, and can stem from the presence and growth of countermovements (Andrews 2002; Meyer and Staggenborg 1996). Tester's (2004) analysis of AIDS activism in the 1980s shows that disease can also be a political threat, especially if governments are unresponsive to the need for research and society stigmatizes those living with the disease. Similarly, research has found that threats posed by environmental degradation inspire environmental activism (Johnson and Frickel 2011; Shriver et al. 2015). Scholars also find that economic threat (e.g., job loss) explains right-wing mobilizations in the U.S., such as the Ku Klux Klan and the militia movement; these mobilizations are understood further as responses to demographic shifts in the form of increased immigration and majority/minority distribution, all of which present perceived threats to the status quo (Dodson 2016; McVeigh 1999, 2009; McVeigh and Estep 2019; Owens, Cunningham, and Ward 2015; Van Dyke and Soule 2002; see also Andrews and Seguin 2015). Lastly, threats can mobilize single constituencies, but can also inspire the creation of coalitions, both within movements and across movements (McCammon and Campbell 2002; Van Dyke 2003; see also Prieto 2018; Staggenborg 1986).

A Limit to the Mobilizing Power of Threat?

Clearly, Jews were threatened by the Nazi regime. They faced what is perhaps the ultimate example of threat: genocide,[6] a threat for which, as Maher (2010) notes, the cost of inaction is lethal. It therefore makes sense that European Jews resisted in response to a threat to their lives. Jewish resistance is still problematic from a theoretical perspective, however. As Almeida (2018) notes, while threatened communities can resist against expected dangers, collective action still requires adequate resources—yet Jews in the ghettos lacked the resources needed for sustained armed resistance.

Even putting resources aside, the concept of threat falls short in its ability to explain this case. That is because scholars have hypothesized a limit to the mobilizing power of threat, positing that extreme levels of threat can actually prevent protest from happening. Some theorists describe a curvilinear relationship between threat and mobilization (Almeida 2003; Eisinger 1973; Lichbach 1987; Muller 1985; Tilly 1978). When threats are low, there is no need to protest, while increasing levels of threat motivate people to act; however, there is a point at which the threats become so great that protest is unlikely. Writing about collective action in repressive contexts, Almeida (2003: 353, fn 5) writes: "The sense of harm . . . has upper boundaries on escalating protest. At some point protest will likely appear too dangerous as the state's repressive actions turn outrage into fear" (see also Eisinger 1973; Goodwin 2001; Tilly 1978). Fear can be a mobilizing force, as Marian Azab and Wayne Santoro's (2017) study of Arab Americans participating in protest post-September 11th finds—but they find a curvilinear relationship between levels of fear and participation in protest, noting that extreme levels of fear actually quell resistance. Broadening the discussion to less repressive situations, and focusing on countermovement mobilization, Meyer and Staggenborg (1996) also posit a curvilinear relationship between threat and collective action: a movement that has the potential to succeed creates a threat that inspires countermovements, but if the movement stands to be so successful that the issue at hand is "closed," then countermovements are unlikely to form (1996: 1636).

While there is no question that Jews interned in the Nazi-created ghettos of World War II faced a grave threat to their existence, the emergence of Jewish resistance is still puzzling. Jewish resistance lies at the hypothesized extreme end of the scale, where collective action is not expected to take place.[7] In such a repressive setting, where any defiance of the Nazi regime was met swiftly with (usually lethal) force, such resistance goes against the proposed "upper boundary" of threat. So, again, why did Jews resist?

Broader Economic Models

Defining threat as the cost of inaction harkens to broader treatments of collective action that understand behavior in economic terms. Rational choice theory (e.g., Olson 1965) posits that unless one is either coerced or receives some kind of selective incentive for their participation, joining protest is irrational; the rational choice, one that minimizes costs while maximizing benefits, is to take a "free ride" on the efforts of others. Following this logic, Jewish resistance seems especially hard to explain, as the costs of armed resistance were enormous. Rather than taking up arms against Nazi forces, a rational decision for Jews in the ghettos might be to go into hiding and hope to survive until the end of the war. Indeed, some people did choose this response. But why did others plan for armed resistance against a much more powerful army—resistance that was costly and had little chance of succeeding?

Work by psychologists Daniel Kahneman and Amos Tversky (1979; Tversky and Kahneman 1981) offers a possible explanation. In a series of experiments, they found that people are risk averse when presented with a gain. For instance, when respondents were asked whether they would prefer a) a sure gain of $240 or b) a twenty-five percent chance to gain $1000 and a seventy-five percent chance to gain nothing, the majority (eighty-four percent) chose the first option; they avoided risk, preferring a secure, lower payoff. However, those preferences switched in the face of loss. When asked to choose between: c) a sure loss of $750 and d) a seventy-five percent chance to lose $1000 and a twenty-five percent chance to lose nothing, the majority (eighty-seven percent) chose the second option, taking a risk to avoid a certain loss (even though that choice presumed a high probability of having an even greater loss) (1981: 454). These same reversals in preference held when the experiment posed questions related to the loss of life rather than money. For instance, in the context of questions about actions during a deadly epidemic, most respondents preferred an eighty percent chance to lose 100 lives over a sure loss of seventy-five lives (1981: 455).

These experiments show that assessments of threat—i.e., whether potential outcomes are seen as losses or gains, and whether something bad and damaging could result from one's choices—matter to decision-making. Applied to the social movement concepts of threat and opportunity, this work shows that people are more likely to do risky things in response to threat (potential loss) than in response to opportunity (potential gain). Yet while these findings proved to be robust across a number of experiments, and have received support in experiments specifically focused on participation in protest (Bergstrand 2014), Jewish resistance during the Holocaust still presents a challenge to these ideas. In the experimental settings, respondents were always given a choice of actions, one of which was more threatening than the other. However, as I demonstrate in more detail in the chapters that follow, the collective, sustained armed Jewish resistance that I seek to explain was not a risky act undertaken to prevent a greater loss from occurring. In other words, resistance was not intended to preserve people's lives. On the contrary, Jewish ghetto fighters believed that death was certain for everyone in the ghetto, whether they fought back or not. Fully believing that they would die in battle, these young activists fought back anyway. The question is why.

Threat Assessments

The case of armed Jewish resistance during the Holocaust is therefore a theoretical challenge to the study of protest, even for social scientists whose work demonstrates the mobilizing power of threat. I argue that the concept of threat can still help explain Jewish resistance, but it needs to be explored in more depth than have previous studies.

Unraveling the puzzle of Jewish resistance requires an understanding of the difference between objective conditions and how people understand them subjectively. Social movement scholars recognize the importance of this distinction. Following Tilly (1978), scholars have stressed the crucial role played by both in the emergence of collective action (see also Choi-Fitzpatrick 2017; McAdam 1982). These developments are in line with other scholars' focus on activists' perceptions of opportunity as a factor that shapes both social movement emergence (Kurzman 1996) and coalition building (Kadivar 2013). I too argue that perceptions of threat are key to understanding collective action. Applied to my cases, whereas the objective threat of genocide was the same for Jews throughout Nazi-occupied Europe, that threat was perceived differently by people in different places, with consequences for sustained armed resistance (or the lack thereof).

This claim might seem surprising. In a dangerous, life-threatening situation, one might assume that threats are clear and understood, not subject to differences in interpretation. Yet even in what are objectively grave situations, some actors may assess the threat differently than others. People might lack precise knowledge about an objective condition, which can prevent them from recognizing it as a threat (Gaventa 1982; Schwartz 1976). Relatedly, they might recognize a potential threat but see it as unlikely to happen or even impossible. As strange as this may seem from the perspective of those looking back on the Holocaust, a historical series of events with a now-known outcome, it is important to remember that actors on the ground do not have the benefit of historical hindsight when interpreting their circumstances. As just one example, Calhoun's (1994) study of the democracy protests in Tiananmen Square shows that the Chinese student protesters did not expect their government to repress them violently, despite the presence of tanks and other examples of force in the Square. Perceptions of threat matter to decisions about action. Potential actors must assess not only what is likely to happen to them if they act, but also what is likely to happen if they do *not* act.

To understand sustained, armed Jewish resistance in the ghettos under Nazi occupation, then, it is crucial to look at how Jews understood their circumstances. That is, we need to look closely at the experience of living in the ghettos, and how people made sense of what was happening to them. A careful look at Jews' understandings of the threats that faced them is necessary because the Nazi regime's plans for mass extermination were not in place at the onset of World War II (Fein 1979; Friedländer 2007; Hilberg 1979), so Jews had to learn about this threat over time. Further, clear information about the threat was hard to come by. It was complicated by an extensive program of Nazi propaganda and misinformation designed to keep Jewish victims in the dark as long as possible. Such misinformation came in the form of letters and postcards from people claiming to have been deported from the ghettos to safe work camps—letters that victims were forced to write before being put to death—as well as stations for arriving transports that were designed to look like normal train stops as opposed to arrival points for death camps (Gutman 1982; Syrkin 1948). As Gaventa's (1982) classic study of power and powerlessness shows, those in power have the ability to present compelling versions of reality that can shape people's sense of their own interests, so that they acquiesce to something that is actually harmful to them (see also Kendi 2019). Further, some Jews under Nazi occupation simply could not believe that they were being targeted for annihilation; that conclusion required them to make sense of the nonsensical, and to believe something (i.e., the murder of all European Jews) that seemed entirely impossible.

Tragically, all Jews throughout Nazi-occupied Europe were eventually targeted for extermination. It would seem, then, that if the concept of threat is to hold the key for explaining Jewish resistance, all Jews should have eventually resisted against the threat to their lives, to the best of their ability. The objective conditions (genocide) should have eventually been perceived as threatening, and as a threat grave enough to inspire resistance. Yet another part of the puzzle of Jewish resistance is that this was not the case, at least as far as sustained armed resistance is concerned. While such resistance did happen in some places (e.g., in the Warsaw Ghetto), it did not happen everywhere that Jews were threatened by genocide. Explaining Jewish resistance during the Holocaust means understanding why it happened in some places but not others. Doing so requires taking a careful look at how Jews understood the threats facing them *and* how those understandings differed across time and space, and either facilitated resistance or prevented it from happening.

Because threat is forward-thinking—"what will happen to us if we fail to act?"—it is based on actors' assessments of both their current conditions and their likely futures. While such assessments have not received much attention from theorists, Thomas Maher's work is one exception. Maher's (2010) study of Jewish resistance in the death camps identifies two important dimensions of threat—immediacy and lethality—and suggests that resistance is likely to occur in a situation of "total threat," one in which the threat is understood to be both lethal and immediate. Together, Thomas Maher and I (Einwohner and Maher 2011) have expanded those dimensions of threat to include five assessments that can help explain variability in action, even in highly repressive settings under genocidal regimes. We argue that rather than viewing threat monolithically, actors assess distinct aspects of threat differently.

When answering the question "What will happen to us if we fail to act?" actors consider different dimensions of threat. For instance, we argue that judgments of the *severity* of the threat matter to the overall assessment: do individuals see the threatening situation as dangerous but survivable, or completely unsurvivable? Second, the *temporality* of the threat is relevant to assessments of threat: do actors see the threat as imminent, or more long-ranging (and, perhaps, not necessarily worthy of action)? A third dimension is *applicability*: a sense of threat may be present but might be seen as something that is more likely to affect distant actors than local actors. Fourth, we argue that assessments of *malleability* factor into broader attributions of threat: can the threat be mitigated in some way through human intervention, or is the looming danger inevitable? Lastly, but crucially, we note that assessments of the *credibility* of the threat may vary. That is, actors may hear rumors of dangerous situations, or may be presented with conflicting information about a potential threat; such information must be sifted through and verified, to the extent possible, before any decisions about collective action can be made. By highlighting different dimensions of threat, and the ways in which each may be understood differently, we argue that threat is dynamic; even at extreme levels, actors' perceptions of threat can vary. My examination of Jewish resistance in the ghettos of Warsaw, Vilna, and Łódź builds on these ideas and pays close attention to how individuals in those ghettos understood the threats facing them—and, importantly, how those perceptions of threat varied over time and across space.

Motivational Framing and Frame Resonance

While the assessment of threat is important, it is not enough to explain collective action. It might be tempting to think that once a threat is identified—especially a threat as grave as genocide—those who are threatened would conclude that they have no choice but to resist. But as Finkel's (2017) analysis of Jewish reactions to the Holocaust notes, choices existed, including the choice of inaction. That is not to suggest that European Jews confined to the ghettos and targeted for genocide enjoyed any freedoms, or that their "choices" of action were not severely restricted by the context. Still, Jewish resistance was not predetermined; even once the threats to their lives were recognized as such, the ghetto fighters still had to decide that armed resistance (as opposed to other actions, such as escape or going into hiding) was the appropriate response to the threat. In a different study of mobilization among individuals facing grave threats to their lives, Gould's (2001) study of militant AIDS activism in the 1980s argues that despite the threat of AIDS, such activism was not inevitable. Drawing on James Jasper's concept of "moral shocks" (Jasper 1997; Jasper and Poulsen 1995) she argues that moral shocks need not always lead to protest; instead, sometimes people can accept a moral shock without resisting.

To understand resistance, then, it is not enough to examine perceptions of threat alone. Decisions about resistance also reflect choices about action, i.e., the best way to act so as to address the threat. Before they can resist, potential resisters need to interpret, or "frame," resistance as the correct response to a threatening situation. In other words, there is a difference between perceptions of threat and the interpretations of a situation that make resistance seem appropriate. While work on the concept of threat helps explain the former, the literature on framing and social movements (Benford 1993; Gamson 1992; Snow et al. 1986; Snow and Benford 1988) illuminates the latter.

Two of the chief theorists in this tradition, David Snow and Robert Benford (1988: 197), posit that movement actors engage in "framing," or "signifying work" by which these actors "assign meaning to and interpret relevant events and conditions in ways that are intended to mobilize potential adherents and constituents, to garner bystander support, and to demobilize antagonists." Framing is performed not only by activists, but also their opponents and other third parties like state actors and members of the general public (Dugan 2004; Noakes 2000). Identifying three "core framing tasks"—diagnosis, prognosis, and motivation—Snow and Benford (1988) note that while a movement can provide a diagnosis of a particular, threatening condition, individuals will not participate in the cause without also receiving a prognosis for the problem, an answer to the question "What is to be done?" Finally, individuals need to see in the proffered framings some "vocabularies of motive" (Benford 1993), or calls to action; as Benford explains further, these messages may speak either to the severity of a problem, or to the necessity, efficacy, and/or appropriateness of action. Because my interest lies in understanding why and how Jews in the ghettos decided to resist, I focus especially on this third framing task: motivational framing, or the rhetorical and interpretive work involved with the "call to arms" that inspires people to act collectively once a prognosis and diagnosis has been made.

A final insight from the framing literature also informs my examination of Jewish resistance. Just as perceptions of threat do not always lead to action, motivational frames do not always mobilize people. On the contrary, as Snow and Benford (1988: 198) argue, sometimes framing efforts can fail, while at other times they may ring true with their intended targets. At issue here is the question of frame resonance, or how well the proffered frame fits with individuals' experiences.[8] Describing frame resonance, Snow and Benford (1988: 207–208) write:

> Does the framing strike a responsive chord with those individuals for whom it is intended? To what extent does it inform understanding of events and experiences within the world of potential constituents? Is it relevant to their life situations?

A frame resonates with an individual when it "makes sense," matching their understanding of their situation. Together with motivational framing, these interpretive tools help explain why people engage in resistance.

My examination of Jewish resistance in the ghettos of Warsaw, Vilna, and Łódź draws on theoretical work on threat and framing. Using these concepts, I build an argument that rests on what I call *critical conclusions* and *resonant responses*. In the rest of this book, I show how *critical conclusions* (i.e., Jews' assessment of the opportunities and threats facing them in the ghettos) and *resonant responses*, or responses to the opportunities and threats that made sense, given the way Jews in the ghettos understood their situation, explain why armed resistance occurred in the Warsaw Ghetto, but not the ghettos of Vilna or Łódź.

Critical Conclusions and Resonant Responses

Although all ghettoized European Jews faced the threat of genocide, they struggled to make sense of that threat, and to reach decisions about how to respond to it. These struggles are understandable. The rampant confusion brought on by oft-changing Nazi edicts, as well as official propaganda that hid the true reason why Jews were interned in the ghettos, made it difficult for Jews to understand what was happening to them, let alone arrive at a plan of action (Corni 2002; Friedländer 2007; Hilberg 1979). Perceptions of threat unfolded over time, as Jews in the ghettos experienced increasing levels of brutality at the hands of occupying German forces and, ultimately, deportations to the death camps. Yet it is clear from eye-witness accounts that the one conclusion that was critical to decisions about resistance was a conclusion about survival: that is, whether people felt that they could survive the ghettos and the war as a whole. As I demonstrate further in the rest of this book, armed resistance emerged at those times and in those places where people reached a conclusion of hopelessness about their survival. Simply put, if Jews felt that they could survive, taking up arms against the Nazis was foolhardy, but a firm belief in the inevitability of their deaths made resistance more acceptable. A conclusion of hopelessness was *critical* to the emergence of armed resistance: without it, efforts at armed resistance did not emerge. However, this assessment of threat was not enough to facilitate resistance. I argue that Jews in the ghettos also had to fashion responses to that perceived threat that matched meaningfully, or *resonated*, with their understanding of their circumstances. Those responses, which were shaped by frames presented by different actors and constituencies in the ghettos, led to different decisions about resistance. I summarize this argument with the theoretical model presented in Figure 2.1.

I use this model to explain the variation across my cases. Jews in the Warsaw Ghetto staged sustained armed resistance, while Jews in Vilna planned for such resistance in the ghetto but were not able to carry it out. In contrast, Jews in Łódź never planned for armed resistance at all. How can we understand these three different decisions, given that Jews in all three ghettos faced the same threat of extermination? Why did the idea of armed resistance resonate and take hold with Jews in Warsaw, but not in Vilna or Łódź?

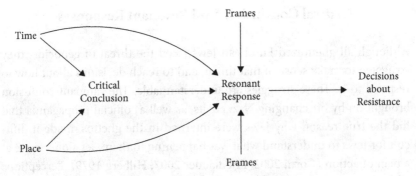

Figure 2.1 Theoretical model.

My answer to that question begins with the Warsaw Ghetto. I show that while Warsaw Jews did not recognize the threat at first, over time they came to realize that they were subjects of a genocidal regime and that they would not be able to survive the ghetto. I argue that this conclusion, which was shaped by both time and place, was critical, for it ushered in a decision to act. Yet the choice of *armed resistance* as an appropriate response to the threat of genocide emerged from framing efforts on the part of youth activists. Framing armed resistance as a means to promote the honor and dignity of the Jewish people, despite their imminent deaths, the idea of armed resistance resonated with these young people and led to the emergence of resistance organizations that planned and carried out the Warsaw Ghetto Uprising in 1943.

Critical conclusions and resonant responses played out differently in the Vilna Ghetto. In Vilna, young activists also reached the critical conclusion of hopelessness and equated armed resistance with honor. However, those assessments were not shared by the rest of the ghetto community. Instead, there were multiple assessments of threat, and different framings that shaped resonant responses to that threat. The story of the Vilna Ghetto therefore shows that assessments of threat not only vary by time and place but can also vary across a community. In Vilna, Jewish activists were unable to attract wide support for the idea of armed resistance in the ghetto. Thus, while resistance organizations emerged in Vilna and began planning for an armed uprising similar to that which took place in Warsaw, activists were not able to achieve those goals.[9] Rather than fight in the ghetto, these activists fled Vilna and participated in resistance as members of partisan units in a different place: in the surrounding forest. Finally, another set of conclusions and responses shaped decisions about resistance in Łódź. Jews in Łódź did not reach the critical conclusion of hopelessness, even though the conditions in that place were particularly dire. Instead, they maintained a steadfast hope for their survival. This prevailing hope worked against the development of an insurgent frame, despite the presence of pre-existing activist groups in the ghetto who might have otherwise been able to promote the frame and try to make it resonate with the broader ghetto population.

Because assessments of threat are dynamic, and vary over time, place, and within a community, the question "Why did Jews resist?" can only be answered by taking the perspectives of multiple segments of the community into account. Youth activists in both Warsaw and Vilna assessed threat in a way that supported resistance, but it was only in Warsaw that the youth's

Table 2.1 Critical conclusions and resonant responses in Warsaw, Vilna, and Łódź

	Critical Conclusion	Resonant Response	Outcome
Warsaw	Ghetto not survivable	Death through dignity	Sustained, armed ghetto uprising
Vilna	Competing conclusions	Competing responses	Sustained armed ghetto uprising planned but not achieved; resistance moved to surrounding forest
Łódź	Ghetto survivable	Work to live	No sustained, armed ghetto uprising

resistance frame resonated with the rest of the community. In contrast, despite the presence of youth movements in Łódź, threat was not assessed in a way that allowed a resistance frame to emerge.

Overall, my comparison of the ghettos of Warsaw, Vilna, and Łódź demonstrates, as this book's title indicates, that hope (or hopelessness) and honor (or some other resonant framing) explain the different resistant outcomes across these three ghettos. This argument is summarized in Table 2.1.

In the chapters that follow, I illustrate and justify this argument by telling the story of the war-time ghettos of Warsaw, Vilna, and Łódź, from each ghetto's establishment to its ultimate destruction. I begin with the Warsaw Ghetto.

3

Fighting for Honor in the Warsaw Ghetto

> *Be well, my friend. Perhaps we shall meet again. The main thing is that*
> *the dream of my life has come true. I've lived to see a Jewish defense in*
> *the ghetto in all its greatness and glory.*
> —Letter from ŻOB Commander Mordechai Anielewicz
> to ŻOB leader Yitzhak Zuckerman, written on April 23,
> 1943, the fifth day of the Warsaw Ghetto Uprising
> (quoted in Zuckerman 1993: 357)

On Monday April 19, 1943, the city of Warsaw had been under Nazi occupation for three-and-a-half years. It was a brutal occupation. In the aftermath of the German invasion in September 1939, Poles had lost all rights of citizenship and were subject to repression at the hands of a regime that considered them, as Slavs, to be racially inferior. As a result, Warsaw's residents endured forced labor, food shortages, inflation, and heavy taxation (Gross 1979; Gutman 1990). Soup kitchens attempted to feed the city's poor but struggled to provide enough food, and with a high enough caloric content, to meet the people's needs. Food, along with other necessities such as fuel, clothing, and shoes were all rationed, expensive, and hard to obtain.

Yet, as if in defiance of the hardships placed upon the city, the sun shined brightly in Warsaw on April 19. Tuvia Borzykowski, a Polish Jewish man active in left-labor political circles, was in the city that spring day—a day, as he wrote in his post-World War II memoirs, when "the sun flooded the ghetto, penetrating all its dark corners with light" (1976: 48).

The "ghetto" to which Tuvia referred was the Warsaw Ghetto, a walled-in area of a little over a square mile in the city's Jewish Quarter. Officially known as the *Jüdischer Wohnbezirk in Warschau*, or the Jewish Residential District in Warsaw,[1] it housed what was officially left of Warsaw's Jewish population by April 1943—some 30,000 to 60,000 people. They did not live there by choice, however. By Nazi edict, all of Warsaw's Jews were forced to live in

Hope and Honor. Rachel L. Einwohner, Oxford University Press. © Oxford University Press 2022.
DOI: 10.1093/oso/9780190079437.003.0003

the Ghetto, no matter where in the city they lived at the beginning of the war, and regardless of what they had to leave behind to move there.

By that sunny April 19, the Warsaw Ghetto had been in existence for two-and-a-half years. Its walls encompassed a gerrymandered series of streets whose jagged outline bespoke the complex logistics of determining which blocks in a bustling capital city would be cordoned off for Jews and which would remain accessible for non-Jewish Poles. When first created, the 1.36 square mile ghetto consisted of two distinct areas, the "Big Ghetto" and the "Little Ghetto," connected by a narrow strip one block wide and several blocks long. The "Big Ghetto" was bordered to the north and northwest by a railway station and the main Jewish cemetery, two sites that would eventually serve as tragic ending points for many Ghetto residents. To the south, across Chłodna Street, lay the "Little Ghetto," in what had been a more upscale neighborhood home to the wealthier ghetto residents who lived there before ghettoization and remained in their homes, at least initially. A bird's eye view of the ghetto borders in 1940 (see Figure 3.1) reveals an irregularly cut landscape, as if the shears used to cut a pattern in a piece of cloth slipped here and there. On its eastern edge, the Great Synagogue on Tłowmackie Street was included in the Ghetto but the area right around it was not. Nearby, an "Evangelical enclave" that included the Reformed Evangelical Church at 16 Leszno Street and the Evangelical Hospital at 10 Karmelicka Street remained outside the Ghetto. In January 1942, German authorities constructed a foot-bridge over the non-Ghetto part of Chłodna Street (see Figure 3.2) to link the two parts of the Ghetto (Engelking and Leociak 2009).

Through a series of changes in its borders, the Ghetto's footprint was reduced greatly over time. By April 1943, the "Little Ghetto" was liquidated, and the remaining ghetto area comprised three non-contiguous patches of real estate, some consisting of only two square blocks. Yet, although the Ghetto in 1943 was smaller than it had been originally, its structure, and purpose, remained the same: a walled-in area to which Jews were forcibly confined. Its boundaries were clear, marked by a ten-foot brick wall topped with barbed wire and broken glass. Its residents' identity was clear as well: in the Ghetto, all Jews over the age of 12 had to wear armbands—white with a blue Star of David—to signify their racial identity. Armed guards controlled the gates. Warsaw Jews referred to the area beyond the ghetto walls as the "Aryan side," a place forbidden to Jews, on pain of death.[2] The Warsaw Ghetto was, therefore, literally carved out of the city, with only a ten-foot wall separating it from the Aryan Side. This wall,[3] along with the armed guards

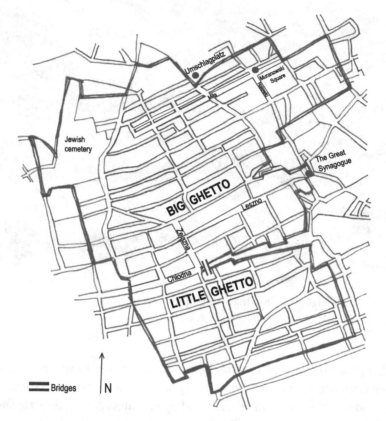

Figure 3.1 Map of the Warsaw Ghetto.
Credit: Elle Rochford

stationed at its gates, was clearly intended to keep Jews in the Ghetto, but did not necessarily keep those beyond the walls from knowing what was happening within its borders. A person standing next to the wall could not see through it, but people living on the upper floors of apartment buildings on the Aryan side could easily observe its goings-on. What they saw on April 19 was remarkable.

Resistance

While the temperatures were warm and spring-like on April 19, the night before had been quite cold. Marek Edelman, a Jewish physician, wore a

Figure 3.2 Bridge over Chłodna Street, June 1942.
Credit: Bundesarchiv, Bild 101I-270-0298-14 / photo: Amthor

red angora sweater to stay warm. He found the sweater in an empty base-ment from which an entire Jewish family had been forcibly removed during a previous *aktion* ("operation"), a round up and mass deportation. He later explained, "It was cold. In April, the nights are cold, especially for those who haven't been eating much. So I put the sweater on" (quoted in Krall 1986: 1).

Like Marek, most of the Jews in the Ghetto had not been eating much. The only regular food distributions came either from official rations or from meals given to Jewish laborers in Ghetto factories, but both were below starvation level. Workers in the "shops" typically received one meal of wa-tery soup per day, and official rations for Jews amounted to 184 calories a day (Gutman 1990; Freilich and Dean 2012)—notably less than the official rations allowed for Polish Warsaw, beyond the wall, which were themselves inadequate.[4] This meant that to survive, those in the Ghetto had to rely on food smuggling. However, there was never enough food for everyone who needed it.

April 19 was notable not only because of the lovely spring weather, but also because that evening was the start of Passover, a religious holiday com-memorating the story of Exodus, during which Jews eat no bread or leav-ened products. Even in the Ghetto, Jews did their best to prepare their homes for the holiday. They had been given special permission from rabbis to make *matzah* (unleavened bread) from non-kosher flour—the only flour available (Borzykowski 1976: 47)—and planned to hold the Seder, the ritual holiday meal. Twenty-six year-old Paula T. was one of many in the Ghetto getting ready for the holiday. Widowed some months earlier when her husband was shot and killed by German soldiers, Paula was still close with her murdered husband's parents and planned to have a Seder with them. However, they never got the chance:

> This was Pesach (Passover), and my mother-in-law said, "Please, I have no-body come to me for the seders." I said, "Sure, I'm going to come to the seder to you." I came to the seder . . . they came, the German, they took away us at that time . . . I never went to . . . never went to the seder, my father-in-law never made the seder . . . they came right away, took us out to Majdanek.

Some 2000 Nazi soldiers, accompanied by tanks, entered the Warsaw Ghetto on April 19 with the goal of deporting—i.e., forcibly removing and relocating—all the remaining Jews to the death camps (Freilich and Dean 2012: 459). The liquidation of the Ghetto was planned as a gift for Adolf Hitler, who was celebrating his 54th birthday the next day, on April 20 (Arens 2011). However, as the soldiers entered the Ghetto on April 19, a surprise awaited them. The ŻOB (*Żydowska Organizacja Bojowa*, or the Jewish Fighting Organization, whose members included both Tuvia Borzykowski and Marek Edelman) and the ŻZW (*Żydowski Związek Wojskowy*, or Jewish Military Union)—were ready to greet them with armed resistance.[5]

The Warsaw Ghetto Uprising

On April 19, 1943, ŻOB fighter Zivia Lubetkin was twenty-nine years old. Dark-eyed and intense, she was a seasoned activist who for years had been a member of HeHalutz ("The Pioneer"), a Socialist Zionist youth move-ment on the left of the political spectrum (see Figure 3.3). Based on her ac-tivist experience, she rose easily in the ŻOB ranks and commanded her own fighting cell.

Zivia and her fellow activists did not know exactly when the Nazis would come to the Ghetto to deport the remaining population, but they knew that

Figure 3.3 Jewish resistance leader Zivia Lubetkin, between circa 1938 and circa 1945.

Credit: Unknown author. Source: National Library of Israel, Schwadron collection. This file is licensed under the Creative Commons Attribution 3.0 Unported license. (https://creativecommons.org/licenses/by/3.0/deed.en). No changes made.

they would do so at some point. They received word of the pending invasion late in the night on April 18, 1943:

> At two o'clock in the morning, while we were discussing problems and making plans for the future, one of our comrades entered. From the expression on his face we realized that something had happened. He approached the table and quietly informed us a telephone message had just been received from the Aryan side. The ghetto would be surrounded that very night and the Germans would open attack at six o'clock in the morning. Even though we were prepared and had even prayed for this hour, we all turned pale . . . But we suppressed our emotions and reached for our guns.

Our messengers ran swiftly through the ghetto informing all the Jews. (1981: 178)

Zivia's comrade in the ŻOB, Simha Rotem, was eighteen years old. With his fair eyes and hair, Simha could pass as a Gentile. His appearance allowed him to carry out his activist work beyond the Ghetto walls, where he went by his Polish code name, "Kazik." On April 19, however, he was in the Ghetto and ready for battle. Describing the view from his post that day, he wrote (1994: 156):

> At four in the morning, we saw at the Nalewki Passage a line of Nazis marching to the Central Ghetto. They walked and walked endlessly. There were a few thousand of them. They were followed by a procession of tanks, armored vehicles, light cannons, and hundreds of Waffen SS on motorcycles. "They're going as to war," I said to my companion at the post, Zippora (Lerer); and suddenly I felt how very weak we were. What were we and what was our strength against an armed and well-equipped army, against tanks and armored vehicles, while we had only pistols and, at most, grenades? But our spirit didn't flag. Here we were waiting to settle accounts with our executioners at last.

All around the Ghetto, groups of fighters stood at the ready. The ŻOB was organized in small fighting cells, each consisting of members of a particular political organization predating the war; these included various leftist and Socialist Zionist organizations as well as the non-Zionist workers' group, the Bund. The ŻZW, in contrast, was organized by youth who were part of the right-wing Betar Revisionist movement, but it also allowed non-affiliated individuals to join its ranks (Arens 2011). Owing to deep-seated ideological differences between their movements, the ŻOB and the ŻZW fought separately. The ŻOB had few weapons: each fighter had a revolver, ten to fifteen bullets and a few hand grenades, and the organization as a whole had only ten rifles and one or two machine guns (Gutman 1982: 366). Some guns that had been purchased on the black market and smuggled into the Ghetto did not even work properly. Still, the fighters did what they could to plan for resistance. Tuvia Borzykowski explained, "Since weapons were so scarce, we taught our comrades to fight not only with guns, but with fists and fingers" (1976: 20).

Jewish fighters supplemented their meager arsenal with homemade weapons, including Molotov cocktails[6] and lightbulbs filled with sulphuric acid, the latter described by Zivia Lubetkin as "a Jewish innovation" (1981: 150). Sixteen-year-old Sol R., a baker's son, had joined the ŻOB with a friend after they had returned to the Ghetto following a miraculous escape from a train bound for the death camp Treblinka. Determined to join the resistance efforts but lacking a gun, Sol R. was taught how to build Molotov cocktails, as he explained during his testimony:

What did they do with the bottles and the petrol?
Putting in petrol and make Molotov cocktails. We had plenty of them. I always call it these Jewish cocktails . . . And I was very eager to do more. I want to learn how to shoot. They didn't have enough guns. They need people like me to do other things. So I was involved in that, in the uprising in Warsaw Ghetto.

Even without a full complement of guns, Jewish fighters stood ready to resist on April 19. Sol L., who also fought as a member of the ŻOB, described the beginning of the fighting:

The first Passover night, the first seder, the ghetto is surrounded . . . SS surrounded, like every ten feet an SS with a machine gun. We knew this is it. And they called out with loudspeakers we should get in the street. Well, nobody went out. Next day, they marched in and we opened fire. The guard was right about ten feet from our house. We were sitting on the roofs. They thought they marched in like usual, like nothing happened, you know. We opened fire. And when we opened fire a few fell and they backed up. They backed out of the ghetto. They backed out and, meantime, a few of us had the order to burn this factory, they went to burn the factory. The factory went up in flames . . . Next day a few tanks appeared at the crossing and we threw some Molotov cocktails from the roof. Two tanks blew up and the Germans escaped through the hatch in fire.

The fighters knew on April 19 that "this was it," as Sol L. put it, in part because they had fought brief battles earlier that year. On January 18, Nazi forces made a similar incursion into the Ghetto, prompting a four-day battle. Fully expecting another, longer period of fighting to follow, the April action did not surprise the Jewish fighters. They were ready—or as ready as they could be, given the circumstances. Continuing his reflections on the beautiful spring weather of April 19—and once he knew that the Germans would return to take the Ghetto that day—Tuvia Borzykowski wrote (196: 48–49):

> It was the day designated by the Germans for the final liquidation of the Warsaw ghetto. Having spent the night in the expectation of tragic events to come, we regretted that the day of the killing of Warsaw Jews was so beautiful. We felt that nature awakening from its winter sleep was also our enemy.

Twenty-six-year-old Warsaw native Adina Swzajger, newly wed when Germany invaded Poland in September 1939, was a Jewish pediatrician. Like her colleague Marek Edelman,[7] Adina was both a physician and a member of the ŻOB. She served the resistance group as a courier, sneaking in and out of the Ghetto, transporting false identification papers and other crucial documents. April 19 found her beyond the Ghetto walls, on the Aryan side:

> The shooting was coming from far away. It was not in our house, nor in our street. I put some clothes on and went downstairs, and I was told that it was in the ghetto. People kept saying: "It has started" . . . I went towards Krasinski Square to be as close as possible to my house. It was as though my legs carried me of their own accord to the wall of the ghetto. There was a fountain there. It stands there to this day. Just an ordinary, bulky, squat street standpipe from the past. At this fountain, in my childhood, I used to wash tears from my eyes and blood from my legs after I had fallen in the street or in the garden. But today I didn't have any tears to wash. I just stood and leaned against this fountain which I knew from my child-hood. A merry-go-round had stood on the square nearby for several days. A working merry-go-round[8] . . . The children were laughing and people going by were smiling. And on the other side of the walls you could hear shooting. (1990: 86–87)

Far outmatched in terms of guns and rifles, the Jewish fighters likely were not responsible for most of the shooting that Adina heard. Still, they did get some shots off: small cells of fighters moved in and out of apartment buildings throughout the Ghetto, firing on Nazi soldiers when they could. They also used their homemade weapons. Zivia Lubetkin recounted the actions of

Zippora Lerer, Kazik's fighting companion on April 19, during the first few days of the fighting (1981: 186–187):

> One of the women in the unit, Zippora Lerer, leaned out the window and hurled bottles of acid on the Germans below. They were so shocked to see a Jewish woman fighting that they cried out in surprise: "Eine Frau kämpft!" ("A woman is fighting!").

The fighters also used tactics of deception. During the fierce battle in Muranowski Square, ŻZW fighter Leon Rodal disguised himself in an SS uniform. He then led some German soldiers in a charge on a building, only to stop them in their tracks, which allowed other ŻZW fighters to shoot at them from the rooftops (Arens 2011).

Other fighters played more supportive roles. Sixteen-year-old Henry L., who had arrived in the Ghetto some years earlier as a deportee from Berlin, helped the ŻOB as a smuggler; his job was to safely ferry parts for a water pump from the Aryan side into the ghetto. Still other members of resistance organizations recovered precious arms and ammunition left behind after skirmishes. Such was Sol R.'s job:

> And I was assigned, and a few more boys, to organize all ammunition. And when one of them get killed, our boys, or the German, I should be able to recover the ammunition and bring it back. Because I was fast, and quick, and didn't give a damn, you know. And, so that's what I was doing. When the tanks came in, got burnt up, and half a truck of Germans got shot, I jumped on them, took away their guns, took away their helmet and knife . . . A few of them still was alive, you know, the Nazis, crying, not to kill me, not kill me . . . And I took one helmet away, I'll never forget that . . . I wanted to wear that helmet. I scratched the swastika and I put a David star on there. Boy, [laughs] I was proud. I thought we won the war, I'm not kidding.

Not everyone in the Ghetto was a fighter or involved with the ŻOB or ŻZW. Of the 30,000–60,000 residents who remained as of April 19, only a small portion, perhaps 750–800 people, were actually members of the resistance organizations.[9] Those who didn't fight went into hiding. Pola I. went to a Seder with her cousin and a friend, but hid in a bunker when the fighting began:

And we are prepared for the Seder, then all of a sudden they start to scream, "To the bunkers, to the bunkers, to the bunkers!" then we went up on this . . . how do you call it?, on the attic. And over there was a lot of feathers, feathers. And we all pushed in under the feathers, we didn't make any more Seder.

As the battles continued, *S.S- und Polizeiführer* Jürgen Stroop ordered his soldiers to set fire to the buildings to flush the Jews out. Kristine T., a 28-year-old Warsaw native who came from an upper-class family, witnessed the fires from the Aryan side. Her husband Michael, whose job with the Ghetto sanitation department required that he leave the Ghetto frequently to transport garbage, used his trips to the Aryan side to develop contacts to help his family escape. In March 1943, he arranged for Kristine to flee the Ghetto and move in with a Polish woman named Marila. While Michael had planned to help the rest of the family flee, when the Uprising began, he was still in the Ghetto, along with Kristine's sister and nephew. Kristine T. recalled:

In '43. And ghetto . . . it started liquidation of the ghetto, uprising. And he [Michael] didn't have time to do anything for my sister, and for her little boy, and for himself. I was on Chmielna Street, it was not far from the ghetto. And I could see the flame . . . the flames. And I knew what's happening there. And Marila was sitting . . . she believed in St. Anthony, that she was sitting and she was praying for my family, for my sister, her little son, and Michael.

Despite the fires, Jewish fighters held out for several weeks, firing shots from one burning building and then moving on to another when the fires became too intense. Non-combatants who were hiding also escaped from burning buildings and sought new hiding places. Those who could not escape leapt from the buildings rather than being captured. As Sol R. explained:

With the General Stroop, that no-good *mamzer* (bastard), he sent one after another one. We were fighting street by street. What can I tell you? People been . . . they set that Warsaw ghetto a fire, like inferno, everything we burning. People for didn't even took part in that Uprising were hidden in the buildings, build rooms, they jumped from the windows, you know. The whole city . . . the whole . . . I thought the whole world is burning in my

young mind. I said, "My gosh, what it's going to be? Everything is in a fire,"
you know, burning people, jumping.

Aware that some Jews were attempting to escape by climbing down into the
city sewers, German soldiers also pumped poison gas into those passages.
They used poison gas to clear out bunkers and fighting positions as well. Gas
is what felled the ŻOB fighters at Miła 18. Trapped in a bunker along with a
number of civilians, some of the fighters took their own lives on May 8, 1943.
Those who died there included twenty-six-year-old Arieh Wilner, who had
been detained by the Gestapo some months previously and was tortured so
brutally that he could hardly walk; twenty-four-year-old ŻOB Commander
Mordechai Anielewicz, and his girlfriend and fellow HaShomer HaTzair
("The Young Guard") activist, Mira Fuchrer, twenty-three. Zivia Lubetkin
arrived at Miła 18 after the gas attack and found some dazed and injured surviving fighters who were able to tell her what happened:

> This is the story the survivors told . . . The enemy arrived and ordered
> everyone outside. The civilians obeyed, and the fighters stayed where
> they were. The Germans repeated their command. They promised to
> send everyone to work and threatened to shoot anyone who refused to
> come out. Our comrades took up positions by the entrance, weapons in
> hands, waiting for the Germans to enter . . . The Germans didn't dare
> enter the bunker, but chose rather to use gas. This evil device destroyed
> our comrades . . . It was not a quick death, either. The Germans used only
> enough gas to suffocate them slowly. Aryeh Vilner[10] was the first to chal-
> lenge: "Let us kill ourselves first rather than surrender to the Germans
> alive!" The sound of shots filled air . . . Someone suddenly discovered a
> way out of the bunker hidden from the Germans' view. Only a few man-
> aged to escape. (1981: 231–232)

Despite the losses at Miła 18, the fighting continued in the Ghetto. On May
13, General Stroop described resistance by a Jewish woman after she was discovered in a bunker:

> After a few of the bunker's [fighters] were brought out and stood waiting to
> be searched, one of the women slipped her hand under her dress in a flash
> and—as has often happened—pulled a hand grenade out of her underwear,
> released the cap, and hurled it at the men who were searching her, while she

herself jumped back quickly and took cover. (quoted in Gutman 1982: 391; additions in original)

Henry L. also described Jewish women scratching and spitting on Germans, resisting with the only weapons at their disposal:

> In 1943 I have seen women jumping on German soldiers, and scratching, and fighting with a bare hand, and spitting on the soldiers, a Jewish women, God bless her, the honor, you know, and who have fought with a bare hand, and spit on the German soldiers who were . . . who's duty it was to hold them on a . . . on a horse-ridden cart, or on a car . . . on a truck, in order to be transported to Auschwitz and to Treblinka. They resisted with their bare hands, and spit on them. They called them *Deutsche*. And *Deutscheland, kaput* . . . but they couldn't really do nothing against armed soldiers.

By the end of May 1943, the Warsaw Ghetto lay in ruins.[11] The uprising led by the ŻOB and ŻZW had been stamped out, and with the exception of some miraculous escapes,[12] the fighters were either captured or killed in the battles and subsequent razing of the Ghetto by German troops (see Figure 3.4).

It is not surprising that armed resistance in the Warsaw Ghetto was eventually crushed. What is surprising is that it happened at all. As these accounts attest, Jews fought back with very few weapons or external support against a much stronger army, against whom they fully expected to fall. Resource mobilization theory, political process theory, and related insights from the field of social movements have a hard time explaining this uprising. So why did the Jews resist?

In this chapter I explain the uprising in the Warsaw Ghetto. I show that in this case, and contrary to what theories of social movement emergence would expect, a lack of opportunity was not a barrier to collective action. Even without an "open door" that invited collective action, Warsaw Jews mobilized for resistance. Moreover, they resisted with precious few resources, fighting back even though they did not have enough weapons to do so. Rather than responding to opportunity or the availability of resources, they fought back because of the gravity of their situation, calling for resistance only once they realized that there was no real chance to survive. I argue that this realization was a critical conclusion that made resistance possible. However, this critical conclusion was not enough to produce resistance. Framing processes were important to the emergence of collective action as well; members of

Figure 3.4 Jewish fighters captured during the Warsaw Ghetto Uprising.
Credit: Unknown author. (Franz Konrad confessed to taking some of the
photographs, the rest were probably taken by photographers from Propaganda
Kompanie nr 689.), Jürgen Stroop. (https://commons.wikimedia.org/
wiki/File:Stroop_Report_-_Warsaw_Ghetto_Uprising_08.jpg). "Stroop
Report—Warsaw Ghetto Uprising 08," marked as public domain, more details
on Wikimedia Commons: https://commons.wikimedia.org/wiki/Templ
ate:PD-1996.

the resistance organizations framed resistance not as something that would
save Jewish lives, but as a way to die with honor and dignity. This frame
emerged over time, following a series of events that unfolded in a particular
way in this particular place. Crucial developments, such as the onset of mass
deportations from the Warsaw Ghetto to the death camp Treblinka, made
this frame resonant and facilitated resistance. To understand armed resistance in the Warsaw Ghetto, however, it is important to examine Jewish life in
Warsaw at the onset of the war before the Ghetto was created.

Before the Ghetto

On the eve of the Second World War, Warsaw was a thriving city. The capital
of Poland, with a population of 1.3 million people, Warsaw was a center of

government, culture, and education. Its Jewish community—around 380,000 people—was not only the biggest in Poland, but in all of Europe.[13] As Irving M. noted:

> There were approximately from 10 to 12 Jewish newspapers, daily newspapers. There was one of them the first thing in the morning, one of them . . . some of them in the middle of the day, in the evening newspapers, still quite a few of them. At the same time, there were Jewish newspapers in the Polish language, which, give a variety of various ways of living in the city itself. There were many Jewish schools and there were Hebrew schools, Yiddish schools, Polish Yiddish schools, and, of course, a lot of Polish schools.

While the city was vibrant, it was also segregated, with much of the city's Jewish population living separate lives from their Catholic countrymen and women.[14] Some neighborhoods were entirely Jewish. Segregation extended to education and the workplace: Jews were limited to certain trades, and some Polish universities limited the number of spots available for Jewish students. Boleslaw L. recalled:

> It was a beautiful city. Yes. And the Jewish neighborhood was also beautiful. Only Jews. Only Jews. And all the . . . the wholesale companies, everything was very . . . of course the . . . the trade was in the Jewish hand. The whole trade was in Jewish hand. I would say, 95 percent was everything Jewish. The stores . . . the stores in the gentile section was mostly Polish, but they bought the Jewish merchandise. They came to the Jews to buy the merchandise. They couldn't buy it somewhere else . . . leather goods, wool, fabrics, you name it. You name it. Everything what is for sale was made by Jews. Because Jews . . . they were trades people. They couldn't get jobs in the city hall. They couldn't be a mailman. They couldn't be a policeman. They couldn't . . . they couldn't work, no. They had to be only in the trade . . . Doctors, lawyers, engineers, architects, they were Jewish also. Yes. Correct. But you could . . . a Jew . . . for a Jew to get a job in the city hall was just impossible. I don't . . . I didn't know any Jews who was working for city hall, you know.

Discrimination against Jews in some professions did not preclude inequality within the Jewish community. Like any sizable minority in a large city, Warsaw's Jews included both rich and poor: professionals, scholars, tradesmen, and workers, along with an underclass. However, this vibrant, diverse community would be changed forever with the start of World War II.

Early in the morning on September 1, 1939, air raid sirens sounded throughout the city of Warsaw, signaling the approaching German aircraft. For days, German planes attacked the city, unleashing hundreds of tons of bombs and damaging or destroying nearly half of the buildings. While the Polish defenses engaged the invader, the Polish government made pleas to the public to assist in any way that they could. In Warsaw, citizens grabbed shovels to dig trenches and fill sandbags, but these efforts could do little against the unceasing bombardment. Overwhelmed, the Polish army surrendered on September 28, 1939, and German soldiers marched into Warsaw on October 1.

With this surrender, Poland's lands were divided between Germany and the Soviet Union, pursuant to the Ribbentrop-Molotov Pact Hitler signed with Stalin in August 1939, before the war. The western section of Nazi-occupied Poland, along the German border, was annexed to the Reich directly, while the central section (including Warsaw) became a German territory of sorts, referred to as the "General Government" and overseen by Governor Hans Frank. Polish Jews now living under Nazi occupation were not sent to the concentration and death campus immediately, as Hitler's "Final Solution" for European Jews had not yet been codified. Nonetheless, Jews living in the General Government were subject to Nazi repression from the beginning of the occupation. Such repression took place in the form of restrictive edicts that limited what Jews could own. Some of these restrictions applied to all residents of the General Government, Poles and Jews alike. Xenia S., who at the start of the war lived in an integrated, upscale Warsaw neighborhood with her mother and grandfather, described how life changed after the Germans arrived:

> So, after the first few days, the Germans . . . started issuing declarations.
> *Like what kind of declarations?*
> Like, for example, that we are going to get . . . in order to buy food you had to have stamps. You were getting so many stamps for meat, for butter, for sweets and so on for a month. And you had to live on this.
> *This was for the whole population?*
> For the whole population. Like, for example, we were not allowed to have radios. We had to surrender all the radios that we owned.

Poles and Jews alike.

Poles and Jews alike. They . . . and then . . . and newspaper. The newspaper was discontinued, Polish newspaper. We had some sort of a little sheet put out by the Germans with the German news. Schools, of course, were closed. Banks were closed. This went on day by day.

Increasingly, though, edicts targeted Jews in particular. For instance, Jews could no longer own businesses or have more than 2000 złotys, or $380 USD, in currency outside bank accounts (Gutman 1982: 20). Furs and other valuables were confiscated. Even before the confinement to the ghettos, Jews' freedom of movement was curtailed: curfews were enacted, and Jews were not allowed to ride street cars or even walk on certain streets (see Gutman 1982; Sloan 1958). As Abraham M. explained:

Well, first of all we couldn't walk after certain hours . . . then there were times that you had to . . . you had to deliver your furs, and your gold, and you . . . everything you have to bring into a certain place, because if you're not you could . . . you could go to jail or whatever, whatever at that time the . . . the law was. Basically, that was the beginning, right off the beginning, from the restrictions.

The edict requiring all Jews in the General Government over the age of twelve to wear identifying armbands came on December 1, 1939 (Gutman 1982: 29). Casimir B. remembered:

We weren't allowed to leave the house unless you had a . . . arm band with a Star of David. We weren't allowed to be on the same street as a German. You had to step off the sidewalk. You're not allowed to ride in a streetcar. You had to be all the way in the back . . . it was still . . . the streetcar had a sign on it, "*Fur Juden*," it means "Only for Jews."

Nazi repression against Jews was not limited to formal, restrictive edicts. In addition, Jews were frequently beaten on the streets and rounded up for forced labor. More humiliating treatment occurred as well: Jews were forced to perform calisthenics, dance naked, or clean Nazi officers' quarters using their own undergarments as cleaning cloths. On February 7, 1940, Ghetto resident and historian Emmanuel Ringelblum, who organized a grassroots effort to document Ghetto life known as the "Oneg Shabbat" archive,[15] wrote in his journal, "Both yesterday and today women were seized for labor . . . They're ordered to wash the pavement with their panties, then put them on again wet" (1958: 17). Religious Jewish men were particular targets of Nazi abuse, as soldiers often cut, burned, or tore their beards off (Ainsztein 1979; Donat 1978; Gutman 1982, 1994; Klajman 2000). As Boleslaw L. described it:

> With the Germans there were always problems. You were afraid to go out, because they can catch you to work to load trucks. And sometimes they took you out very far and to load stones or bricks or something. You never know what's happened . . . what can happen then. You know, this is number one. Number two, you . . . you could see such cases on the street that they caught, let's say, those religious Jews with . . . with the *peyos* (side locks) and with the beards, you know. And they was cutting the beards, and the . . . and pulling them by the *peyos* and making . . . making all kind of jokes and making the pictures of them, you know. Those scenes, listen, it was a terrible period of time for a Jew, you know, because they were outlaws, the Jews, and they . . . they could with the Jew everything, whatever they wanted. They killed Jews on the street if they . . . if they didn't like him, you know.

Even greater repression was to come, however, in the form of the Ghetto.

The Creation of the Warsaw Ghetto

Plans for the ghettoization of Jews throughout Nazi-occupied Poland began to form soon after the German invasion. Within the General Government, Jews from the countryside and smaller towns were relocated to the larger cities and forcibly confined to ghettos. In Warsaw, intermittent rumors about a ghetto began as early as November 1939, but the community did not receive the official proclamation until some eleven months later, on October 12, 1940 (Gutman 1982: 49, 52). Boleslaw L. explained:

> There was . . . there was an announcement. They started to build the walls from brick . . . And on the top of that wall you had broken glass and wires, you know. And there was an announcement that on that and that day, from to, you have to . . . to leave the outside area, the Gentile area, and everybody has to go to the ghetto.

Once constructed, the wall was eleven miles long (Freilich and Dean 2012: 456). Yet, the exact placement of that wall did not proceed smoothly. The goal of locating the Ghetto in the city's traditional Jewish Quarter was complicated by the fact that there were Polish citizens who lived in that area or nearby, and who had interests in keeping their homes, businesses, and places of worship out of the Ghetto borders (see Gutman 1982: 56–61). The 140,000 Poles who actually lived in the Jewish Quarter would need to be relocated, as would the 60,000 Jews living outside the Quarter who would have to move into the Ghetto once it was created (Sloan 1958: 72).

The announcement of the Ghetto set off a mad scramble among Jews to find new housing arrangements. However, given the oft-changing Ghetto borders, it was unclear where exactly to search.[16] Some people had to move several times because once they found a new apartment within the Ghetto borders, those borders changed again. Abraham M. described moving to one area of the Ghetto and then being forced to relocate to another area so that Polish families could move in:

> There was . . . at the beginning there was one ghetto. And there wasn't enough room in that ghetto. So what they did, they built a second part, which you had to go over a bridge to go to the other ghetto. So they called a small ghetto and a . . . and a big ghetto. We lived actually in the first ghetto but . . . we had to move out. It was take—it was taken away by Polish people . . . So we had to move out, and we had to move in . . . more into the ghetto area, which is . . . which at that time it became already very . . . very hard to get an apartment. It's different when you spread out through the whole city . . . and you go in . . . So we had to move in with another family.

Casimir B., who was nine years old when the Ghetto was created, recalled moving several times. With each move, though, Casimir was sure to bring along his teddy bear:

> My recollection of that [first] place was it was overrun with bedbugs. That place was . . . it had vermin all over the place. The bedbugs . . . we used to wake up in the middle of the night and kill them. I mean, the walls turned red from all these bedbugs. But it was a . . . we . . . it was already the ghetto. We were not allowed to move. Everybody had to wear armbands. There was some resemblance of . . . of living. We had some aunts living nearby and they came in to visit, because we . . . I had no idea what's coming on. We

just accepted it because my mother said that's the way it is. And we lived there . . . I don't exactly remember the amount of time. I know that it was reasonably . . . reasonably comfortable under the circumstances . . . and then . . . that part of Warsaw was then declared to be outside the ghetto. All of a sudden the Germans declared that this part of the city was going to be excluded from the ghetto, and all Jews living within this part of the city had to go to another section of town, much smaller, much more congested. So, within . . . I remember they gave us, I think, 15 minutes to get out. Leave everything behind and go.

What did you take with you personally?

Again, my teddy bear, and whatever my mother took for me. But my teddy bear went with me. That was inevitable.

Life in the Warsaw Ghetto

By the end of 1940, Warsaw's Jews—about thirty percent of the city's population—were confined to a 1.36 square-mile area, which represented only 2.4 percent of the city (Gutman 1982: 60). They were eventually joined by Jews from surrounding small towns and, later, from elsewhere in Nazi-occupied Europe, all of whom were forcibly deported from their homes and relocated to the Warsaw Ghetto. At the height of its population in the summer of 1941, the Ghetto housed nearly 500,000 people. Thus, to say that the Ghetto was "crowded" does not come close to an adequate description of the living conditions. Murray M., who was deported to the Warsaw Ghetto from his home in Grójec, 48 kilometers to the south, recalled:

I remember of Warsaw Ghetto so being overcrowded that people were living anywhere, in basements. We lived in a hallway. We could not find anything. The situation there was terrible. People begging in the street.

David S. said simply, "Living in ghetto was hell on earth." He continued:

There was very little food. And many times no food at all. There were people literally dying in the street. There are pictures of people dying in the street. You would see every day people being gathered in the hundreds to the cemetery . . . they shipped all the Jews from all over Poland and Germany into the Warsaw ghetto. There was no room to live anymore. Instead of like living three or four people in an apartment, we had 10 and 15. And every community and every *shul* (synagogue) had people living in there. And people were living in the street.

Irving M. also described his family's crowded living situation:

We got an apartment. It was the . . . the room was 7 feet by 24. It was a converted from a store. It just to be a little store, a grocery store, but the store was no more a store and it was on Elektoralna Street. We moved in . . . there was one large bed, so I and my sisters and my father slept in one bed. And it was like on the floor was my grandparents, my mother, and a aunt stayed with us too. She was sleeping sitting up. We used to joke that she's a . . . a sitter sleeper.

Living in such close quarters, and with insufficient water and bath facilities, hygiene was difficult to maintain; ultimately, disease became widespread. Typhus, a disease spread by lice, was a particular problem. Wladyslaw Szpilman's memoirs about life in the Ghetto[17] described how his mother met him nightly "with a bowl of spirits and pair of pincers" to remove and destroy lice that he picked up during the day (1999: 18–19), while Janina Bauman, who was confined to the Ghetto with her family as a teenager, wrote, "Physical contact with strangers was what we tried most to avoid . . . The homeless, tattered, undernourished people we brushed against in the streets were covered with lice and often suffered from infectious diseases" (1986: 40).

Hunger was widespread as well. People could not take much with them when they relocated to the Ghetto; further, once confined to the Ghetto many were cut off from their jobs and traditional ways of earning a living. Therefore, most Ghetto residents had quite limited means. While there were official food rations, these were woefully inadequate, estimated at less than 300 calories per day (Kurzman 1993: 23). Even wealthy Jews who managed to bring some currency and valuables to the Ghetto found it difficult to buy food, given the Ghetto's isolation. Writing on November 19, 1940—three days after the Ghetto was sealed—Emmanuel Ringelblum described the situation:

[It] was terrible . . . Jewish women found the markets outside the Ghetto closed to them. There was an immediate shortage of bread and other produce. There's been a real orgy of high prices ever since. There are long queues in front of every food store, and everything is being bought up. (Sloan 1958: 86)

With time, hunger grew even worse. It became typical to see starving people lying in the street; as Sol R. remembered, "There's a lot of Jewish people been suffering in ghetto. The streets were full with dead people, starving. The belly were swollen, lay in the ditches. Nobody would pick them up." The sight of corpses, often naked or covered with paper because their clothing was more valuable to their surviving relatives, became commonplace:

Michael V.:
At that time we were really starving. Ah, we used to eat only soup, which was water and maybe a couple of potatoes. And, ah, when I used to eat the soup, after I finished, I used to lick the bowl, just like a dog. And, ah my mother got very skinny. My father was very skinny. We all were skinny. We were sleeping late, so we wouldn't have to eat, so we weren't hungry. And we used to go to bed early. And, if you went outside, all you could see is people starving to death right in front of you. All the streets in Warsaw were full of corpses, dead people who were dying from hunger. And they would put paper over them, and bricks, a couple of bricks, the corners of the paper. And they couldn't pick them up fast enough, to bury them.

Beggars were everywhere. Desperate for food, some people became *khappers* or "snatchers" who grabbed food away from others on the street and ate it before they could be caught (Gutman 1982; Kurzman 1993).

Abraham M.:
To get a loaf of bread you had to stay all night long in a line to barely . . . to get the money if you could get a loaf of bread. There were times that . . . even myself, at one time I was so hungry that I saw somebody take—getting a loaf of bread . . . [sighs] and young kids . . . it was a woman, she got a loaf of bread from the bakery. And as she walked away, she didn't realize that she should have put it right away under shirt, she kept on . . . she hauled it and she walked away. And there was a bunch of kids jumped on her and got the bread out of her. It's just like animals in the wild . . . When you're hungry nothing matters. And we . . . and I was one of them that jumped on that woman to take a piece of bread away from her. And if I got two bites out of it, it was a lot of it. But when you're hungry you can't help it.

Others turned to smuggling[18] to obtain food. Adult smugglers typically bribed guards at the Ghetto gates or threw goods over the wall, but small children were also adept at smuggling because they could fit through small holes in the Ghetto walls.[19] Larry L. was a food smuggler as a child:

> I would sneak out of the ghetto as a kid, through holes in the wall. And I was just like ten years of age. Usually take some clothing, or linen, or something my parents gave me. And I would go out and sell it to the Poles, and then . . . or trade it for potatoes, or carrots, and put it in my shirt, and then smuggle back through the holes, into the ghetto.

Such activity was extremely risky, however. Jack Klajman, who was a ten-year-old boy in Warsaw in 1941, described the actions of a Josef Blösche, a German guard known among Jews in the Ghetto as "Frankenstein":[20]

> He guarded the area in a jeep with a mounted machine gun. As children would climb the wall, Frankenstein and a German assistant would zoom in from out of nowhere on their killing machine . . . Once you were spotted there was no time to hide—it didn't matter whether you were in the process of climbing or just near the wall and getting ready. It took him only seconds from the time he eyed you until the moment he murdered you with a spray of bullets . . . If you were a smuggler, you were terrified of him. But you had no choice. You had to eat. (2000: 21–22)

Community Organization

Despite the crowding, disease, and starvation in the Ghetto, life was not entirely chaotic. In fact, there were various forms of community organization in place. Some of these were imposed by the Nazis themselves. In Warsaw and in ghettos throughout occupied Poland, Nazi authorities created *Judenraete*—Jewish Councils—that were charged with carrying out German orders (Gutman 1982: 36). Typically, leaders of the pre-war community, including religious and business leaders, were coerced into joining these bodies; in Warsaw, Adam Czerniakow, an assimilated Jew who was an engineer by trade, was installed as the Chairman of the *Judenrat*. Despite their official status these individuals had little autonomy and faced threats if they refused to comply with the demands of the German authorities. Such demands ranged from the collection of taxes to the provision of Jewish men for hard labor; notably, German officials pressed the Warsaw *Judenrat* to provide the capital as well as the labor to create the Ghetto wall.[21] The Warsaw *Judenrat* also oversaw the distribution of food, work permits, and living space. As a result, most of the community resented and mistrusted the *Judenrat*. The Nazis also decreed a Jewish police force, which operated as part of the *Judenrat*. This agency was particularly controversial, and, like the *Judenrat*, was disliked greatly by other Jews in the Ghetto. Jewish police did not carry weapons (save nightsticks) but acted authoritatively in the Ghetto, enforcing curfews, carrying out arrests, and, eventually, participating in the roundups and deportation of their fellow Jews to the death camps.

Sol R:
And the Jewish police . . . They was police, and they were wearing green bands on their head, they had a whistle, they bunch of *putzes* and a little stick. And they were like collaborators, I don't know, a bunch of *mamzers*. I used to have a lot of different scrimmages with them [laughter].

While these organizations were imposed by the occupiers, Jews in the Ghetto also organized themselves in various ways to provide needed community services. They held clandestine schools and religious services, which had to be done in secret because both were prohibited by Nazi decree. Political organizations also operated underground, sometimes using soup kitchens to hold secret meetings (Gutman 1982, 1994; Kurzman 1993; Zuckerman 1993: 44).

Vladka M.:
In the ghetto, in the Warsaw Ghetto itself, over 2,000 house committees were created by the Jews themselves . . . Illegal Jewish culture organization was created, and we, the young people, started to have seminars. I recall that . . . and later assigned to places to go after the curfew and to have lectures for the people of the houses, which were closed up. So I, a 16, 17 year old, went to such lecture, and I recall it was on Pawia 30 and I was talking about Peretz, about *Bontshe Shvayg*[22] at this particular lecture, and two young people, children, were outside, the windows were covered in case a German will come and knock to have time that we will be able to disperse.

Religious life also persisted, despite its illegality. Mordecai G. explained:

> Day in the ghetto was a hard time. You didn't know if you'll come back or
> whatever you go. It was very hard, but still there was a great friendship be-
> tween one and each other. We tried, you know, to be together to have serv-
> ices, to learn and so on. So when we had a service, my brother and I were the
> look out, you know, to see if somebody's coming, the Nazis are not coming.
> And we *davened* (prayed) in the basement.

Other community organizations provided "self-help," in the form of soup
kitchens and other vital services. Many of these predated the war, but
remained active in the Ghetto's early days; they included the National Society
for the Care of Orphans (CENTOS) and the Institution for Vocational
Guidance and Training (ORT). These were supported initially by funds from
the American Joint Distribution Committee;[23] they were later kept going, at
least for a while, by donations from relatively solvent Jews in the Ghetto when
contributions from the Joint fell off as America entered World War II. Each
apartment building also had a building council, which provided assistance
to needy families and helped represent residents to the *Judenrat* and other
authorities (Gutman 1982: 45). Those confined to the Ghetto could also still
receive mail from friends and family from the outside, at least until June 1941
(Gutman 1982: 112); for some, the mail brought desperately needed food and
money. Casimir B. was one of the lucky recipients of care packages from afar:

> Amazingly, even in that particular ghetto, that particular house [on Leszno
> Street], we were still receiving some subsistence packages. They were
> coming from the west, from the free world. Since then I found out my father
> was sending them.
> *What was in these packages?*
> Well, there were sprats, sardines, chocolate. Somehow, somewhere, I don't
> know how, my father managed to put in money in these packages. Till this
> day I don't know how he has done it, or who did it for him. We used to
> be very careful when we used to open a chocolate bar. There was a piece
> of . . . piece of money in it, either a $20 bill or something of that nature.
> A gold coin in a cocoa box or open a can of sardines, there was a gold
> ring . . . Never have I figured out how it got there. But I didn't care. But we
> ate the sprats and sardines and very careful to make sure that my mother

took out whatever . . . But then, towards . . . as the time progressed, nothing came through.

By May 30, 1941, an estimated fifty percent of the Jews in the Warsaw Ghetto were starving to death. In July 1941 there were 5500 deaths, compared with only 454 deaths among Warsaw's Jews in May 1938 (Ainsztein 1979: 2–3). People of all ages suffered from hunger, but there was an especially large number of children begging on the street. On December 21, 1941, Ghetto resident Emmanuel Ringelblum wrote:

> A terrifying, simply monstrous impression is made . . . [by] the wailing of children who . . . beg for alms or whine that they have nowhere to sleep. At the corner of Leszno and Karmelicka Streets, children weep bitterly at night. Although I hear this weeping every night, I cannot fall asleep until late. The couple of *groschen* (pennies) I give them nightly cannot ease my conscience. (Sloan 1958: 241; emphasis added)

Halina M., who worked as a waitress[24] in a café that served Germans and Poles of German descent, often had to pass starving children on her way to work:

> I started working in the café as a waitress. You have to be young, you have to be pretty, you have to be smart, and you have to be from a very good background, and with good manners, a good home, to get the job. More difficult than ministerial high job in . . . in England now, I assure you. Anyway, I got the job . . . but the . . . the worst part of ghetto life was me walking from . . . from small ghetto we lived in . . . from my small ghetto to my work in the big ghetto, there and back, when I was passing the streets. I'm not talking about the dead people covered with the newspapers in the morning because they were dead. But the children faces . . . you have to turn your head against those skeleton faces with those big eyes looking at you, staring at you. And then what do you do? How can you feed all those children, and the old people, and the old men, sitting, those skeletons? What do you do about it? If you still can, perhaps give a little, you should really. You should. And if you do, how far . . . you know it's useless, and you know it's . . . you can't everybody, and you know that it would last only a day, or two. And then you don't see those children two, three days after anymore. They're dead.

A Prevailing Sense of Hope

Despite these daily horrors, many Jews in the Warsaw Ghetto shared a sense of optimism, remaining hopeful that the Nazis would lose the war and that life would return to normal. Vladka M., for instance, noted how cultural activities in the Ghetto helped maintain some semblance of normalcy and hope:

> I still remember the atmosphere, the uplift that, in the ghetto, with so much starvation and the typhoid epidemic which started, and hunger and misery, we were talking about literature. And a young girl was talking to older people and they were listening and somehow it was . . . they thought, they hoped that this will pass. It is a time that will not remain forever. And this kind of hope was constantly in the life of the ghetto.

Others based their hopes on positive news about Nazi war defeats that occasionally filtered into the community. Chaim Kaplan's diary, a near daily account of his experiences in the Ghetto until his death in August 1942, repeatedly describes such hopes. On June 7, 1942, he wrote:

> The Nazi sword rests against our throats, wreaking havoc amongst us. But we were always a nation bound by hope—and so we shall remain . . . The English radio, whose listeners endanger their lives,[25] strengthens our hope . . . Every word gives us courage; every small detail that points to any military weakness is carried through the length and breadth of the ghetto as though on eagles' wings, with even children talking about it. When the news doesn't tell us what we want to hear, we twist and turn it until it seems full of hints, clues, and secrets that support our views . . . A stubborn people! (Katsh 1999: 347)

A well-known Ghetto adage—"Don't give up the bread card"—bespoke this optimism as well. As Abraham M. explained:

> And there was a . . . there was a word going around in Jewish . . . and I'm sure the people that will ever see that and understand, *gebn nesh u di boneh*, which it means don't give up your rational [sic] card because once you give up the . . . ration card you're dead. So try to live and don't give up your ration card.

Responding to Information from Afar

As these quotes suggest, Jews in the Warsaw Ghetto generally believed that they were subjects of a war-time occupation that, brutal as it was, would end at some point. This was especially true in the Ghetto's early days, when death camps had not yet been constructed and Germans were not yet implementing the "Final Solution." At that time, Jews in Warsaw could not know what their future held. As Boleslaw L. said:

> So it was a big tragedy in ghetto. It was terrible. Terrible. But people hoped that one day it will come to an end and we will be free, but nobody believed on that end [genocide]. Nobody. I . . . I . . . I personally don't remember that somebody talked about such end, that this can happen to us.

War-time deaths made sense, given food shortages and disease. Even cruelties against Jews and random killings could be understood as the product of a vicious occupying regime. However, the idea of actions explicitly designed to murder all Jews in a particular region was unimaginable. In June 1941, after Germany invaded the Soviet Union and began mass killings of Jews in newly conquered territories, both rumors and hard evidence of mass killings began to trickle into the Ghetto. However, many in Warsaw did not believe the reports—or did not believe that such killings could take place in their community. As Berysz A. explained, it was hard to accept the concept of genocide:

> That time nobody knew that the people go into the gas ovens, you understand, because it was hidden and there was no in and out and nobody knew. There was a gossip, you know, but nobody knew . . . They didn't understand . . . because the brains and the human nature could not understand it, you know . . . So, why I'm stressing this point is . . . That the Jewish people never could learn thing what was unexpectantly . . . you cannot learn from history what there never exist before.

Similarly, Joseph S. said:

> Basically, there we were, the ghetto. And then you begin to hear stories that so many Jews were executed. When I say "eastern Poland," I mean the part of Poland closest to Russia. That villages just disappeared and all you

heard was stories, because there was no such thing as getting on a train and going someplace. You heard of mass executions and stories. But the mass executions and the stories were so preposterous that you didn't believe it. I mean, you couldn't believe that 1,000 Jews in a little town were executed. I mean, it's a . . . it just didn't make any sense.

Elsewhere (Einwohner 2009) I have used the term "cultured ignorance" to refer to a group's inability to accept a horrible truth. "Ignorance" in this sense is non-judgmental, and simply means a lack of knowledge. Similarly, this "ignorance" does not imply some "deficit" in a group's culture. Instead, I call this lack of knowledge "cultured ignorance," following work on culture and cognition (Cerulo 2006; Clarke 2006), which examines how people use their accumulated experiences to interpret the cues from their environment in order to make sense of their surroundings. This research shows that it is hard for people even to imagine, much less accept, something that goes beyond the limits of their experiences. In the early 1940s in Nazi-occupied Europe, mass genocide against Jews was an unprecedented horror, so seemingly far-fetched that it could not be believed. As ŻOB leader Yitzhak Zuckerman wrote in his memoirs:

> If I had considered, even for a moment, what we hadn't seen in our worst nightmares, I would have thought: "Yitzhak Zuckerman, go to the mad-house!" Because you had to have a sick imagination to come to such conclusions. (1993: 72)

As time wore on, people's understanding of their situation began to change—but not as quickly as one might think. For instance, Warsaw Jews heard the news of massacres of Jews outside Vilna, the Lithuanian capital city 400 kilometers to the northeast, in the summer and fall of 1941. Still, they did not realize at first that all European Jews would eventually be targeted for death. For many, the news from Vilna did not seem to apply to Warsaw. Regions to the east were different, Warsaw reasoned; further, the Warsaw Ghetto was simply too big for all its inhabitants to be killed. Vladka M. noted:

> We in the underground heard that, for instance . . . there are vans where people are being gassed. But we didn't realize it. We thought groups of people. Even I didn't realize that it really is that people, whole cities and towns are being wiped out. I thought that it is in camps, in the beginning,

in resettlements in other ghettos, in other cities. And this was the main thought of the majority of the people in the Warsaw Ghetto. In the Warsaw Ghetto, people also thought that Warsaw is the capital, and it is open for the whole world, and there are embassies, and how can they do even the same thing in such a big city with so many Jews, a half a million Jews in the ghetto, what they are doing in a small town? So people didn't believe that it's really going and being deported to nowhere or being killed.

Similarly, Dawid Wdowinkski, who became a member of the ŻZW, explained:

People consoled themselves with the thought that the Eastern districts were recognized as Russian territory, but other laws prevailed in the General Government and that Jews in this part of Poland would therefore be saved. Many believed that it would be impossible to exterminate the half a million people of the Warsaw Ghetto . . . It was self-deceit, to be sure, but how could it have been otherwise? (1985: 53–54)

Thus, life in the Warsaw Ghetto went on. However, the events of late July 1942 changed everything.

Turning Point: The Great Deportation, July–September 1942

On July 22, 1942, German soldiers began mass deportations in the Warsaw Ghetto, sending several thousand Jews to the death camp Treblinka every day for a period of six weeks. *Judenrat* Head Adam Czerniakow had heard rumors of impending deportations and queried a number of German officials for confirmation but was assured that the rumors were without merit. Clearly, these assurances were false, and Czerniakow committed suicide on July 23, the second day of the roundups.[26] Kristine T., who, like Halina M., worked in a café in the Ghetto, saw him a few days before then:

And then I was working in the coffeehouse. And this is the incident, you know, I had. One day, in one corner of the table, were sitting a few gentlemen and talking. I could see that their faces were very serious and very sad. Among them was the president of the Judenrat, Czerniakow. And I remember serving him cup of tea. And maybe after three or four days he committed suicide. Sitting there, they probably discussed the orders, which German were issuing.

It is hard to overstate the shock and fear that overtook the Ghetto once the mass deportations began. Deportees were taken to the *Umschlagplatz*, the holding area adjacent to the railways in the northern part of the ghetto, where they were loaded onto cattle cars and, for the most part, never seen again. Between July and September 1942, more than 260,000 people were deported (Freilich and Dean 2012: 459). Joseph S. described what he saw:

> And every day, maybe for a month or a month-and-a-half, I saw those crowds going to the railroad stations. And that is the closest that I was to the railroad station, because I could hear the railroad whistle, and the rumbling of the cars in the background. Especially late in the evening. And you ... you saw ... you could see, as far as your eye can see, people, six, seven across, you know, just walking with their little knapsacks, carrying a suitcase.

Halina M. described the shock of the mass deportations:

> This deportation, this sort of finishing of . . . of the ghetto, of all of us, and so on, came like a bomb. There came like complete change, a complete cataclysm, because that ghetto life was in a . . . in a way, now, if you can call it normalized. But it was, in a way, with the death, and with hunger, and what was going on. But in a way it was bad. There were bad things going on and . . . and good things going on, and life was going on. Cabarets with . . . with songs, with, creation was . . . was going on, was . . . was people making with love affairs, with lives going on. But then, suddenly, it all stopped. Suddenly, there was end of it all. Here you are; you're going through this.

Falsely believing that one could avoid deportation simply by proving one's worth—i.e., as an able-bodied worker who could contribute to the German war effort by working in one of the Nazi-run Ghetto factories—many in the Ghetto scrambled to find employment. Ghetto resident Alexander Donat wrote, "Everyone in the Ghetto frantically set about getting papers to prove employment . . . Instead of saying 'Hello' or 'How are you?' people now greeted each other with 'Are you covered?'" (1978: 58). Vladka M. also described the mood at the time in her memoirs:

People exchanged reassuring words, perhaps seeking to delude themselves as much as to console one another. The clouds would yet disperse . . . It was necessary to find work, to obtain an employment card;
then, according to the German edict, one could be sure of being permitted to stay in the ghetto. The ghetto put its trust in the printed word;
workers would not be deported. Life might be hard, but still bearable.
(1979: 15)

Even among those without work permits, hope prevailed. Some held fast to
the thought that deportation simply meant relocation. This view was perpetuated by rumors as well as Nazi propaganda such as letters and postcards
from people saying they were sent to work camps—letters that victims were
forced to write before being put to death (Gutman 1982; Syrkin 1948). Halina
R. noted that her aunt voluntarily reported for deportation because she could
not take the pressures of ghetto life anymore; presumably, conditions would
be better wherever the trains would take her. Yet, there was the troubling reality of what was to become of those who could not work—such as children,
the sick, and the elderly.

Irving M. recalled the day Nazi soldiers took his younger sister away. He
ran to the *Umschlagplatz*, and found that people there did not understand
what was going on:

She was a baby yet. She must have been about nine to ten years old. Nine
years old. And she was gone. And I stood there and cried and chased
and everybody . . . some people . . . everybody had their own problems.
Everybody lost everything and they were sitting for transport to be
shipped. They didn't know where. There was nothing. Nobody knew exactly what . . . what's happening. And people have the imagination because
they have hopes, so everybody told you a different story. This transport
is going here, and this one to Białystok, which wasn't true, but they didn't
know any better.

How is it possible that, even with thousands of people being deported daily,
some Jews did not recognize that they were being targeted for mass murder?
As previously discussed, Nazi propaganda played a large role in shaping Jews'
persistent misunderstanding of the true meaning of the roundups. Notices
posted around the Ghetto promised bread and marmalade to those who went
to the *Umschlagplatz* for deportation, where trains would take them to work

camps. For starving Jews, reporting for relocation to a work camp—with bread and marmalade, no less—seemed preferable to staying in the Ghetto.

Sol R.:
And then, 1942, September, August, it really got tough. Then when they start and evacuating the Jews, relocating the people, tell them to send them away somewhere. And we believed it. I did too. My parents too.
You believed that people were being sent where?
I believed that they're going to relocate us, send us to factories, working. I really did believe that. There had been rumors going on, they're doing bad on the Russian front, and all that. They need workers and they're going to send all the people . . . relocate them . . . you know, everybody.

Casimir B.:
And all I remember just this gathering on the *Umschlagplatz* was called, where the Jews were being herded like cattle. I remember seeing it, and the people being packed in these cattle cars, screaming and crying and being hit by whips and bayoneted. It was not far from where I lived, staying . . . the *Umschlagplatz* was nearby . . . Of course the German propaganda was that they're going to take us to a labor camp, they're going to give us a piece of bread and we're going to go work and everybody's going to be fine. So . . .
What did you personally think was happening?
All I remember is crying. I didn't want to go. But I told my mother, "If you go, I go." I just didn't want to leave my mother. There was some debate whether my mother should go because there was some part of it that . . . my mother began to believe that maybe the German propaganda is true, maybe . . . no matter where we go, maybe it would be better than where we are. They will give us some help, they'll give us some bread, they'll give us some food.

While the true meaning of the deportations may have been unclear to many at first, as the *aktion* (round up) progressed, hopes for survival dimmed, even for the able-bodied workers. Kaplan's diary entry of August 2, 1942 began, "Jewish Warsaw is in its death throes. A whole community is going to its death!" (1999: 396).

On August 5, 1942, a particularly heartbreaking scene played out in the Ghetto. A slim man, bald and bespectacled with a trim beard and mustache, walked slowly through the Ghetto on his way to the *Umschlagplatz*. He was part of a small caravan of people, mostly children, who held hands as they made their way to the trains. The man was none other than Dr. Janusz Korczak, a renowned Warsaw pediatrician, author, and children's advocate who ran an orphanage in the Ghetto; the children were his young charges. Dr. Korczak was deported, along with the children and staff from his orphanage. Famously, he refused several offers of help to escape, insisting on accompanying the children on their journey so that they would not be frightened. Rena Z. was one of many eyewitnesses to his deportation:

> I saw Dr. Janusz Korczak walking with the children to the *Umschlagplatz*. And this was a scene what I will never forget. He had four children in his hands, two in each hand and two under the arms, six children, and the rest follow him. It was something unbelievable. I can tell you . . . whenever I remind myself, today it breaks my heart, how this Dr. Korczak went with those children to the *Umschlagplatz*.

Alexander Donat pointed to Korczak's deportation as clear evidence that everyone in the Ghetto would eventually be killed:

> Why had the *Judenrat* tried to save Korczak? If the two hundred children were really going to be resettled somewhere in the East, wasn't it perfectly natural for their teacher and shepherd to go along with them? What we had suspected all along—but could not or did not want to believe—was now confirmed . . . This was not resettlement; this was deportation to death. (1978: 71)

The Assessment of Threat

Warsaw's Jews did not resist collectively during the Great Deportation in the summer of 1942. As Joseph S. explained:

> There was very little resistance, you know, because what resistance could you . . . people were numb. They didn't know what was going on. They just went. And it's beyond me now, as an adult, and this has always plagued me, that there was no resistance.

Joseph S.'s words echo the usual discussions about Jewish resistance: why didn't the Jews resist? His answer is telling. As the survivors themselves note, when the Great Deportation began, many Jews in the Warsaw Ghetto did not realize what was happening. They did not understand that they, and all others like them, were being sent away to their deaths as part of a mass genocidal undertaking.

Yet, while individuals may not have initially understood the terrible fate that awaited those who were deported from the Ghetto, after six weeks' worth of forced removal, shootings, and other atrocities, the message was clear to those who were lucky enough to evade the roundups. The story of the Warsaw Ghetto is marked by this event: the Great Deportation changed the remaining Jews' assessment of their situation. This change was critical to the emergence of resistance.

As the testimonies show, before the onset of the roundups, many people in the Warsaw Ghetto believed that survival was possible. That is not to say that survival was easy. To survive, one needed to find employment, and enough food and shelter to live—difficult tasks, fraught with uncertainty and danger. Certainly, some people in the Ghetto believed that they would succumb to hunger and illness, as illustrated by Kristine T.'s testimony:

Some people who lost faith that they will survive, they were going, you know, very quickly. Very quickly. For instance, my husband had a cousin. He was a brilliant man. He was a lawyer. He played beautiful piano. And I remember, he came to us and he said, "It's the end." And in a few days' time he was gone. You know, people who had belief that they can survive, they very often survived. But the people who . . . and that was very difficult, to believe in the survival in the conditions like that.

Still, before the Great Deportation, many Jews in the Warsaw Ghetto assessed their situation as one that was life-threatening, but potentially survivable. This assessment of threat—the answer to the question, "What will happen if we don't act?"—had implications for resistance. As long as survival was a matter of enduring the ghetto conditions, dire as they were, until Germany lost the war, collective resistance was unnecessary at best, and life-threatening at worst (Ainsztein 1979). In his memoirs, Stanislaw Adler, a member of the Jewish Ghetto police, wrote:

The Jewish population had two choices: to engage in a heroic fight irrespective of the outcome and without any chance for even partial success, or to engage in a terrible race with time, a race which seemed to give some hope of survival. The kind of heroism required by the first choice *nobody* in the whole world would attempt as long as one spark of hope existed that they could last out. The overwhelming majority was overcome with an immense desire not so much to endure to the end of the war as to see with their own eyes the Nazis collapse. The community as a whole ardently and fanatically believed that this would happen though no logic could justify such a belief . . . Therefore, this community, whose pre-war condition had compelled them to constant compromises and deprivations, persisted in their will to outlive this trial. (1982: 80; emphasis in original)

On the other side of the wall, though, at least some people understood the enormity of what was happening. Xenia S., who was living on the Aryan side with the assistance of Polish friends, in an apartment overlooking the Ghetto, said:

The Germans in uniform would start kicking and beating people. I remember I saw one . . . this is when that wall was still showed the people walking. There was a crowd of people running and there was a small child with the people, with the Jewish people running, and a German was herding them and, the child fell down and he just grabbed that child by the ankles and threw him against the wall.
What were the others doing at this time?
They were running.
And what about . . .
Because they were being rounded . . . they are being rounded up for the trains.
Did you . . . did you know where the trains were going?
No. They told us . . . they . . . okay, by that time we knew they were going to a extermination camps, but there were several possibilities. I mean, this was . . . this was the time when Auschwitz was going full, full blast, and so was Treblinka. So we guessed that the trains were going to Auschwitz or Treblinka.
What did you know or what did you hear about Treblinka or Auschwitz?
That people never came back from there.
Did you believe it?
Yes.

As the Great Deportation wore on, those who remained in the Ghetto came to realize what Xenia S. knew: that they would all eventually be taken away to their deaths. Moreover, they came to believe that they could not survive these circumstances—that there was no way to protect themselves, no place to escape. Not only was this interpretation—shaped by the sequence of events in the Ghetto and marked by the Great Deportation—a drastic change in the Warsaw Ghetto residents' understanding of their situation, but this new assessment of threat was a *critical conclusion*, one that was necessary before resistance could emerge.

The Critical Conclusion of Hopelessness

Before the mass roundups began, Ghetto residents were focused completely on day-to-day survival, and would hardly have begun planning for armed resistance when life was such a struggle; the way to survive was to secure food, shelter, and safety for oneself and one's family, not to take up arms against one of the strongest armies in the world. Even those who were oriented toward radical collective action—notably, the young activists in the Ghetto, representing a variety of youth movements—busied themselves with the ideologically driven work of their movements, rather than calling for armed resistance against the Germans. Zivia Lubetkin, the HeHalutz activist, explained that at the beginning of the Ghetto, her movement was focused entirely on work with youth, most of which consisted of seminars and sharing educational materials to prepare youth to join *kibbutzim* in Palestine; anti-Nazi activism was never their goal.[27] Describing life early in the Ghetto, she wrote (1981: 36):

> Despite the cruel restrictions and prohibitions, there was still a feeling in our hearts that "We will outlive our persecutors! We will not allow them to overcome us!" We felt that we would lose many to the Germans, to starvation and disease, but most of us would remain alive. Therefore our role was to ensure that the survivors, particularly the youth, would remain healthy in mind and body so that they could carry on their duties after the war.

However, by showing those who remained in the Ghetto (activists and non-activists alike) that all Jews were targeted for death, the Great Deportation

changed everything. Now believing that they had no chance to survive, Warsaw Jews had to respond differently to the Nazi threat. Henry
L. explained:

> My mother was deported in 1942 . . . and later, we heard already the rumors,
> what . . . in Treblinka, exactly what was going on. I didn't know . . . we only
> know they are not going to come back, they are probably going to be mur-
> dered. Some people who were bigger than I probably knew . . . Now, the
> group which I belonged, like all the other groups who worked outside, we
> were already organized. Most of them belonged to Zionist organizations.
> Others belonged to other democratic or socialist movements . . . politically
> motivated to resist. We had already the desire to do something, you know,
> to . . . because we knew we had nothing to lose. When we knew that our
> family was deported, we organized, or we started organizing.

Yet although the realization of genocide was critical to the eventual calls
for revolt, resistance itself was not a foregone conclusion. After the onset
of the Great Deportation, a debate within the Ghetto ensued: what was the
best course of action? Young activists called for armed resistance, speaking
passionately about the need to fight back against the Germans. However, it
was difficult to get other segments of the Ghetto community to recognize
the threat, much less resist against it. Others believed that resistance was too
risky and could make the Jews' situation even worse by increasing Nazi repression. At a community meeting on July 24, 1942, two days after the mass
deportations began, Hirsch Berlinksi, a member of the youth organization
Left Poa'lei Zion, argued for resistance:

> In one way or another, deportation means annihilation. It is therefore better
> to die with dignity and not like hunted animals. There is no other way out,
> all that remains to us is to fight . . . We realize that our armament compared
> with that of the enemy reminds one of a fly facing an elephant. But we have
> no alternative—annihilation faces us in one form or another. (quoted in
> Ainsztein 1979: 36)

Older Ghetto leaders disagreed. Dr. Isaac Schipper, an historian and Zionist
leader, said, "To defend ourselves is tantamount to bringing annihilation
upon the ghetto," while Rabbi Zysie Frydman, the leader of the Orthodox
group Agudath Israel, said further:

I believe in God and I believe that a miracle will take place. The Lord will not allow His people to be annihilated. We must wait, we must wait for a miracle. To fight the Germans does not make sense. The Germans will wipe us out in a couple of days . . . Dear friends, persevere and have faith and we shall be rescued! (quoted in Ainsztein 1979: 37).

Although the views of the Ghetto elders prevailed at that meeting, as the *aktion* continued throughout the summer more people began to support views like Berlinski's. With first-hand evidence of the German authorities' plans either to kill outright or forcibly deport Jews from the Ghetto—not just the old, the young, and the sick, but also able-bodied adults who, presumably, could contribute to the German war effort—plans for action gained support.

The young activists had actually been interested in resistance much earlier, after receiving the news about the mass killings of Jews at Ponar, a wooded area near Lithuania's capital city of Vilna, in the summer and fall of 1941. As noted earlier, many Jews in Warsaw who heard this news dismissed it. In contrast, the activist youth found it credible—and, importantly, realized that similar killings could take place in Warsaw. Zivia Lubetkin wrote, "Our feeling was that Vilna was the beginning of total annihilation" (1981: 85).[28] Similarly, Zivia's comrade and eventual husband, ŻOB leader Yitzhak Zuckerman, a Vilna native himself, recalled:

The harsh crisis in our group erupted at the end of 1941, not because of anything the Germans did in Warsaw, but because of the news from Vilna, and later, from Chelmno,[29] which shocked us. I think I was paralyzed when I heard. In 1942, I was on the brink of madness. (1993: 95)

As a result of the news from Vilna, Zivia and Yitzhak's Dror/Frayhayt movement began spreading the word about the killings, in meetings and through a newly created underground newspaper, *Yediyes* ("News").[30] They also attempted, along with other activists, to mobilize political organizations in the Ghetto into an armed resistance force. Some organizations joined their coalition, but the Bund (the Jewish Worker's Union) refused to do so, due to differences in political ideology.[31] However, because the Bund had important ties to the Polish Socialist underground, it was seen as an organization crucial to the nascent Jewish resistance coalition; with the Bund's participation, Jewish resisters hoped to gain recognition, as well as material support, from Polish groups (Zuckerman

1993: 169). The Bund's unwillingness to participate initially harmed efforts to create resistance organizations. Another blow came on April 17, 1942, when Germans killed fifty-two Jews in the Ghetto as part of an effort to terrorize the underground and put a halt to the underground newspapers. While the newspapers continued, these events did force activists like Zivia and Yitzhak (the latter of whom was targeted on April 17, what became known as the "Bloody Night") to be more cautious, and put a damper on their efforts (Gutman 1982; Zuckerman 1993). Yet, the onset of the Great Deportation renewed their calls for resistance, despite the dangers and difficulties involved.

The Emergence of Resistance

By the end of September 1942, two organizations dedicated to armed resistance in the Warsaw Ghetto had emerged: the ŻOB and the ŻZW. Each formed from the Ghetto's network of activist youth. Activists from a variety of youth groups on the political left such as HaShomer HaTzair, Dror, and, eventually, the Bund, joined the ŻOB (see Zuckerman 1993: xvii–xviii for a description of these and other organizations), while the right-wing Betarim youth of the Revisionist Movement established the ŻZW (Wdowinski 1985).

The timing of the creation of these organizations is instructive and helps illustrate the role of the Great Deportation and the changing assessments of threat among people in the Ghetto. The ŻOB was formed at an activist meeting on July 28, 1942, at the end of the first week of the Great Deportation, during which the youth discussed how to respond to the roundups. Some at the meeting talked about trying to save as many people as possible by arranging for their safe passage out of the Ghetto. Zivia Lubetkin, who was present, recounted:

> We rejected this idea. How many Jews can we save that way? Very few. Is there any point in trying to those few when millions are dying? No, we all share the same fate and it is our duty to stay with our people until the very end. We must try once again to organize a resistance. *It was absolutely clear to us that time that if we did nothing, the entire Jewish community of Poland would be murdered without having uttered a cry of protest* . . . (1981: 111–112; emphasis added)

Zivia's words illustrate assessments of threat. Eventually, both groups decided to prepare for armed resistance against the Nazis and embarked upon the difficult task of obtaining weapons.

Importantly, activists reached the decision to stage armed resistance without the resources necessary to carry out such action. In fact, as of July 28, 1942, the ŻOB only had two pistols.[32] Their decision to act flies in the face of dominant theories of social movements and collective action, such as resource mobilization theory. So how did the fighters prepare for resistance?

The Ghetto was a confined, restrictive place; of necessity, all guns and ammunition had to be purchased from the outside and smuggled in. Those activists who could pass as Gentiles slipped out of the Ghetto to try to obtain arms, while those who could not leave safely stayed behind to plan and train for armed resistance. Vladka M. headed to the Aryan side:

> We didn't have any arms. I belonged to the first group of the so-called fighters' organization [ŻOB]. We didn't have any arms at that time. It was a need to get arm. It was a need to prepare ourselves . . . they turned to me, it was the Bundist youth group, that because I look like a Polish girl, there are a few others on the other side of the wall, or the other side of the ghetto wall, to get out and to work in the underground on the Polish side to try to prepare to buy on the black market guns . . . whatever it's possible. And also to prepare some hiding places for children, if it's possible there to find out. And this is how I got out of the ghetto.

Vladka M.'s job, and that of other activists working beyond the Ghetto walls, was immensely difficult, for a number of reasons. First and foremost, weapons were costly. In addition to the monetary cost of the weapon itself—Ghetto fighters had to pay three times the going rate for arms because of the risks that Polish arms smugglers took if caught helping Jews[33]—there was the cost of bribing Ghetto guards to allow safe passage back and forth over the wall. These financial expenditures were exacerbated by the human costs, in terms of the fear and danger involved in weapons smuggling. Vladka M. described one of many harrowing experiences smuggling dynamite into the Ghetto:

> And it was a ladder put at the wall of one side on the Polish side of the . . . on the ghetto wall. And I was at that time already I talked . . . to mine group people, to the youth, where I am going to smuggle in. And

this were packages of 5 kilo dynamite put in, in greasy paper to look like I am smuggling butter. Usually the smugglers paid a certain amount of money, the foreman and he was staying near the ladder, and they gave him the money, went up the ladder on the other side and jumped on the other side of the wall into the ghetto. And the smuggler was going on and it was my next, and I gave also the money the foreman and I went up with mine package . . . while I was on top of the wall, shooting started. And I was on top and shooting started to come closer. The foreman snatched away the ladder and I was not able . . . not to go back to the Polish side and I didn't see anybody on the Jewish side. And I was afraid to jump, not knowing too much about dynamite, that maybe this could explode . . . So I was on top and the shooting came closer and I was sure that I am done. But suddenly the two people who were waiting for me saw me there on top and they made a human ladder from the ghetto side and brought me down, and we run away just in time.

Not only was the act of smuggling dangerous, but even when on the Aryan side, far away from the wall, activists were at great risk: any Jew caught outside the Ghetto could be put to death. Resistance fighters working outside the Ghetto were particularly fearful of blackmailers (*shmaltsovniks*) who extorted fees from Jews in exchange for not turning them in to the Gestapo (Rotem 1994; Zuckerman 1993). These blackmailers targeted anyone whom they suspected of being Jewish. Irene I. was not a resistance fighter but escaped to the Aryan side after her mother died of pneumonia in the Ghetto. She too was subjected to extortion:

Once . . . once on the street, somebody approached me, you know, "You are Jewish" and so on. He wanted money. I didn't have money. I gave him a ring.
How did he know you were Jewish?
Black hair, black eyes, I don't know?
So didn't you just deny it? If you gave him a ring . . .
I was so scared, I couldn't.
Really? I mean, that was more or less admitting it, wasn't it, by giving him a ring?
Yeah. Yeah.
You must have been frightened after that.
Frightened like hell.

Larry L., who fled the Ghetto for the Aryan side in 1942 and resorted to stealing food to survive, described similar experiences:

> I met Polish kids, bad kids, thieves, and street kids, and whoever. I would hang around with them. And they knew that I am Jewish. And obviously, I befriended them. So they kind of didn't like the Jews, but still tolerated me to some . . . some way. Because I was stealing with them. When the train would come, the farmers would come with bags, and baskets with bread, and eggs, and apples, fruit . . . And I would steal from the basket, picked like hand—what you call, a pocket-picking, you know . . . Those kids, they, even though they were bad and they hate Jews and all this, they tolerated me, as I said. But every once in a while, their joke on me was holding me against the wall, and saying, "Go to the policeman and tell him that we have here a Jew." This was the . . . because a Jew was a fugitive from the law, to be shot immediately, you know, to be caught on the Polish side. And they would go over to a Polish policeman on the corner, across, and ask him what time it is, you know, or something, then came back, "He's coming right away to pick you up." And this was the joke. In the meantime, I was dying inside.

Given the dangers on the other side of the wall, resistance fighters needed to conceal their Jewish identity at all costs. Yet while the armbands that Jews were forced to wear could be removed easily, other identity markers were harder to hide. In the context of Nazi-occupied Eastern Europe, certain facial features, eye color, and hair texture were stereotypically associated with Jewishness. Further, because Yiddish was the first language of most Jews in Poland at that time, having poor Polish language skills and/or speaking Polish with a Yiddish accent identified Jews as well (Engelking 2001; Gutman 1982; Rotem 1994). Boleslaw L. explained:

> The Poles, they know who is a Jew and who is not a Jew, because every fourth person was Jewish in Warsaw, they know the Jews exactly. It was easier to survive among Germans than among Poles. They know even a Jew how he walk. A Jew opened his mouth, they know right away.

Resistance fighters working on the Aryan side therefore had to look, and sound, as if they were not Jewish. Beyond their appearance and language skills, these activists performed the "identity work"[34] of masking their Jewishness in a number of ways, such as obtaining forged identification

papers and assuming Polish, non-Jewish names and nicknames. For instance, Vladka M.'s real first name was Feigele; "Vladka" was a nickname
for her assumed name of Wladyslawa Kowalska. Similarly, ŻOB activists
Simha Rotem, Arieh Wilner, Yitzhak Zuckerman, and Tovye Shaingut went
by Polish nicknames "Kazik," "Jurek," "Antek," and "Tadek," respectively
(Meed 1979; Rotem 1994; Zuckerman 1993). Yet, a new name and identity
card meant nothing without the ability to pass as a Pole. To pass successfully,
Jewish resistance fighters on the Aryan side also had to demonstrate cultural capabilities that a Polish person would embody—including the ability
to perform the rites and practices of Catholicism, Poland's dominant religion. Irving M., who smuggled food into the Ghetto as a child, was the lucky
beneficiary of a kind-hearted Polish woman who taught him how to recite
some Catholic prayers. He described an exchange he had with another Polish
woman while attempting to pass as a Gentile on the Aryan side:

> "So, by the way, are you Jewish?" I said to her, "No! What makes you think?"
> "Can you pray?" So I start praying. She says to me, "You don't . . . you don't
> sound . . . it doesn't sound . . . it sounds funny." I . . . she went out and I was
> afraid she might go for the police and whatever. I picked myself up and
> escaped.

Passing was difficult for both Jewish women and men, but men faced a
particular challenge: while all Jewish men were circumcised, this practice
was not shared by most other religious and ethnic groups in Europe at the
time. A Jewish man's identity was therefore easily revealed in a strip search.
Simha ("Kazik") Rotem, a ŻOB fighter who worked on both sides of the wall,
described a close call with his Polish landlady on the Aryan side:

> One evening as I returned home, the landlady asked me, "Are you really
> a Pole? I think you're also a Jew." She looked at me obliquely. I burst out
> laughing and replied on the spot, "I'm willing to prove it to you, madam."
> She said, "Please, sir, prove it!" I unbuckled my belt, unbuttoned my fly,
> and pulled down my pants; when I was down to my underwear, she turned
> around and walked out. This was the kind of "existential problem" you came
> across on a normal day; it was not unique at all. (1994: 85)

Kazik's tale illustrates another performative strategy used by activists, one
that shows a connection between identity and emotion for Jews on the Aryan

side. Had his landlady called his bluff, Kazik's Jewishness would have been clear; apparently, his confidence (as evidenced by his burst of laughter, lack of hesitation, and willingness to expose his body) was sufficient to maintain his cover. More broadly, a lack of fear helped maintain the illusion that he was a Gentile. The converse was also true: public displays of fear—especially during everyday activities, which no non-Jewish Pole should have feared—were visible indicators of one's Jewishness. As Vladka M. explained (1979: 194):

> "Your eyes give you away," our Gentile friends would tell us. "Make them look livelier, merrier. You won't attract so much attention then." But our eyes kept constantly watching, searching the shadows ahead, glancing quickly behind, seeing our own misfortune and foreseeing even worse to come. Haunted by fear of betrayal, our eyes betrayed us and this knowledge only increased our fear.

Like fear, sadness was another emotion that could reveal Jewishness and had to be managed carefully on the Aryan side. In fact, the ŻOB explicitly forbade fighters from crying in public. Working in pairs was one strategy for managing sadness; for example, ŻOB courier Adina Szwajger (1990: 83) noted that it was important for her to be with another young woman at all times when in public, for "if one of us went out alone, she might forget herself, and have 'sad eyes,' eyes that betrayed the pain within."

Paying for Weapons

Above and beyond the costly identity work on the Aryan side, weapons cost money. To raise the necessary funds, resistance fighters turned to those few remaining Ghetto residents who were known to still have money and valuables. By late 1942, the people who had such resources were mostly smugglers who had profited from the Ghetto's isolation and members of the Jewish police who had availed themselves of valuables left behind by those Jews they helped deport (Kurzman 1993; Rotem 1994; Szereszewska 1997). While some of these individuals voluntarily donated money to the resistance efforts, others did not; in such cases, ŻOB and ŻZW members exacted taxes and used force to get the desperately needed funds. Sol L. witnessed one such "expropriation," as the ŻOB called it (Rotem 1994; Zuckerman 1993):

About three or four people from the Underground comes into my . . . they ring the bell, come into my uncle's place and they say, "You Yisroel Grauman?" "Yeah. Yisroel Grauman." . . . They were asking for some money to buy weapons, because my uncle was considered a rich man, in the ghetto. No, he wouldn't give them any money. They took one son, the middle one . . . They blindfolded him, took him away for two weeks . . . Anyway, he [my uncle] gave them some money.

ŻOB fighter Tuvia Borzykowski also wrote in his memoirs (1976: 38):

Our enforcement bodies were particularly severe towards members of the Jewish police, whom we taxed extra heavily. The policemen were among the richest Jews in the ghetto because they appropriated much property left by Jews who fell victim to the German extermination actions. Many were arrested for not responding to the demands of the tax collectors; there was even one case when a Jewish policeman was shot when resisting fighters who came to collect money.

Yet while the expropriations generated some cash and valuables, weapons were still expensive and difficult to obtain. Members of the Polish Underground, who were themselves mobilizing for resistance against the Nazis, were largely unwilling to sell weapons to Jews, due to the Underground's lack of confidence in Jews as fighters.[35] To supplement the small volume of arms that they were able to purchase on the black market, Jewish resistance fighters turned to what they could fashion from the materials at hand in the Ghetto, including pipe bombs, Molotov cocktails, and light bulbs filled with acid. Berysz A., who fought in the Ghetto as part of the ŻOB, described taking materials from empty houses to build small explosives:

So, we didn't have enough money. But we had people who used to be genius, used to be . . . people who used to study before the war chemical things. And they knew how to make, what do you call it, material . . . in Polish it called *materiały wubochowe*. Material where they can . . .
Explosives? Explosives?
Yeah, to make grenades. To make grenades. So what we did, we went . . . every organization sent out people and cut off all the pipes from the building, you know. More or less, not the very big pipe, but the minimum pipe . . . we cut them into pieces, that it . . . let me say, 10 inch or so, or 15 inches . . . We

put a . . . we put a cover under the . . . we put the material . . . the material was a can . . . we tried to find any pieces of material to put inside, nails, screws . . . now I'm just . . . it's a fact of life. We made grenades because we couldn't supply enough with . . . was very expensive in that time. Any Polish person who wants to sell a gun or something, it was so expensive that you . . . we didn't have enough money to buy.

By January 1943, the ŻOB had obtained only a few grenades and a few dozen pistols (Ainsztein 1979).[36] After the Jews' brief battles with Nazi soldiers in the January Uprising, the Polish Underground was more willing to sell arms to the Jewish fighters because the Jews had demonstrated that could indeed fight back (Zuckerman 1993: 292; see also Lubetkin 1981: 164–165). By the start of the April Uprising, each ŻOB fighter had a pistol and a few home-made hand grenades, while the ŻZW had pistols and grenades as well as twenty-one submachine guns, eight machine guns, and eight rifles (Ainsztein 1979: 97–98; Gutman 1982: 344, 348). Given the conditions under which they were amassed, these arsenals were impressive; still, they were hardly enough for the Ghetto Jews to fight effectively against the much better armed German soldiers. As Syrkin remarks (1948: 203), "The Jewish fighters were rich only in daring and the readiness to sell their lives dearly."

Spreading the Word

The activist youth had reached the critical conclusion that the Ghetto was unsurvivable even before the Great Deportation, after hearing about massacres in Vilna. However, they recognized that resistance depended on their ability to help others reach this same conclusion. Zivia Lubetkin wrote:

> We knew very well that our greatest enemy was the false hope [for survival], the great illusion, which we would have to destroy through our movement newspaper and personal contact. We would have to tell people the truth. (1981: 92)

To do so, the activists had to counteract the prevailing belief that work would save lives, as fomented by the Nazi propaganda claiming that deportees would be given food and resettled to work camps, and convince the community that deportation led to death. Both the ŻOB and the ŻZW posted signs in the Ghetto streets calling on Jews to resist or hide, rather than go to the *Umschlagplatz* willingly. Berysz A. was one of the activists who produced the signs:

> Firstly, we made literatures, we printed leaflets and we called out to the people that go on that train, don't go out to the . . . don't yell out to the work to work for the . . . they say you're going to work for the army, this is a . . . to make people not to get people tricked, because not everybody believed it yet. We didn't have a printing machine. We had some sort of little printer what you could print a few words. Secondly, we made some lectures, we call people to come to lecture and explain it to them.

Signs posted in the Ghetto were a start, but the young activists also knew that to convince the community to heed their calls for resistance, they would have to do more establish their authority. Adam Czerniakow's suicide at the beginning of the Great Deportation created a leadership vacuum, but young activists did not yet have enough standing for the rest of the community to follow them. Jack S. recalled the first days of the roundups:

> Everybody was busy with themselves, how to get . . . how to survive day by day. Who was in charge? Nobody was . . . everybody was in charge and everybody was not in charge at that time. It was all mixed up already.

To establish their authority, the youth also had to demonstrate that Jews did have the power to fight back. They did so by targeting the Jewish police who were facilitating the roundups. The first attack was on Josef Szerynski,[37] the Chief of the Jewish Police in the Ghetto. He was shot and wounded on August 20, 1942, by, of all people, a former member of the Jewish Police: ŻOB member Israel Kanal, who had resigned from the police force earlier in the Great Deportation. After the attack, the ŻOB posted announcements taking credit for the assassination attempt. Interestingly, the Ghetto community believed instead that a Gentile carried out the attack, because they did not think that Jews had guns.[38] However, additional attacks and announcements helped the resistance fighters demonstrate their capabilities. Another attack, this one successful, was carried out against Jakub Lejkin, Szerynski's deputy and replacement. Lejkin was assassinated by three members of HaShomer HaTzair (which became part of the ŻOB) on October 29, 1942. The ŻOB posted the following announcement the next day:

ANNOUNCEMENT

It is hereby made publicly known that as a result of the indictment of the directorship, officers and functionaries of the Jewish Order Service [Jewish Police] in Warsaw, about which notice had been given in the announcement of 17.8, the sentence passed on *Jakub Lejkin* was carried out on 29.10 at 6.10 p.m.

Further drastic measures will be applied with the utmost severity.

(quoted in Kermish 1986: 588; emphases in original)

Other assassinations followed. Tuvia Borzykowski wrote:

The first bullets were fired at Jews who sold out to the enemy. Thus our people executed the commandant of the ghetto police, Laikin, and the liaison man between the Judenrat and the Gestapo, Fuerst.[39] After the executions were carried out, the Jewish Fighting Organization publicly announced that its members did away with traitors . . . The Jewish community realized that a new force had arisen in the ghetto, taking upon itself the burden of leadership. (1976: 20)

Still, not everyone in the Ghetto accepted the resistance organizations' authority at first. Ghetto resident Helena Szereszewska was one skeptic:

One morning we were shattered to hear that the Jewish Council's safe had been raided. Melamud,[40] the Council's cashier, lived with his wife on Kurza Street. Someone knocked at the door at two in the morning. He was afraid to open the door so Mrs. Melamud got up out of bed. "Open up!" they heard someone shouting in Yiddish. In the end she opened the door. Six of them came in and they each had a revolver. Melamud said to them from his bed, "You're Jews, aren't you? What are you doing? Have you gone mad? Isn't it enough that the Germans . . . " They didn't let him finish but put their guns to his head. "Where are the keys to the safe?" And when he'd handed them over they said, "Right then, Melamud. Get dressed and come with us." They forced him to go with them. He opened the safe for them with his own hands. They took out 100,000 złotys. "Tell the Chairman," they said as they were leaving "that the Jewish Fighting Organization has taken the money from the safe to buy machine guns." (1997: 169)

Szereszewska was unimpressed with the ŻOB's actions; she wrote that similar "robberies" continued and that the Ghetto was "gradually becoming slack" and "sailing into the unknown like a rudderless ship" (1997: 167). Others opposed the ŻOB's attempts more openly. For instance, on at least one occasion ŻOB flyers were torn down (Zuckerman 1993: 197). Nonetheless, the Ghetto eventually accepted the resistance organizations and answered their call to action, either by joining fighting units or by preparing bunkers and hiding places[41] (Gutman 1982; Klajman 2000; Szwajger 1990). Ghetto resident Janina Bauman's diary entry from November 2, 1942 read:

> They say, "Fight." Yes, of course, it's the only way, though there won't be much chance of survival if we do. But what else can we do? There is something called "dignity," much forgotten these days. Yes, I'm ready to join at once . . . I've been trying to find out the people behind those three letters [ŻZW]. (1986: 84)

Resistance as Honor: A Resonant Response

Once Jews in the Warsaw Ghetto realized that they were targeted for extermination, with no hope for survival, they decided to resist—with the Jewish youth leading the way. Further, they arrived at this critical conclusion of hopelessness over time, following a sequence of events marked by the Great Deportation in the summer of 1942. This conclusion alone was not enough to produce armed resistance, however. An assessment of threat is only part of the process that ultimately leads to action; as framing scholars (Benford 1993; Snow and Benford 1988) have argued, the frames that guide collective action provide the "vocabularies of motive" that render a given action plausible and appropriate. Even with a grave recognition of certain death, armed resistance against the Nazis was only one potential course of action. For instance, Jews could have called for mass suicide,[42] or mass prayer, each of which could have been resonant responses in the hands of the right framers. For the youth in the Ghetto, however, resistance became the preferred response.

Importantly, the fighters did not choose resistance to save their lives.[43] On the contrary, they were sure that they would all perish. When asked if he expected to survive the Uprising, Henry L. answered:

No, not really. Nobody really did. I told you, when we came out on the bunker we expected to be shot. Nobody expected to survive . . . When you go and you take resistance up, and you take weapons, you're doing illegal thing, it's a hundred percent. You know, how can you survive the Nazis when you know that your family already . . . But we wanted to . . . we made efforts but we didn't expect to survive . . . We were willing to die. We never expected to live, to with everything, because we had nothing for to live, you know.

Sol L. described an encounter with a resistance fighter, who expressed a similar pessimism:

Then I met this guy in the street. I say, "Feivke, what . . . what is all about this . . . ?" He says, "We have an underground and we're going to fight the Germans. I know we're not going to win, but we're not going to go [to the trains] anymore." He say, "Would you like to join?" I say, "If you'll explain to me, I will join."

Even ŻOB Commander Mordechai Anielewicz did not think he would survive the Uprising. Commenting on a conversation he had with Anielewicz, Emmanuel Ringelblum wrote:

He gave an accurate appraisal of the chances of the uneven struggle, he foresaw the destruction of the Ghetto and the workshop, and he was sure that neither he nor his combatants would survive the liquidation of the Ghetto. He was sure that they would die like stray dogs and no one would even know their last resting place. (quoted in Kermish 1986: 600)

Even the brief triumphs during the fighting did nothing to change the fighters' overall sense of their chances. Tuvia Borzykowski wrote of his experiences on April 19, the first day of the Uprising (1976: 51):

Rivka, a lookout girl, arrived with the news that the enemy had retreated; not even one soldier remained in the street. Our commander went to survey the scene, and came back radiating joy. The Germans had left several dozen wounded and dead, while we had not suffered even one casualty. The message was circulated to all positions arousing enthusiasm everywhere. However, we did not let this victory deceive us; we were aware all the time that the uprising meant the death of us all. We were just happy to have the satisfaction of inflicting damage on the enemy before we died.

Fighting for Honor

With no hope for success, and, in fact, a firm belief that they would all die, why did Warsaw Jews resist? Their uprising is hard to understand in light of theories that argue that a sense of efficacy is a necessary ingredient for collective resistance. Even Kahneman and Tversky's explanation of risky behavior—i.e., their findings that people make risky choices to avoid loss—cannot account for the Uprising, because the fighters believed that there was no way to avoid the loss of their lives. However, the fighters' decision makes more sense when we look at how they framed their call to action: namely, by equating resistance with honor. By resisting, they would surely die, by they would do so by choice—that is, by choosing the *way* they would die. Since death was a certainty, it was better to die in battle than to submit meekly to being slaughtered. As Emmanuel Ringelblum wrote in October 1942, after the Great Deportation had ended:

> The Jewish public understood what a terrible error had been made by not offering resistance to the SS. It was argued that if on the day the Warsaw "resettlement action" was announced, everyone had rebelled, if the Germans had been attacked with knives, sticks, spades, and axes, if hydrochloric acid, melted tar, boiling water, etc., had been poured over the Germans, Ukrainians, Latvians, and Jewish Order Service, in short if men, women and children, the young and the old, had begun a mass rising, there would not have been three hundred and fifty thousand murdered in Treblinka, but only fifty thousand shot in the streets of the capital . . . Oaths were sworn aloud: Never again shall the German move us from here with impunity; we shall die, but the cruel invaders will pay with their blood for ours. Our fate is sealed, people were saying. Every Jew carries a death sentence in his pocket, handed him by the greatest murderer of all time. Thus we must think not so much of saving our lives, which seems to be a very problematic affair, but rather of dying an honourable death, dying with weapons in our hands. (quoted in Kermish 1986: 594–595)

The main goal of the resistance was not to prevail over the German forces in battle, nor was it to prevent the final liquidation of the Warsaw Ghetto from occurring; no one thought either was possible. Instead, the goal was to act, and die, honorably. Describing the Uprising in an interview with a journalist, ŻOB leader Marek Edelman noted one point at which he and his fighters shot at some German soldiers and missed them, saying, "We missed but it didn't matter." When asked to explain, he replied:

The important thing was just that we were shooting. We had to show it. Not to the Germans. They knew better than us how to shoot. We had to show it to this other, the non-German world. People have always thought that shooting is the highest form of heroism. So we were shooting. (Krall 1986: 3)

The idea of fighting for honor also resonated with activists who were in relative safety on the Aryan side at the start of the Uprising and therefore did not necessarily have to fight. Leon W. was one:

Now, matter of fact, I was in the Uprising in the other side, because it was Pesach [Passover], before Pesach. I was in the other side. It was a mobilization. Every member from . . . should come over, it's a mobilization. This was sacred. And I went in voluntarily. I could survive the Uprising. Being in this side had nothing to do with this. But I was always a patriot. I was always a . . . I was . . . I love the Jewish nation. And I feel like a grown-up man. If I lived to this moment, and God gives me the strength, and I'm still healthy, why shouldn't I take part in such a *historische* moment, to stand up. And once we'll all take part in an Uprising, with these people, where they took away mine parents, my brother, and sister. What they made from the Jewish nation make them dust! No matter what I'll do I'll do something, pay him back. For this alone brought me back to report to my group.

Similarly, according to Arens (2011: 136), the following exchange took place between Shoshana (Emilka) Kossower, a Jewish woman passing as a Pole who worked as a courier for the *Armia Krajowa* (AK, or Home Army), a Polish resistance organization, and ŻZW Commander Pawel Frenkel, at the ŻZW headquarters at 7 Muranowska Street:

Looking at Frenkel, she said, "You know, you look like a Pole and speak per-
fect Polish. You could leave the ghetto and live in relative safety on the other
side, and help your organization from there." "I will stay here until the end,"
he replied. Emilka had known that, but still she could not keep herself from
saying to Frenkel: "So you want to die as a hero." "No," Frenkel replied, "I
don't want to live at any price. I want to die as a man."

Further, by resisting—even in the belief that it would lead to a certain death—
the Ghetto fighters would preserve not only their own honor and dignity, but
also that of the Jewish people as a whole (Cochavi 1995). A notice posted
in the Ghetto by the ŻOB made this goal clear; it read, "To fight, to die, for
the honor of our people!" (Kurzman 1993: 93). Recounting the start of the
fighting on April 19, Henry L. said:

Really . . . I was thinking hard, because at the moment, I mean, all of us were
thinking of the exit of Egypt. In a way it was similar except that the Jews in
Egypt were not in quite a danger. But we saw like a fate of the Lord, that we
were something parallel, something . . . I had that feeling, that this is a re-
vival of the exit of Egypt. But we didn't know we [laughs] were exit, you see.
The Moses wasn't there. We didn't see the freedom, where we can run out.
But I could feel, there's a certain parallel in Jewish history, you know . . . The
main thing was the spirit. You keep your Jewish pride, and you have the
force and the pride to resist, to the God, almighty, and Nazi army.

While the idea of resisting to die honorably originated with the young
activists of the ŻOB and the ŻZW, it was eventually adopted by non-ac-
tivist segments of the Ghetto population as well. Jack Klajman wrote in his
memoirs:

Perhaps the devastation of the Aktion was the final straw, but people in
the ghetto finally realized death was certain to come sooner or later, and
that there was nothing to lose by resisting. With no fear of death, we were
energized to fight to the best of our abilities. Everyone knew the chance of
victory was zero, but winning wasn't the goal. We just wanted to die with
dignity. (2000: 62)

Equating resistance with honor provided some of the "vocabularies of motive" that compel participation in protest. According to Benford (1993: 200)

such "vocabularies" consist of "rationales and justifications . . . [that] provide participants with 'good reasons' for identifying with the tools and values of the movement and for taking action on its behalf." Framing resistance as honorable in this case illustrates the motivational vocabulary of "propriety," or frames that cast the movement's issues in terms of participants' moral duty and ethical responsibilities to themselves and their communities (Benford 1993: 207). These themes are particularly evident in Zivia Lubetkin's (1981: 91) summary of the call to resistance:

> We said to ourselves: "We must see the truth for what it is. The Germans want to annihilate us. It is our duty to organize ourselves for defense, and struggle for our honor and the honor of the Jewish people" . . . This conviction was the motivating force behind our self-defense, our approaching battle.

Framing their resistance as a fight for honor may also have been a resonant response because by doing so, the Ghetto fighters made a statement about who and what Warsaw Jews were: strong and proud people, not the weak "subhumans" portrayed by Nazi ideology. In this sense, resistance was a resonant response to the threat of genocide because it was the enactment of an identity. As scholarship on a variety of cases of resistance shows, including work on Tiananmen Square (Calhoun 1994) and women's resistance in squatter settlements in Brazil (Neuhouser 1998), people may be moved toward extremely costly, "high-risk" activism because doing so enables one to enact a valued, positive identity. Simmons' (2016) examination of community mobilization in response to threats to water access in Cochabamba, Boliva provides a similar example. In her case, water was not simply a material resource but one that was deeply ingrained in the community's history and identity; a threat to that resource constituted a threat to the community's identity. One large event, during which protesters blockaded major roads in the region, was known as the "blockage for dignity" (2016: 92).

Perhaps most importantly, framing resistance in the Warsaw Ghetto in terms of honor applied not just to Warsaw Jews, but to the Jewish people as a whole.[44] As Henry L. explained:

> There was nothing to lose. I remember, that the people who organized that uprising, this was only what was left of the overwhelming, I would . . . eighty percent of the Jewish population was already shipped out. So after this, we

saw . . . just before we shipped out we saw the Germans, that we want to defend our honor, for the name . . . and for the holy name of the sake of the mem—in the memory of our lost family, and for the sake of all the Jewish people of the world, for the honor of the Jewish people in the world.

Again, however, it is important to remember that resistance did not emerge until well after Warsaw Jews were subjected to the brutalities of the Ghetto. Despite the motivational force of an honor-based frame, the timing of the resistance cannot be explained simply as a response to dishonor. Instead, the Uprising depended on both the critical conclusion of hopelessness *and* a resonant resistance frame. Indeed, framing resistance as honorable became compelling in part because the Ghetto fighters were certain that they would die. As Zivia Lubetkin wrote, "We all desired a different death, a death which would bring vengeance upon the enemy and restore the honor of our people" (1981: 123). These assessments of threat, which formed the basis for the critical conclusion of hopelessness, must be understood in the context of the Ghetto's brief history—namely, in the aftermath of the Great Deportation. The desperate situation in which the Ghetto residents were placed—and of which they eventually became aware—therefore created a context in which an honor-based frame resonated with potential resisters and motivated collective action.

Thus, it was not simply the *risk* of death that made armed resistance in the Warsaw Ghetto honorable or compelling. Other scholars (Loveman 1998; McAdam 1986; Wood 2001) use the term "high-risk activism" to refer to situations where protest participants risk beatings, torture, and even death, and argue that the dynamics of high-risk activism require different explanations than other forms of collective action. While the Warsaw Ghetto Uprising may be thought of as a case of high-risk activism, what distinguishes this case from others is not simply that the Ghetto fighters risked death, but that they believed they were *certain* to die; further, they felt that they would die *regardless of their decision to resist*. Had Warsaw Jews the option of either resisting or continuing to live in the Ghetto under German occupation, perhaps the Uprising would not have taken place; indeed, the fact that no collective resistance took place before July 1942 supports this conclusion. Henry L.'s words support this conclusion as well:

As I mentioned it again, mentioned a few times, there was a official, how do you call it, poster on the walls, in the ghetto, that we should bear arms.

We should prepare ourself for uprising. There is nothing to expect from the German. Only an uprising will defend our honor, and we have nothing from them. That's it, and that's what we . . .
Did everybody agree?
I think everybody, yeah, as far as I know. I didn't know what everybody, you know [laughs] . . . But obviously, if this was under the nose of the Germans, this . . . we didn't expect to live, or else we wouldn't have done it, okay?

Conclusions

The armed uprisings in the Warsaw Ghetto show that European Jews did not always submit meekly to Nazi aggression. They also teach us something new about collective resistance, in that Warsaw Jews' decision to stage resistance is the opposite of what opportunity and resource-based explanations of social movement emergence would expect. Instead of responding to opportunity and the availability of resources, these activists resisted despite a lack of both. How can we explain the resistance? I argue that Jews fought back in the Warsaw Ghetto *precisely because* they lacked opportunity and resources. With few resources, little opportunity, and no hope for survival, they reached a critical conclusion of hopelessness that, ironically, made resistance possible. At great cost, they set out to mobilize what resources they could, never attaining enough to stage a successful revolt. Of course, not only was it impossible to mobilize enough resources to defeat the German forces but doing so was never the goal of the Uprising in the first place.

Another aspect of this resistance that runs counter to what social movement theory would expect is that the Warsaw Ghetto depended not on hope, but on hopelessness. With an attribution of threat so great that they believed their deaths to be inevitable, resistance—framed in terms of an honorable death—became the preferred way to die. Young activists promoted this resistance frame, which resonated with the remaining Ghetto community because it spoke to the propriety of collective action and promoted a positive collective identity.

It was only in the context of widespread, systematic genocide that armed resistance made any sense. When Jews realized this was the case—that is, once they reached that critical conclusion—they still had to decide how to respond to the threat. Because the threat was perceived to be unsurvivable, resistance became a possibility. It then became a reality when it was framed in terms of honor, in a way that resonated with the remaining Ghetto residents. Its main goal was resistance itself: to fight back, knowing that they would die in the process, and believing that such death was honorable. As Ghetto survivor and Israeli historian Israel Gutman (1994: 259) concludes in the final paragraph of his book *Resistance*:

> In the darkest hours of the Warsaw ghetto, when all hope was lost, when none had a chance to survive and the end was certain, young Jews arose to fight. They chose to die in freedom rather than cower before an overpowering enemy. They refused to surrender, preferring instead to fight to the death and thus preserve their honor even then they could no longer defend their lives.

Given everything we know about social movements, resistance in the Warsaw Ghetto seemed impossible; remarkably, it happened. But if an armed uprising could happen in Warsaw, why didn't similar uprisings emerge in Vilna and Łódź? An examination of these cases gives further support for my explanation. Critical conclusions and resonant responses played out differently in Vilna, as I show in the next chapter.

4

Competing Visions in the Vilna Ghetto

*Let us not go as sheep to the slaughter! It is true that we are weak and
defenceless, but resistance is the only reply to the enemy! Brothers! It is
better to fall as free fighters, than to live by the grace of the murderers.
Resist! To the last breath.*

—From manifesto delivered in the Vilna Ghetto
by FPO leader Abba Kovner on December 31, 1941
(quoted in Shneidman 2002: 48)

*The basis for the existence of the ghetto is work, discipline, law and
order. Every resident of the ghetto who is capable of working is one of
the pillars on which the ghetto rests. There is no room among us for
those who shirk work and who by devious means engage in criminal
activity.*

—Announcement made to the Vilna Ghetto community on
July 12, 1942 by Ghetto Chief Jacob Gens (quoted in
Tushnet 1972: 173)

In April 1943, while the ruins of the Warsaw Ghetto lay smoldering, some
250 miles to the northeast, another major ghetto was very much intact. The
wooden fences surrounding the Vilna Ghetto still stood. There had been no
fires, poison gas, or tanks in the streets. The Warsaw Ghetto was no more, but
in the ghetto of Vilna, Jews were still alive, eking out a meager existence and
doing their best to survive ghettoization and everything that went along with it.

In April 1943, some 20,000 Jews lived in a cramped ghetto in the narrow
streets of Vilna's old Jewish Quarter. Under Nazi occupation, it was, like the
Warsaw Ghetto and the hundreds of other ghettos throughout occupied
Europe, a temporary holding place for Jews, the place in which they either
succumbed to hunger or from which they were forcibly relocated to other
places to be murdered directly. Simon T. was a relatively new arrival to the

Hope and Honor. Rachel L. Einwohner, Oxford University Press. © Oxford University Press 2022.
DOI: 10.1093/oso/9780190079437.003.0004

Vilna Ghetto, having been forced in March 1943 to relocate from a smaller ghetto in Smargon, a town of 6000 people fifty miles away, where he lived with his parents, brother, and grandmother. What he saw when he first came to the Vilna Ghetto shocked him:

> I do remember coming into . . . into Vilna . . . and seeing the legions of people walking out of . . . of the gate, this was in the morning, and they looked like . . . you know, walking ghosts. They were so pale, because, naturally, this was the city and they . . . they were going to forced labor and they didn't have much to eat. And there it . . . we still looked more or less robust, because [in Smargon] we were in . . . in the open more, and we still had managed to find more food. So this was a great shock to me. Like I felt like this is going to be the end here. And it sure enough it was the end for many.

Simon T.'s observations captured the daily experience of Vilna's Jews quite accurately. By April 1943, most Jews left in the Vilna Ghetto were workers, the lucky bearers of *scheinen*—official work passes—that permitted them to leave the Ghetto on a daily basis and work in Nazi-run factories and other sites throughout the area (Arad 1982; Shneidman 2002; Tushnet 1972). Each morning, Jewish work brigades lined up near the Ghetto gates and were escorted out to their workplaces; they were then marched back to the Ghetto at the end of each day. Ted S. described this daily routine:

> The conditions in the ghetto were, of course, bad. Like I remember where we . . . in the apartment there was . . . I think we had cold water somewhere. No toilets, in a room for about 3–400 square feet, if I'm not mistaken, there were about three, six, nine, twelve, fourteen people sleeping in five beds . . . four beds. Like where I slept, there were three people sleeping in different . . . different directions. And . . . but we would get up five o'clock in the morning and walk to work, about two three miles to this particular working camp.

When walking to and from the Ghetto on their way to work, Jews were, of course, easily identified by the yellow Jewish stars[1] that they were forced to wear, by Nazi decree. Still, working beyond the Ghetto walls gave some the opportunity to buy or trade for food with Poles and Lithuanians. Such activity was dangerous, as Jews were observed closely while working and also had to get past guards when returning to the Ghetto at the end of each day;

if caught smuggling food back into the Ghetto they were subject to beatings, jailings, or worse. But the risks were necessary, given the dire food shortages and inadequate rations. Michael M. recalled:

> My first job was in city hall. The city hall had a department, to take the furniture of the Jewish homes and put them into a central station . . . So we used to . . . in the morning a officer used to come from the city hall and pick the twenty people. We used wait for him already, and take us in big wagon, and used to come into a house, a big apartment house, yeah. And we used to go in and *schlep* (drag) their furniture, the pianos, the chairs, everything, what belong to the . . . even the kitchen, and everything now. The outside, there were nonJewish people waiting for us, we should give him like a mirror or, you know, something smaller we used to give them. And later we got smarter. We used to . . . "You want this mirror? A piece of bread. You want this . . ." . . . so, sort of speak, wasn't a bad job, from the point of view of organizing some food . . . So in the evening, we used to come [back] in [the Ghetto] with food here and food . . . if they . . . by the gate, if they got us, they have to give the food back. If they smuggled through we had food.

Some Jews even stole food from nearby farmers' fields to survive.

> Lucie C.:
> I used to work outside the ghetto. I used to work at the railroad station . . . I always wanted to stay out of the ghetto, because I said there is maybe a possibility I can steal some food. And say steal . . . that was actually stealing that we were doing to survive. You were running out from the railroad where you worked, to the fields, and take a few potatoes. But that was everything for survival.

Other jobs also provided the opportunity to obtain food. Aron K., a twenty-two-year-old married father of one, held the enviable position of Ghetto chimney sweep:

> And that was the best job a Jew can have . . . a doctor . . . a doctor wasn't good, a professor wasn't good, but a chimney sweep was one of the best jobs.
> *Why so?*
> Because we had certificates that we could go wherever over the whole town, because we were chimney sweeps, you know. We could go everywhere we

wanted to without . . . usually, Jews when they went out from ghetto to work, they need . . . they needed somebody to lead them, you know. We were with . . . we were individuals, like individuals. So by having this kind of liberty we could go and buy and sell and do whatever we wanted.

But you had to be back at the ghetto by a certain time.

We had to be in ghetto by a certain time. That's true. And we still . . . we still were treated as Jews, because we still had the . . . the yellow . . . the yellow stars, but working as chimney sweeps nobody saw the yellow stars, because it was all black with . . . with, you know . . . so they . . . so we had real . . . quite free movement.

Working outside the Ghetto also allowed Jews to hear what was going on elsewhere in Nazi-occupied Europe. As William T. explained, this is how some learned about the Warsaw Ghetto Uprising in April 1943:

> Now, in April we find out that the fighting in Warsaw. How did we know that they're fighting in Warsaw, in the ghetto, Warsaw ghetto? People worked on the railroad. So some railroad men who was on the . . . who was Warsaw–Vilna in the trains, told that the Jews are fighting in Warsaw.

One Vilna Ghetto resident who was especially pleased to hear the news about the fighting in the Warsaw Ghetto was a twenty-five-year-old activist named Abba Kovner. Tall and slim, with a long face and a curly, wiry mop of hair, he had the heart of a fighter but the soul of a poet.[2] A longtime activist, Abba was member of a coalition planning for armed resistance in the Vilna Ghetto. On April 30, 1943, he wrote in the small pocket diary he always carried with him that the Warsaw Ghetto Uprising had begun (Porat 2010: 110). Perhaps he noted this news in his diary because it made him proud; after all, he and his comrades were the very ones who had sent the word about their own plans for resistance to Warsaw, calling on their fellow youth activists in Warsaw and elsewhere to take up arms against the Nazis.

Abba Kovner was the Deputy Commander of the FPO (*Fareynikte Partizaner Organizatsye*, or United Partisans Organization).[3] By April 1943, the FPO had been in existence for more than a year, and it was quietly collecting weapons and planning for armed resistance. Given the danger of their work, and the certainty that they would be put to death if discovered by the Nazis, they worked secretly, in small cells of fighters; few knew anything about operations beyond their own small group. As Deputy

Commander, though, Kovner had a broader sense of the organization's plans. He served as one of two Deputy Commanders; the other, Josef Glazman, was a former Ghetto policeman. Both answered to the FPO Commander, Yitzhak Wittenberg. Born in 1907, Wittenberg was in his mid-thirties and therefore older than Kovner, Glazman, and most of their fellow activists; however, the younger ones looked up to him and respected him as a leader. These three men represented different political movements and ideologies—Wittenberg was a Communist, Kovner was a member of the left-wing Zionist group HaShomer HaTzair, and Glazman was a member of the right-wing Zionist group Betar—but they worked well together, planning for an uprising exactly like what was happening at the time in the Warsaw Ghetto. Understandably, the news about the fighting in Warsaw gave them hope that they too would be able to fight back when the time came.

Things did not go as planned, however. Within a few short months, Yitzhak Wittenberg was dead, without ever having issued the call to fight. Abba Kovner and Josef Glazman were gone as well—not dead, but gone from the Ghetto, having escaped to join partisan units carrying out acts of anti-German sabotage in the nearby forests. By mid-September 1943, the FPO, as it had existed in the Ghetto, was no more. By September 24, 1943, the Vilna Ghetto was liquidated entirely.

In the previous chapter I showed how young Jewish activists in the Warsaw Ghetto staged an armed uprising, despite a lack of opportunity, resources, or hope for success. Young activists in Vilna were in a similar situation, and they also organized for armed resistance. Although a small splinter group managed a brief exchange of fire with Nazi soldiers on September 1, 1943, no one achieved the goal of a longer uprising in the Vilna Ghetto. Why not? If armed resistance could both emerge and be sustained in the difficult conditions in the Warsaw Ghetto, why didn't that happen in Vilna?

The story of the attempted uprising in the Vilna Ghetto provides more support for my overall argument about critical conclusions and resonant responses as explanatory factors in collective resistance. In this chapter I demonstrate that in Vilna, as in Warsaw, young resistance fighters had neither the resources, opportunity, nor hope that they would succeed. Their decision to attempt armed resistance in the Vilna Ghetto was not based on these factors; instead, it reflected a critical conclusion of genocide and the belief that armed resistance was the proper response.

Yet while the young activists in the Vilna Ghetto reached the critical conclusion and resonant response necessary for resistance, they could not convince the rest of the Ghetto community to join them in battle. The story of the Vilna Ghetto illustrates that threat is dynamic: it can change over time and place, and it can also vary within a community. There were, in fact, different ways to make sense of the threats facing Vilna's Jews: multiple assessments of threat led to different, competing conclusions and responses, which were too much for the FPO fighters to overcome. Without more widespread support for their critical conclusion (i.e., that everyone in the Ghetto would eventually be put to death) and their response to the threat (i.e., an armed ghetto uprising)—in other words, without an assessment that resonated more broadly with the community that they hoped to lead in battle—the fighters called off their plans for an uprising in their ghetto and turned to alternate venues and forms of resistance.

In this chapter I tell the story of the Vilna Ghetto. I emphasize the role of critical conclusions and resonant responses in people's decisions about resistance. But the narrative of this ghetto also reflects how time and place shaped these dynamics. As I show, a transformative event in the Vilna Ghetto marked a turning point in assessments and responses that made the erstwhile Ghetto fighters rethink their strategy and pivot from a ghetto uprising to acts of armed resistance in the nearby forests. Indeed, Vilna's proximity to the forests, and the presence of partisan units operating therein, was part of what made this tactical shift possible.

Vilna: The Birthplace of Everything

According to Israeli historian Dina Porat, Abba Kovner wrote, decades after the end of World War II, that "Vilna was the birthplace of everything" (2010: 17). Taken out of context, it is not clear whether he meant that the city was the birthplace of Jewish resistance during the Holocaust, or, more generally, the birthplace of a rich, vibrant Jewish community—but both were certainly true.

Vilna, a medieval city near the convergence of the Negris and Vilnius rivers in the southeastern part of Lithuania, had a population of 195,100 in 1931—54,600 of whom were Jewish (Arad 1982: 27). It was, by all accounts, a beautiful city. Sol A., a Vilna native born to a family of tailors, described it as "a beautiful city with mountains all around," while David B., who was eleven at the start of World War II, said:

The city was an old city, but it had a lot of beautiful things, like . . . for an example, churches, tremendous churches. And I remember when there was . . . the streets were big wide streets, and if you walked and you went through that particular street and there was a church, you had to take off your hat, whether you were Jewish or Christian or whatever . . . that I remember, because I used to sometimes walk with my father and we had to take off our hats. It was no problem. But it was a beautiful city. They had beautiful, beautiful synagogues, old but beautiful.

As suggested by the city's multiple names—Vilna in Russian, Wilno in Polish, and Vilnius in Lithuanian—Vilna is a city whose nationality changed frequently in the first half of the 20th century (Porat 2010: 15). Bernard D., a Vilna native, joked about the city's shifting national identity when answering a question about the year he completed college:

In 1941. I started and studied in Poland and I finished in Germany [laughs]. I didn't go any place, they came to me. In '39 the Russians came.

Despite changing hands among different sovereign nations, Vilna traditionally had a large Jewish population, and remained a center of Jewish religious and intellectual thought throughout the 17th, 18th, and 19th centuries. Lucie C. referred to the Vilna of her childhood as "a cosmopolitan city" that was "the cradle of Jewish life." Similarly, Abram Z., another Vilna native, described his city as "full of Jewish life":

And in that center of the city, where the Jews have been nearly ninety percent, it was at a city where . . . full of Jewish life, Jewish life in all walks of this, in secular and in religious.

Unparalleled in Europe for its strengths in Jewish thought and scholarship, the city was the home of the Gaon ("genius") of Vilna, the renowned 18th century rabbi Eliyahu ben Shlomo Zalman, as well as numerous *shuls* (synagogues) and *yeshivas* (centers of Jewish religious study), all of which led Vilna to become known as the "Jerusalem of Lithuania" (Arad 1982; Harshav 2002; Shneidman 2002; Tushnet 1972). The city also housed YIVO, the Jewish Scientific Institute (*Yiddisher Visnshaftlecher Institut*), established there in 1925, as well as the Strashun Library, the most famous Jewish library in Europe, named for the Jewish scholar and book collector Mathias

(Mattityahu) Strashun. Founded in 1892, the library had more than 35,000 volumes (Arad 1982: 2) and was well used; Porat (2010: 7) writes that "Every thinking young person . . . in Vilna found a seat at one of its long tables." Numerous Jewish newspapers, in Yiddish, Hebrew, and Polish, were also published in the city—and read. Michael M. said proudly,

> Vilna produced seventeen daily Jewish newspapers a day. This was the most popular city in the Jewish world, and non-Jewish world, that produced in a population of 300 thousand, 1,000 Jews, seventeen newspapers daily, twenty-six weeklies and monthly, all kind of magazines. I want this should be known for the future history, that no city *in the world* produced so much material to read.

Not surprisingly, Jewish political life thrived in the city as well. Political movements abounded, representing the spectrum from left to right, and from Zionist (focused on reviving the Hebrew language and establishing a homeland for Jews in Palestine) to Yiddishist (focused on Yiddish language and culture, and advocating for the rights and protections of Jews, especially workers, in Europe) (Shneidman 2002). As Aron K. explained,

> There were many Jewish political youth organizations, were all kinds of Zionist organization, with left Zionists and right Zionists and middle-of-the-road Zionists and maybe a half a dozen more. And there was the Bund, which was a Socialist organization against the Zionist organization. Then was the Jewish Communist organization, which was against the Zionists and the Socialist . . . Socialist organizations.

The downside of such a large, vibrant, and visible Jewish presence in the city was overt anti-Semitism at the hands of some non-Jews. In this regard, Vilna was no different than Warsaw or other cities. Esther M., who was thirteen at the start of World War II, described anti-Semitism as a child growing up in Vilna:

> Ever since I was a child, we always had to fight because they always used to approach us, "Bloody Jew, dirty Jew," things like this. "Jews, go to Palestine." This you heard on every step. I was six years old when I was . . . it was the end of school. I was walking back with my older sister and a cousin in my age. And suddenly I felt hot in the back of my head. And the blood started

to run over my neck. I was hit with an iron, from a boy, on the back of my head. That's how bad it was.

And you were doing . . . what at the time?

Nothing, we were just walking. And we were speaking Yiddish. And I even didn't know who the boy was, and he didn't know who I were, that he only heard us talk Yiddish. And that was the reason he . . . and I saw the blood running over my neck. I got so scared. All . . . the three of us were screaming and we ran home, naturally.

Yet while many Vilna Jews experienced anti-Semitism before the onset of World War II, they could not anticipate what was to come.

The Start of the War: September 1939

Vilna, located northeast of Warsaw, lay in the region ceded to the Soviet Union in 1939 as part of the Molotov-Ribbentrop Pact. When World War II began, Vilna Jews were therefore initially under Soviet, not German, oc- cupation. While the Soviets briefly restored sovereignty to the independent state of Lithuania, with Vilna/Vilnius as its capital, in October 1939, they annexed the area again on June 15, 1940. Importantly, because it was located in Soviet territory at the beginning of the war, Vilna (along with other major cities northeast of Warsaw, such as Białystok) was a seemingly safe destina- tion for Jews in Nazi-occupied Poland. Thus, at the beginning of World War II, thousands of Polish Jews fled east, seeking refuge from Nazi abuses, and Vilna's Jewish community absorbed a number of refugees. Zula S. described Vilna as a "haven" for refugees from areas occupied by Nazis in 1939:

They came from Warsaw. They came from Poland. They came from Germany. They came from different way. Any way they could get in, they got in. They knew there is a . . . a haven in our town, that it was . . . they were accepted. Because one-third of the town was Jewish, so they had enough room for them to be accepted and welcome.

The refugees who streamed into Vilna shared news of what was happening in Western and Central Poland, where Nazis had begun the ghettoization and deportation of Jews. The Vilna Jewish community was sympathetic to their fellow Jews' plight but did not see it as applicable to themselves; after all, they were in the Soviet zone, and not subject to Nazi abuses. David B., describing what he knew about treatment of Jews in Nazi-occupied Poland at the time, said:

> But we heard there was going on bad things over there that they were taking them to ghettos and camps, but we didn't . . . you see, and a lot of people from those cities, like Warsaw or Łódź or Kraków, or places like that they used . . . they ran away from there, as many as they could, and they arrived in Vilna because it was still free. And they were telling us all these stories what they had to go through there until . . .
> *What did you think when they were telling you these stories?*
> We thought it was terrible, but in our . . . we didn't know that it's going to ever happen with us, you know, in our city, because here the Russian just made a deal with the Germans, and who knows whether . . . what kind of deal they make and we assumed that this is okay.

Youth activists from Poland were among the Jewish refugees. Two thousand members of HeHalutz came to Vilna, of which 700 were members of HaShomer HaTzair—including Mordechai Anielewicz, who would later return to Warsaw to lead the ŻOB in battle (Arad 1982: 18; Porat 2010: 18–21). In fact, many youth groups moved their headquarters to Vilna, especially when the city was part of Lithuania in the first year of the war, because it was seen as safer there—better to be in an independent Lithuania than under the control of Germans or Russians. The relative safety was short-lived, however; when Russia took the city back from Lithuania, all non-Communist political organizations were outlawed, forcing HaShomer HaTzair and other youth movements to go underground. Further, due to the repression under Russian occupation, some activists—mostly, older community and Zionist leaders—left the city. Another, distinct segment of the Jewish community also had reason to fear the Soviet occupation of the city: upper class Jews. As capitalists, they were sent away to Siberia. Zofja L., who came from a wealthy family, described how her father went into hiding at the time:

> During Stalin, he got together most of the professional people in Vilna and sent them off to . . . I believe that most of them were sent off to Siberia. My father was in hiding there.
> *Your father.*

My father was in hiding. And then he joined us again after all that. Because as I said, it didn't last forever.

Yet, despite the restrictions that went along with Soviet control, things were relatively calm for Jews in Vilna—that is, until the summer of 1941. As Boris K., a baker's son who was nineteen years old at the time, put it:

This is when all the *tsuris*, all the trouble started . . . This is when the war started for us.

The *Real* Start of the War: June 1941

When German bombs first fell on Vilna on June 22, 1941, there were 57,000–60,000 Jews in the city (Arad 1982: 28; Porat 2010: 36; Rojowska and Dean 2012: 1149). German tanks soon followed the aerial attacks, arriving on June 24. Chaos reigned in Vilna's streets in the first few days of the new occupation. Along with the arrival of the troops, a wave of anti-Jewish violence ensued, as some Lithuanians suspected[4] Jews of being Communist and Soviet supporters. Abram Z. recalled:

And Tuesday, the 24th of June, 1941, the first Germans come into Vilna. And even before the first Germans come into Vilna, some parts of the Lithuanian army, what have been under the Soviet, start to attack Jews. And we have been living just opposite where it was, a part of the Lithuanian army. And they start to come and look for Jews in our flats. So, my brother-in-law, what was about twenty-five year older than myself, have to stay for forty-eight hours between . . . hiding between two doors.

In those early days of the occupation, both German and Lithuanian forces kidnapped Jews, either killing them or using them for forced labor. Seventeen-year-old Abraham S. was grabbed and forced to work, but was later returned to his family:

One evening, by 7 o'clock, it was a very hot day, it was a very hot summer, two Lithuanians came and walked in, in the house, armed with rifles . . . They gave me a shovel. There was another Jew . . . [And there] were sturm . . . young storm troopers . . . swearing on us, "You dirty Jews," in German, and so and so . . . It was very hot. They were standing over us and harassing us, pushing, touching with the butts of their rifles, with some like hard whips. "*Schnelle, schnelle, schnelle*" [fast, fast, fast]. I was younger, so I finished first. So they made me to help the other guy. Two in one hole was impossible. The handles from the shovels were, so every time he took a shovel, he hit me. Every time I took . . . and they were standing and laughing, you know, and making fun. Shortly, when we were ready, said to me, going in the other hole . . . and made the other one to bury me up to here. When I was buried, the two Lithuanians buried the other one. They were keeping us in the ground. They were inside, drinking and singing. And then one older guy, in a brown uniform, walked out, and he gave us a small spot, "Dig out yourself." So I was the first, I dugged on myself. Those two Lithuanians took me and they brought me back home. The whole family was sitting and crying already.

Soon after taking control of Vilna, German authorities instituted a number of restrictions. On top of food rationing and the requirement to wear identifying badges, Jews could no longer buy, sell, or transfer property. In addition, Jews could no longer use public transportation, nor could they walk along central streets; instead, they had to use side streets. They could not own radios or telephones, and they were banned from theaters and coffee shops. They were even prohibited from greeting non-Jews (see Arad 1982: 56–58; Shneidman 2002: 11).

Michael M.:
Right away, the restriction came out. Every second day a new restriction. The first restriction was to wear . . . stars. Then white bands. Then, after a couple days, you couldn't walk on the . . . you had to go on the street, not on the sidewalk. Another day, six o'clock, no Jew can go in the streets, he has to be home. And a couple days later . . . and everything was officially written, you know, on pape—on the street. And if you don't follow the instructions, their orders, it's dead by killing. And they took out a couple Jews and they killed them in the middle of the city. And they said, "This is what will happen if you don't listen to our orders." And the dead bodies were laying there for a couple days. And everybody had to go and look at the bodies, to see what will happen if they do not obey to their restrictions, to the new orders. This was a big . . . big downgrading to us. All of a sudden, overnight, you become not a human being. And another thing, when you

see a German you have to take off your hat. This was also . . . not insulting, I don't even have the English expression, how to express myself.

Sol A.:
The first order they gave to the people was that everybody must turn in their radios, if they had a radio. If anybody is going to be caught with a radio at home, he's going to be shot . . . And right away they gave cards for the people that they could buy bread and some kind of pro—in other words, you couldn't buy any food just as much as you want. You had to buy a certain amount and give part of your card to the . . . to the store where you bought it. Now, the Jews had on their card a "Z," which is *Žydas* in Lithuanian, and Polish is *Žyd*. Now, if you had a card with the "Z" on it, you only could get half of whatever the portion was for the Poles, and the others, the Jews got half. But, somehow, this wasn't the worst yet. I mean, you learned to live with things and you learn to do things to . . . to . . . to . . . in other words, if we didn't get enough bread, so had, maybe, potatoes or whatever it is. And this wasn't the worst part.

The worst part was what was happening at a place called Ponar.

The Killing Fields of Ponar

In Warsaw, mass killings of Jews—i.e., the Great Deportation—began after the establishment of the Ghetto. Events unfolded differently in Vilna. In Vilna, the killings began first, and the Ghetto followed. In fact, Lithuania was one of the first places in Eastern Europe where Jews were killed en masse. In this sense, the "birthplace of everything" took on another, tragic, meaning.

For the Jewish communities of both Warsaw and Vilna, the initial experience of Nazi occupation was the same. Jews were subject to violence and harassment as well as restrictions on their property and movement; further, Jewish men in both cities were frequently snatched off the streets and taken away, either to prison or for forced labor. Arrestees in Vilna were sometimes told to pack a towel and soap, ostensibly for use in a labor camp. However, more often than not they were taken to the Lukiszki prison in the city's Jewish Quarter. From prison, most were never released back to their families, and in fact were never heard from again. Claire G., who was nine years old at the start of the war, lost her uncle to these early roundups:

[W]hen the Germans came in, the first thing that has happened, they were telling us that they were rounding up some of the men and sending them to work, which my uncle was sent. And there was no clue, disappeared, basically completely disappeared overnight. Never heard from him, even though they said they sent him to work.

Ann K. also remembered people being taken away. What she remembered was how it sounded:

It was . . . it was horrible. You could hear at night, especially when they came and took the people away.
What would you hear at night?
Crying. "Don't take me," or whole families, "Don't take my brother," or, "Don't take my father," or . . . you know, they divided families.

Where were these men taken? Unbeknownst to the community at the time, many of those arrested were eventually relocated to Ponar, a wooded area eight miles to the south. In happier times, Ponar was a well-known vacation and recreation spot for Vilna residents, the site of pleasant childhood memories for many people, such as Zula S.:

It was . . . outskirts of Vilna, which was a very nice . . . it was a beautiful forest where we used to go sled riding there, because there were beautiful hills.

Yet under Nazi occupation, this lovely, verdant place became a killing field, the final resting place for tens of thousands of Jews. As a result, the name Ponar—also known as Ponary (in Polish) and Paneriai (in Lithuanian)—became synonymous with mass murder.

When Vilna was under Soviet occupation at the beginning of the war, Soviet forces dug large open pits at the Ponar site; these were originally intended as storage for fuel tanks (Arad 1982: 75). Sadly, they also facilitated mass murder. Jews taken to Ponar beginning in the summer of 1941 were lined up at the edges of the pits and shot, both by the German *Einsatzgruppen* (mobile killing forces, tasked with murdering Jews throughout Germany's newly occupied lands) and the Lithuanian *Ypatingas Burys* (special troops). Ten thousand Jews were killed in this manner in the month of July 1941 (Rojowska and Dean 2012: 1148).

Zula S.'s father was rounded up and arrested in the early days of the German occupation; miraculously, he was released. Yet as she noted, he was affected terribly by what he saw:

> And when he came home, he was just hysterical for three days. He said, "The worst thing was, is not what they were, but they made . . . " before they were taking the people to Ponary, they put out a line of German soldiers, or Lithuanian soldiers . . . with big clubs, and beating everybody to death. So when the people went to Ponary, they were so . . . uh, so depressed and so beaten up, that they . . . they could not possibly fight them. That's what they did. Everybody said that the Jews don't fight them, that they did in such a way. They prepare the Jew in such a way that he couldn't fight them. And my father was really hysterical, I would say, for three days.

Zula's father was lucky; many others were not. Importantly, though, those who evaded Ponar in the early period of killings did not recognize that the imprisoned and disappeared were the victims of mass murder. Indeed, it would have been hard for anyone to know exactly what was happening, given the chaos and uncertainty at the time. Moreover, because mass killings of Jews during World War II began in Lithuania—the "birthplace of everything"—Vilna Jews of necessity could not know what was happening, as there was no precedent for such killings during the war, or during any war. Here again, a form of "cultured ignorance" (Einwohner 2009) took hold: it was hard to see the roundups as the prelude to mass murder, because Vilna Jews had nothing to compare it to (Arad 1982; Porat 2010). Instead, many took the Nazi officials at their word, believing that the imprisoned deportees were being taken away to prison and/or work camps. Mass murder—genocide—was unprecedented, and therefore unthinkable. Unfortunately, though, the unthinkable was happening, and kept happening for the rest of 1941.

The Creation of the Vilna Ghetto

In the eyes of the Nazi regime, the use of the Ponar woods as a killing field did not preclude the need for a ghetto in Vilna. On the contrary, killings at Ponar went hand-in-hand with the establishment of the Vilna Ghetto. The area that was designated for the Ghetto was not large enough to accommodate all the Jews that would need to be moved there. To create room, the Nazis had to remove some of the residents who were already living in what would become the Ghetto. Ponar served that purpose.

In fact, Jews who were sent to the Ghetto when it was first created entered homes that had clearly been occupied by people who left in a hurry. New arrivals found many belongings that were left behind; in some cases, they even found half-finished meals. Ruzka Korczak, a youth activist who later became a member of the FPO, recalled her first apartment in the Ghetto: "The room was still alive, and from all sides the shadows of those who lived there stared at us" (quoted in Porat 2010: 56). Similarly, Sima S. described her move to the Ghetto, and what she found there:

> [M]y sister lived at the end of the street. They went first . . . and then came our turn. Knock on the door, "Get out, *raus, raus, Jude raus, verfluchte jude raus.*" [out, out, Jew out, cursed Jew out]. And we . . . we were taken all in the same way . . . And my sister stood at the gates and finded and she took us to them. On the floor, that was our bedding. That was our bedroom. And we finded . . . before we came, we finded people were eating meals of . . . frying food or cooking food. And everything was left. They took out these people and . . . they put us in . . . in their houses, in their dwellings.

To continue to create needed space in the Ghetto, Nazi officials turned to a new ruse: they began falsely accusing Jews of murdering German soldiers, and instituted mass arrests as punishments for these "provocations." On September 1, 1941, officials posted flyers proclaiming that German soldiers had been ambushed, and that the shots fired at them came from Jews. The occupying army used this "incident"—later referred to as the Great Provocation—to justify rounding up Jews living in the Old Jewish Quarter from August 31 to September 3, 1941 (Arad 1982; Shneidman 2002; Tushnet 1972). Unlike the arrests and disappearances during the early weeks of the German occupation, which targeted Jewish men, women and children were rounded up as well. Further, these roundups were done systematically: soldiers went house by house, clearing out the residents of one side of a street on one day and the other the next. The deportees were taken to Ponar as well. Thousands of people were killed during these weeks, including 3700 on September 2 alone (Arad 1982: 103–104).

Into the Ghetto

The Vilna Ghetto was announced on September 6, 1941. On that day, Nazi soldiers went door to door throughout the city, ordering Jews to gather their belongings—only what they could carry—and head to the Ghetto by foot. Typically, they gave families only fifteen minutes to vacate their homes.

> Aron. K:
> They . . . they came from door to door and . . . they told us, 15 minutes. You have to be out with your packages, whatever you can . . . whatever you can handle.
> *And then everything they had . . . people had to leave behind.*
> Everything else you had to leave. Everything else you had to leave . . .
> *So you remember them actually coming to the door and saying to you . . .*
> Yes. Yes.
> *. . . 15 minutes.*
> Not only do I remember, but I . . . I got so scared that I . . . I got 39 degree . . . that's probably like . . . that's Celsius . . . that's probably like 102 or something temperature.

With only minutes to gather their belongings, people frantically grabbed valuables and keepsakes. Mira H. recalled:

> The Germans came to our apart—our apartment to take us. I was home, my mother and my grandmother. And when they came they gave us about ten, fifteen, twenty minutes . . . very short, to gather the things, what we want to take with us to the ghetto. So my mother took something, my grandmother took a pillow . . . and I grabbed my doll . . . And there was on the table an album with pictures, and I grabbed the pictures . . . when the Germans came to the apartment I was holding the pictures with a doll. He took away the doll from me. It was a beautiful doll if he wanted probably for himself. But the pictures I took with me and that's what I have until today. I saved them, the pictures. This is my only remembrance from my childhood, from everyone who was alive before the war.

September 6 was an unseasonably warm day. Some Jews donned multiple layers of clothes, so as to transport extra clothing as easily as possible (Arad 1982). Yet, the late summer heat complicated matters, forcing some people to remove and abandon the garments. Others simply grabbed too many things to carry and had to drop them along the way.

Ida K.:
I had my fur coat on. And it was September. It was very hot and I had to take it off and leave it on the street, and carry only my sweater underneath, with a skirt, and dropped a lot of the other things. Mostly warm clothes, and shoes to change, and underwear, and bread. Bread, salami to keep us alive.

Michael M.:
What did I take? We lost our heads, we took the unnecessary things . . . I remember, I put on like three suits, all kind of shirts, all kind of what my mother gave me. And my sisters put on all kind of dresses, like five dresses on themself, and stockings, and extra shoes on you . . . We came into the ghetto in the hundreds of people. The march for the ghetto was impossible to even describe . . . On the side there were soldiers with dogs, with guns. And they were watching us, we shouldn't run away or do something. A lot of things . . . a lot of people couldn't even carry anymore. They took so much . . . after five minutes, ten minutes, it becomes very heavy, so you drop it. So on the sidewalks were non-Jews grabbing the things, and yelling, and insulting, "Good for you," "You don't belong with us," all kind of insults. But they actually were going and picking up our belongings.

Struggling to carry their belongings in the late summer heat, Vilna's shocked and saddened Jews made their way to the narrow streets of the city's old Jewish Quarter. There, they found that the neighborhood had been carved into two distinct, fenced-in ghettos, separated by Niemiecka Street (see Figure 4.1).

Each ghetto was surrounded by a tall wooden fence and had a single gate for both entry and exit (Arad 1982)—clearly designed to limit Jews' movement in and out of the ghettos. Further, the ghettos were designed to keep Jews from observing what was happening beyond the walls: windows that looked out on the rest of the city were boarded up. As Aron K. described it,

They put up . . . they put up fences. At the beginning of the street, where it started, they put a fence and a gate for people to be able to get in and get out. And then all the houses which were in the ghetto and had doors and windows on the outside of ghetto, they boarded them. They put up boards like . . . like . . . wooden boards. So if you had a room, if you lived in a room with your window outside the ghetto, they board it up and you didn't have any daylight in there.

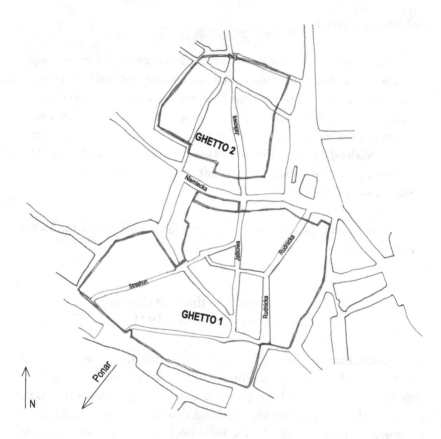

Figure 4.1 Map of the Vilna Ghetto.
Credit: Elle Rochford

As if the journey to the Ghetto was not traumatic enough, once they arrived in the Ghetto, Vilna's Jews were faced with the difficulties of finding housing in a severely crowded environment. Even with the early roundups and arrests before the establishment of the Ghetto, there was not enough room to accommodate the 40,000 people—ten times the size of the population that used to live in the neighborhood—who now needed housing (Rojowska and Dean 2012: 1148; Tushnet 1972: 148). As Claire G. said:

> I remember marching into the ghetto, and ended up in a small little apartment of two rooms with seven different families, all sleeping on the floor. And when you tried to go to sleep, forget it, if you had to go to the bathroom. I mean, you just had to crawl over people.

and Mira H. recalled:

> it was very crowded. Each of us slept on the floor because we were so many
> people that we had to have place. No beds, nothing. The conditions there
> were not . . . people were all nervous. Everyone was screaming, a lot of fights
> between the people because no one . . . no one was so . . . aggravated with
> everything that if somebody would say a word, the other one . . . if you were
> talking too loud. Some . . . they had all kind of nasty people so they would
> scream at you, "Don't talk, don't run, don't move." Everyone was very . . . the
> tension was very high.

As the new Ghetto residents were to see, though, crowding was the least of
their problems.

Further Roundups in the Two Ghettos,
September–December 1941

Once sealed, the two ghettos functioned independently; for instance, each
had its own *Judenrat* and police force (Porat 2010: 58). This seeming ineffi-
ciency did not matter for long, however. The second ghetto, which was the
smaller of the two, was quickly liquidated in a series of three *aktionen*, or
roundups, and was emptied by the third week of October. Sol A. initially
lived in Ghetto 2, because that is where his family's home was before the war.
Thanks to his tailoring skills, he got a work pass and a job in a hospital where
he mended soldiers' uniforms. His job saved his life because he was at work
during a roundup. However, he lost his entire family:

> [W]hen I came from work . . . when I came from work I would go to the
> smaller ghetto. One day, when I was at work, one . . . the German . . . the
> German who was, by the way, a nice man who was in charge of us, so he
> took . . . took us on a side, a few of the people, including myself, and said,
> "Don't go back to the ghetto, to the small ghetto." Just told us. He didn't
> say . . . he wouldn't say anything more, but he said, "Don't go back to the
> small ghetto." And we decided to stay overnight in the hospital, because
> they didn't know . . . and we did. And the next morning the people from
> the big ghetto came to work, to that hospital, and they told us that the little

ghetto was completely liquidated. The German knew about it. And we
didn't know what happened.

After the liquidation of Ghetto 2, a new rule was put in place: workers could
list a spouse and two children on their passes. With this allowance, Ghetto
residents used creative strategies to find life-saving passes even if they could
not find work. As Paula N. explained,

> Being able to go to work was a very important thing . . . for instance, at one
> point I was married to a friend of ours who had a pass like this. Later on
> my . . . whether . . . it was, of course, a fictitious marriage, but I appeared on
> his pass. At some later point I didn't need to be married to him anymore, he
> was married to my school friend.

Zofja L. also got married, on paper, to someone she did not know:

> It was not easy to get a job. And one just managed to survive the best one
> can. And in the ghetto they used to do clearings, where they took all the
> people, and then they took babies. And then at one stage they were going
> to take all the unmarried women. And in that time my parents managed to
> marry me off. I don't know whom they married me to [laughs] but we had
> some documents, that somebody was willing to marry me. So what was it?,
> '41. I was sixteen. I was a married woman.
> *Had you met your husband?*
> No [laughs], I don't know who my husband was.

Marriage saved Toby W.'s family as well, but for a different reason. Her grandfather, a rabbi, was gifted a precious work pass for performing a wedding:

> They were sending men out to work. So one day a young man came over to
> my grandfather with his girlfriend. Then he said to him, "Rabbi, I'd like you
> to marry us [begins to cry] because . . . ," excuse me, " . . . I don't know what
> tomorrow can bring and I feel that I want to be married to this girl." So of
> course, my grandfather married them. And he thanked . . . the man thanked
> him, and thanked him. And he says, "How much do I owe you?" My grand-
> father said, "I don't, I'm not going to charge you anything. Just have good
> luck. And I hope your luck stays with you." So the man turned around, he
> says, "You know, I'm authorized . . . " And I don't know how he got to it or

how he did it, " . . . to give you a permit, a working permit. So if the Germans come through the door and want you to go to work or they want to get you out of your dwelling, you'll show them the permit and they will leave you alone." So my grandfather of course accepted it. So he filled in his name and he gave him his permit. And that was another lucky break.

While work was important for survival, it was anything but easy. Typically, Jews did hard, manual labor: digging ditches and chopping trees, carrying bags of cement, or cleaning. Further, as Abram Z. explained:

> And it was not only work. You know, they beat us. The guy was . . . especial made us do very hard things. Still, we have been happy because we got a special papers that we are working. And only the people what have these papers could stay on in the ghetto.

Of course, Jews were not paid for their labor. Rather, they received small amounts of food, along the right to live. Under the circumstances, though, this arrangement was welcome. Helen Z., who was fourteen when she was sent to the Vilna Ghetto, said,

> You know, it was very bad in the Vilna ghetto. We used to go to work, and we used to get . . . I can't remember what I used to get for working, some bread and what else? Anything, a little bit of soup, every day they used to give us.

Work was all important, because it protected the worker from being sent away, as Theodore F. stated:

> A pass was equal to gold. Anybody who had a pass could survive as long as . . . more than anybody else.

Yet although the work passes seemed to hold the key to survival, they were at best a means of delaying the inevitable. Worse, once the Ghetto community put its faith in the power of work passes as protection, the Nazis could use the seeming legitimacy of the passes to facilitate additional roundups and killings. After the liquidation of Ghetto 2, officials announced that all extant work passes had to be traded in for new passes, printed on yellow paper. The problem was that only 3000 passes were available, which could protect up to 12,000 workers and "family" members—not anywhere near the number needed to cover the 28,000 people left in the Ghetto at the time (Arad 1982: 145). Those without coverage were rounded up and taken away, in what became known as the "Yellow Pass Aktion," on October 24, 1941. Knowing that some Jews without passes had gone into hiding—fashioning *malines*, or hiding places, for themselves—another announcement on October 30 proclaimed that all Jews without passes could relocate to the now-empty Ghetto 2. But those who did so were killed in another *aktion* there. This process played out several times throughout the rest of the year; a second "Yellow Pass Aktion," following an announcement that the yellow work passes had to be exchanged for new yellow passes, took place between November 3 and 5; and a "Pink Pass Aktion" captured and killed more people between December 20 and 22. By the end of December 1941, some 33,000 people—about half of Vilna's Jewish population at the beginning of the German invasion—had been taken away (Arad 1982: 217).

The Assessment of Threat

How did Vilna Jews make sense of the roundups, constant changes in protocols for work passes, and the ever-shrinking Ghetto population? Clearly, they saw the roundups as dangerous, something to be avoided if possible; the *malines*, creative and desperate efforts to secure work passes, and other strategies were proof of this. Yet, as of mid to late 1941, most Jews in the Vilna Ghetto had no precise knowledge of the fate that befell those who were taken away. All they knew for sure was that those individuals were gone.

Benjamin A.:
They [soldiers] start, at night, taking out people, taking out, and taking them away. We didn't know where. They was taking out . . . you didn't see them anymore.

While it was not clear exactly where the arrested and disappeared Jews were taken, most who remained in the Ghetto believed the Nazi officials' claims that the roundups were based on work productivity. The later *aktionen* seemed to confirm those claims: people with work passes were allowed to stay in the Ghetto, and those without (seemingly, those unable to work, such as children) were taken away. The proper response to the threat of deportation, then, was to secure employment that would allow one to stay in the Ghetto. The corollary was that nonproductive people had to hide.

> Zula S.:
> We had to survive, so we had go out to work . . . But you always had to watch out, that older people could not go, and children could not go. Because the Germans, the first thing is they took . . . is if you were thirty, or over thirty, you were already a old person. Because my parents was only in their forties and they were . . . to them, to the Germans, they were old. They wanted strong, and they wanted to have them make believe . . . it really was a lie but this is the way they did it. And they also, uh, liquidated as many children as they could. If they saw a child, the child was always in danger. So you had to hide the children.

Again, though, while people knew that being taken away was bad, they did not know exactly how bad it was. Many people in the Ghetto did not, or could not, believe that the deportees were being killed en masse. Once women and children were taken away to clear out the area that became the Ghetto, Vilna's Jews thought it strange—but still could not imagine, or believe, mass killings, as Esther M. suggested:

> Even the Germans said that they're taking them for work. When they took my brother, they said they are tasked to take a towel and a piece of soap, and they are going for work. But when they took out the people from this place, where it's supposed to be the ghetto, we knew that we are women and children, you don't send them to work. So that was not good. But still, you didn't want to believe that you can take out women, and children, and men, and take them and just kill them; you just couldn't believe that. Even, we knew it's happening, but you just couldn't believe it.

Eventually, word about the killings at Ponar made its way to the Ghetto. Incredibly, some of this news was delivered by people who managed to survive the killing fields. Though it is difficult to estimate how many survived, there is clear evidence that some individuals were wounded, but not killed, in the mass shootings, and were able to make their way back to the ghetto to tell their stories. However, many people in the Ghetto did not—or, more accurately, could not—believe what these survivors were telling them (see Arad 1982: 172–178; Porat 2010: 60–61). Toby W. recalled one such incident:

I think two or three people survived it [Ponar], because they fainted while the shooting was going on. They fainted before the bullet hit them. And they came back to the ghetto. And they told some women. They were talking about it and people didn't want to believe them. I remember, two women got into a fight, like . . . or really so upset with each other because they didn't want to believe it.

Sol A.'s next door neighbor also survived Ponar. Yet while Sol believed his neighbor's story, others did not:

He was wearing a black coat . . . When he opened his coat he was in his underwear and all the underwear was bloody. And we asked him, "What happened?" He said, "They took us from the ghetto out and took us in Ponary and they put us against a very deep ravine. And they shoot every one of us. And I fell into the ravine without catching a bullet." . . . He said, "My wife was lying next to me . . . " He had four sons between the ages of 4, 5 to 12. They were all around him dead. He said, "And I crawled out and crawled out and when they put us next to the ravine, they told us to take off all our clothes, so I saw a black coat. So I got the black coat and I crawled out, crawled out and I come here." . . . Anyway, we took him in the middle of our group and brought him at night back into the ghetto and presented him to the people from the *Judenrat* . . . and he told them the whole story. Believe it or not, nobody believed him . . .
. . . *Did you believe him?*
I had to believe him, because I saw . . . I saw when he opened the coat the blood was all over him. He was completely in blood . . . We had to believe it. But nobody believed it, because you just couldn't believe that people are taken out and being shot. I mean, who would do it? We never heard of anything like it in the worst places.

Lucie C. also described how Jews in the Ghetto did not believe the news about Ponar:

One day a woman, a young woman escaped, and she came back to the ghetto. She crawled out from under the dead bodies and she went to a Polish peasant and she gave her clothes and she came to the ghetto. And people wouldn't believe her that she came out from Ponary. But that was true. You always had the hope that you'll survive. And whatever they tell you, they used to tell you they take the old peoples to a old age home, people believed they take them to an old age home. They take you to work in another city, people believed. You believed everything because the urge to stay alive.

Lucie's words provide further illustration of the concept of cultured igno-rance: an inability to accept a horrible truth that goes against one's instinct to stay alive. Further, as William T. explained,

They . . . the Germans never arranged plain, "I'll come. You'll be killed." They always had a deception. And the deception was so good and the survivor instinct is so strong that you believe deception. You cannot talk today . . . you cannot explain to a normal person who is on death row he shouldn't believe that something will happen. Every . . . the whole popula-tion was on death row and it was no appeal. But somehow you hoped that something, big miracle will happen.

Activist youth saw things differently, however. As in Warsaw, these activists' assessment of threat proved to be critical to calls for armed resistance.

Youth Activists' Critical Conclusion

In the terror and confusion of the German invasion of Vilna in June 1941, Abba Kovner, the young HaShomer HaTzair activist, drew on his activist network to find shelter. Thanks to help from Irena Adamowicz and Jadwiga Dudziec,[5] two courageous Polish Catholic women active in the Scout move-ment (Batalion 2021), which had an affinity for HaShomer HaTzair, he was hidden in a small Polish convent of Dominican nuns five miles from the city (Arad 1982: 188; Porat 2010: 45). Abba was not the only HaShomer HaTzair activist who received shelter there. Joining him were sixteen others, in-cluding Arieh Wilner, the activist from Warsaw who would later die at Miła 18, and Chaika Grossman, another fiercely committed activist who later played a crucial role in an uprising in the Białystok Ghetto (Batalion 2021; Porat 2010: 45). While in hiding, these young activist Jews became especially close with The Mother Superior of the convent, Anna Borkowska; in fact, they called her *Ima*, the Hebrew word for mother. Abba Kovner in particular developed a strong friendship with the Mother Superior, and spent hours with her, discussing his activist ideology and even teaching her some Hebrew (Porat 2010).[6]

With the HeHalutz brain trust in hiding at the convent, other youth activists came by from time to time to visit with them. Importantly, they shared rumors from the Ghetto about the killings at Ponar. The activists in hiding also received word of the killings from a priest named Zawecki, a frequent visitor to the convent (Porat 2010: 62). The tragic news about Ponar hit Abba Kovner particularly hard, as he learned that his longtime girlfriend, twenty-one-year-old Hadassah Kamianitski, lost her life there (Porat 2010: 49). The news was devastating to Abba not simply because of Hadassah's death, but because he correctly surmised that the murder of Vilna Jews at Ponar would only become more widespread and would eventually affect all European Jews under Nazi control. Despondent, he initially considered committing suicide, but then decided against it because killing himself would only further the German regime's goal of killing Jews (Porat 2010: 63). Instead, Abba and his comrades reached a decision: if all Jews were eventually going to be murdered, it was better to resist, even if that led to a certain death, than to die at the hands of the Nazis.

Just as in Warsaw, the conclusion of genocide was critical to the decision to resist. Nonetheless, the idea of genocide was so far-fetched and unprecedented that it was a still a difficult conclusion to reach, even for the activists. FPO member Ruzka Korczak later wrote that this position required a "conceptual revolution" in order to make sense:

> How many people are capable of following the reasoning behind such an idea? Every human being wants to live and does so convinced until the very last moment that it will never happen to him! (quoted in Porat 2010: 72)

Nonetheless, Abba Kovner went to the Vilna Ghetto, determined to share the activists' conclusions and decision to resist. The terrible news he had heard while hiding in the convent was corroborated by similarly horrific stories he had heard from people he met in the Ghetto. On September 4, 1941, he jotted in his ever-present pocket diary, "The first greeting from Ponar: Trojak"— in reference to an eleven-year-old girl named Yehudit Trojak who survived Ponar and managed to make it back to the Ghetto, where she told her tale. Describing Kovner's meeting with her, Porat (2010: 62) writes:

Yehudit behaved quite maturely and was precise when she told her story to Kovner and the others present. Members of the various movements met six other survivors in the ghetto hospital and methodically wrote down their stories and found them almost identical. The reports spread throughout the ghetto: Jews who were brought to Ponar were shot.

The youth activists increasingly believed the stories about Ponar, even though others in the Ghetto did not. Knowing what was happening at Ponar solidified their decision to fight back.

A Call to Arms

Having arrived at the devastating, but critical, conclusion that European Jews were systematically being put to death, the young activists in the Vilna Ghetto began preparing for armed resistance. Firmly believing that all European Jews faced the threat of genocide, they wanted to share what they knew about Ponar with youth activists in other ghettos. Individual activists who came to Vilna were sent back to their respective ghettos, carrying the news of genocide as well as the Vilna activists' call to action. Henryk Grabowski, another Polish scout with ties to Jewish youth activists in Warsaw, arrived in Vilna in October 1941 (Arad 1982: 222–223); upon his return to Warsaw he brought the news of massacres and resistance efforts in Vilna that proved so important to the Warsaw activists' decision to fight back. Arieh Wilner also left for Warsaw, traveling separately from Grabowski. Chaika Grossman went to both Białystok and Warsaw, before returning to Białystok to organize for armed uprising in that ghetto (Arad 1982: 243; Batalion 2021).

Meanwhile, those who remained in Vilna continued to discuss strategies for resistance. While all the activists understood that Jews in Vilna faced extermination, they voiced different responses to the threat. Some, such as Mordechai Tenenbaum-Tamaroff,[7] argued for leaving the Vilna Ghetto and moving to safer ghettos that had not experienced roundups and mass killings; in contrast, others agreed with Abba Kovner that the proper response was to stay in Vilna and fight, as it would be wrong to abandon the Vilna Jewish community (Arad 1982: 226–234). These differences of opinion and strategy centered on uncertainty about the dimensions of the threat (Einwohner and Maher 2011)—namely, how severe it was, and whether it was malleable and/ or applicable. That is, the assessments of threat were dynamic, and varied among the activists. They were not sure how bad things were (i.e., whether the threat was lethal or survivable) and whether the threat could be mitigated in some way; further, they were not sure whether the killings were a local problem facing only Vilna (or Lithuania more generally) or something more widespread, that would affect all of Europe's Jews. Abba Kovner argued strongly for the broadest applicability and highest severity of the threat, and of the need for action. At a HaShomer HaTzair Council meeting in late December, he said:

> Everything that has happened so far means only one thing: Ponar, that is to say, death. And not even that is the whole truth . . . Vilna is not only Vilna, and Ponar is not merely an episode, it is a complete system. (quoted in Porat 2010: 66–67)

The activists continued the debate at another meeting, held on New Year's Eve 1941, at a soup kitchen at 2 Strashun Street. There, Abba Kovner read from his now famous manifesto:

> Jewish youth!
> Do not place your trust in those who deceive you. Of 80,000[8] Jews in "Yerushalayim de Lita," only 20,000 are left. Our parents, brothers, and sisters were torn from us before our eyes. Where are the hundreds of men who were seized for labor? Where are the naked women and the children seized from us on the night of fear? Where were the Jews sent on the Day of Atonement?[9] And where are our brethren of the second ghetto?
> No one returned of those marched through the gates of the ghetto. All the roads of the Gestapo lead to Ponar. And Ponar means death. Those who waver, put aside all illusion. Your children, your wives, and husbands are no more. Ponar is no concentration camp. All were shot dead there. Hitler conspires to kill all the Jews of Europe, and the Jews of Lithuania have been picked at the first line. Let us not be led as sheep to the slaughter!
> True, we are weak and defenceless. But the only answer to the murderer is: To rise up with arms!
> Brethren! Better fall as free fighters than to live at the mercy of murderers. Rise Up! Rise up until your last breath.

Kovner read the manifesto aloud, powerfully, in Yiddish. Following him, Tosia Altman—a member of HaShomer HaTzair from Warsaw who had arrived just days before, and who would later fight in the Warsaw Ghetto Uprising as a member of the ŻOB[10]—did the same, reciting the text in Hebrew. Together, they created what was, according to Porat (2010: 68–69), "an event everyone present and still alive after the war never forgot":

> "I remember every detail," said Haim Morocco (later Marom), a Hano'ar Hazioni member, "the noise of the celebrations being held outside the ghetto, the snow, the scores of members who had stolen inside, the excitement of hearing Kovner read the manifesto in his deep voice." "We were electrified," said another individual. "His face radiated light," wrote [Ruzka] Korczak, who later kept the manifesto as a treasure, in the forests and until she reached Eretz Israel [the land of Israel], "and his voice was strong and full of the pain he felt." "Ponar means death," said Littman Moravtchik (later Mor), "and it hit me like a ton of bricks. I was in shock: Ponar means death." The room was silent for a long time after Kovner finished reading, and then they expressed their feelings in a quiet song: "To put our necks under the knife—no, no, never."

As Abba Kovner and Tosia Altman proclaimed, all Jews were targeted for death—in Vilna and throughout Europe. Further, although they had little means by which to fight back, fight back they would; with little hope for success, their goal was to fight, and die, honorably. Thus, Jewish resistance in the Vilna Ghetto, the "birthplace of everything," was born.

The United Partisans Organization (FPO)

While the New Year's Eve meeting marked the powerful recital of the manifesto, the FPO itself was not founded formally until another meeting several weeks later, on January 21, 1942. One of the articles adopted at that meeting, which was central to the organization's ideology, read "Defense was a national act; a struggle of a people for its honor" (Arad 1982: 236). Yet while the FPO's focus on resistance as honor was similar to that of the Warsaw youth activists—who modeled their own calls for resistance in part on what they learned from their comrades in Vilna—its organizational structure was different. In Warsaw, ideological differences prevented the ŻOB and ŻZW from joining forces. In contrast, in Vilna the FPO represented the entire political spectrum and included Communists, Zionists on both the left and the right, and, eventually, members of the Bund (Arad 1982; Porat 2010). Further, while both the FPO and the ŻOB were organized into small fighting cells, in Vilna, the cells—known as "fives," because they had five members each[11]— were composed of representatives of various pre-war movements, whereas in Warsaw and elsewhere, fighting units were comprised entirely of members of a single pre-existing activist organization (Porat 2010: 90). Although the Vilna "fives" were diverse with respect to activist ideology, the FPO generally only accepted youth who were part of pre-existing political organizations, and required a loyalty oath (Arad 1982: 239).

Even with activist credentials, it was not always easy to be accepted into a fighting cell. Abba Kovner, the "head of recruitment," interviewed people and put them through rigorous tests, and not everyone was chosen (Porat 2010: 89). Once accepted, though, fighters were part of a committed collective. Given the political diversity in the fighting cells, the activists took care to build and enhance trust among the fighters. One way they did so was by creating a commune of sorts in the Ghetto, where activists spent time together listening to lectures and discussing politics. Their bonds were further strengthened as they enjoyed the excellent cooking of Rosa Kovner, Abba's mother, who lived nearby and did what she could to feed the youth, despite the food shortages in the Ghetto (Porat 2010: 89–90).

The FPO's breadth was also reflected in its name: the *United* Partisans Organization. However, the "partisans" moniker was less reflective of the organization's actual position on what kind of resistance they wished to undertake. Although they chose "partisans," in a nod toward the Communist members' general desire to support the Red Army in its fight against the Nazis, the activists agreed-upon goal was armed resistance in the Ghetto, led by Jews, as opposed to fighting as part of the anti-Nazi resistance that Soviet partisan units carried out in the nearby forests (Arad 1982; Porat 2010). Further, the plan was to resist only when the Nazis began the final liquidation of the Ghetto. Abram Z., a Bundist member of the FPO, described the coalition's perspective:

We didn't have any illusions. We know what the Germans are prepared to do with the Jews. And in January, '42, was a meeting from youth organizations who decided that they will organize a resistance. Question from the resistance, in the start of . . . from the United Partisan Organization was . . . when will we start the fight. That was one of the very important questions: Should we go out now and start the fight with the Germans? We know that this will bring annihilation from all the Jews around us. So we decided that we should fight there when it will come to the final liquidation from the ghetto.

Still, the fighters had to be ready to resist when the moment came. Yet because they had to work in secrecy, the activists could not turn to the Ghetto populace for money or valuables to purchase weapons. Instead, FPO members used whatever coins, jewelry, or other valuables they had managed to hold on to during ghettoization; they also ingeniously sold forged ration cards to support their resistance efforts (see Arad 1982). They used these funds to purchase weapons from Poles or Lithuanians and smuggled them into the ghetto. Weapons that could not be purchased could be stolen—a risky proposition. The FPO members working in munitions factories were instrumental to such efforts (Arad 1982: 255; Shneidman 2002: 52). Remarkably, some weapons were even stolen from German soldiers. Sol A., the tailor who worked in a hospital mending soldiers' uniforms, was able to obtain weapons this way:

[L]ike where I work in the hospital, they would bring in people, I mean, German soldiers that were half-dead already . . . they had like a railroad going in . . . directly into the hospital. So, when the Germans were wounded, they would put them on trains and bring them right into the hospital . . . and we had the yellow patches as Jews, the people that run the hospital, the Germans, said . . . would not to make angry the soldiers or whatever, they would tell us to take off the [stars] . . . because we would take him out from the . . . from the trains and bring him into different places where they would . . . where they would treat their wounds. So, many of them were wounded to a extent that they wouldn't know what's happening with them. And they had some weapons on them and we managed either to take it off of them or leave it . . . or they would leave it in the wagons themselves. We tried in some way to steal all those weapons and bring it into the ghetto . . . and we were quite successful, because many of those Germans they didn't know what's happening with them anymore. So we did bring in some of the weapons, some of the bullets.

Even if they were able to buy or steal weapons, though, such success was not enough; the resistance fighters still had to get those weapons into the Ghetto.

FPO members used a number of creative strategies. Weapons were hidden in toy chests and coffins and smuggled into the Ghetto. On at least one occasion, FPO activists, posing as city sanitation workers, removed a manhole cover from a street outside the Ghetto and placed a pipe in the sewers; other activists later crawled into the sewer from the Ghetto side and retrieved the pipe, which had rifles hidden inside (see Arad 1982: 254–262). Gentile allies also provided support. Anna Borkowska, the Mother Superior of the convent where Abba Kovner and other activists hid early in the occupation, remained loyal to her young activist charges; in January 1942, she gave Abba his first hand grenade, a precious commodity that she hid under her habit and hand-delivered to the Ghetto gate (Porat 2010: 51; Shneidman 2002: 52). As in Warsaw, the youth activists also supplemented their weapons by creating Molotov cocktails and other home-made devices.

Given the need for secrecy, activists could only work with those whom they trusted. Bernard D., trained as an engineer, built a radio to listen to BBC broadcasts; he was not a member of the FPO himself but still shared information with them:

Now, how the heck are you going to get organized where every second Jew is a . . . they'll tell on the other guy . . . *mamzer* . . . So, I met a couple of guys from college that we went together. And we decided to get organized. Okay? Because those guys I could trust. So, first of all, they had to know what's going on in this world. So I built a short-wave radio. Okay? And we used to listen to the BBC every night when I come into the ghetto, about seven, eight o'clock at night . . . Well, then I used to write out the information and give it to the FPO . . . So we would know what's going on in this world.

As part of their secrecy, FPO members also chose a code phrase, *Liza ruft* ("Liza is calling"), as a call to action and a signal that the uprising had begun. It honored a fallen comrade: Liza Magun, an FPO member who was caught, tortured, and eventually killed at Ponar in February 1943 (Arad 1982: 241). Her name lived on in other ways as well; for instance, FPO fighter Baruch Goldstein named his weapon after her (Porat 2010: 92).

Having reached a critical conclusion of genocide, along with a response—armed resistance—young activists from across the political spectrum were hard at work, secretly planning for an uprising (see Figure 4.2). Meanwhile, life went on in the Ghetto.

Figure 4.2 Some members of the FPO, July 1944. Abba Kovner is in the back row, center. Ruzka Korczak is standing next to him, to the right. Vitka Kempner (partially obscured) is standing in the back row, second from the right.
Credit: Yad Vashem Photo Archive, Jerusalem. 120EO9

Life in the Vilna Ghetto, 1942–1943

After the completion of the *aktionen* in the last months of 1941, the Vilna Ghetto settled into a somewhat "normal" existence. Of the 20,000 Jews left in the Ghetto, three quarters were over age fifteen and therefore, ostensibly, able to work (Porat 2010: 82). In fact, teenagers were considered working adults, while anyone over forty was considered elderly, largely because the harsh conditions caused people to age rapidly (Shneidman 2002: 36). Yet even with the reduced population, people still lived in crowded conditions; even with the large proportion of workers, people never had enough to eat. Paula N., who was sent to the Vilna Ghetto from another town in the winter of 1942–1943, recalled:

[W]e were so lucky, because an average apartment would hold five, seven, eight families. One bathroom. We had a space which was made into a room, but we had a private room for ourselves. It was probably about eight foot wide and a little longer. It held one double . . . it wasn't a bed, it was a piece of plywood on . . . for mama and papa and another piece of plywood where my aunt and I slept, oh the baby slept with my parents. And we were sitting on our bed and there was another piece of wood . . . saw horse? Which . . . which was used as a table. The rations was very . . . they were very, very skimpy, but we added. Now, what did we eat? We had a lot of cabbage.

Remarkably, no one died of starvation in the Vilna Ghetto, and there were few suicides (Porat 2010: 85; Shneidman 2002; Tushnet 1982). Food smuggling helped feed the community; the *Judenrat* also organized soup kitchens for the hungry, along with agencies to help people find housing and firewood (Arad 1982).

Interestingly, cultural life was strong as well. The Ghetto's Cultural Affairs department supported theater and other performing arts; there was also an orchestra and music schools (Porat 2010: 86).

Zula S.:

And the life in ghetto was, uh, I wouldn't say, let's say, normal. My father would, uh . . . in . . . in order to . . . thing . . . he was a very good chess player, so he would go and play. We had cafés, that you could go during the day, and play chess. We had theater. We had a pretty good cultural life in Vilna, in the ghetto. We did the best we could with what we had. So, uh, the . . . the . . . we didn't know what will be tomorrow, so you just live for the minute and for the day.

Ghetto residents were also active readers and users of the public library, which had 5000 visitors in July 1942 alone; at the end of that year the Ghetto celebrated the 100,000th volume being checked out from the Ghetto library (Arad 1982: 320; Porat 2010: 85).

While cultural activities gave Ghetto residents a needed respite from the sadness of Ghetto life, not everyone supported them at first. Members of the Bund and other activist organizations distributed leaflets proclaiming "Theatrical Performances Should Not Be Held in Cemeteries." However, even these activists eventually accepted the performances (Arad 1982: 321–322; Tushnet 1972).

Michael M.:

After a couple months the Vilna culture, the Vilna *geist*, the Vilna spirit woke up by these people. And actors, an artist organized a theater. Musicians organized a symphonic orchestra. Writers formed a club of writers. All kind of professions. There were . . . there were in the evening there were lectures. Can you imagine, in a ghetto, where people were suffering or working so hard, we were going to lectures, and they were going to symposiums, and they were going to . . . discussions. And the culture life became very, very active in Vilna Ghetto.

Equally impressively, the Ghetto staved off the crowding-induced disease that had plagued the Warsaw Ghetto, as Zula S. explained:

We did not have really epidemics and this in the ghetto. The ghetto was pretty clean. We did not have any lice in the ghetto, let's say, like the Germans said, and so on . . . But we did not have it; we did not have the problem.

The relative cleanliness and health of the Ghetto during this period was in no small part due to Jacob Gens, the "ghetto representative" to the Nazis, or the recognized ruler of the Ghetto administration (Porat 2010; Shneidman 2002; Tushnet 1982) (see Figure 4.3). When the Ghetto was originally formed in September 1941, Gens was the Chief of Police of Ghetto 1, but was installed as the Ghetto chief (which included the role of Chief of Police) in July 1942, after the *Judenrat* was dissolved (Rojowska and Dean 2012: 1150). With this new power and position, Gens instituted a number of policies that produced some remarkable successes (see Arad 1982: 315–318). Fearful that widespread disease would lead to the Ghetto's liquidation, the Ghetto administration created a Sanitation Department, which employed residents and helped keep the community clean by giving

Figure 4.3 Vilna Ghetto Chief Jacob Gens.
Credit: Yad Vashem Photo Archive, Jerusalem. 3380/137a

lectures and providing information on ways to avoid the spread of disease. There were laws against dumping garbage, which were enforced. People had to produce certificates saying they had bathed in the past month in order to receive food rations (Porat 2010; Shneidman 2002). Vitamins were available, thanks to successful efforts to manufacture them within the Ghetto; there was also a working hospital[12] and health clinic (Porat 2010: 83; Shneidman 2002). Anna D., a twenty-four-year-old woman who was close to finishing her doctorate in biology before the war began, got a job with the Sanitation Department:

> [A]t first I was in the sanitary police. I mean, we took care . . . there should be kept . . . you know, were so many people in one room, the hygiene, taught them to be . . . keep clean things, and to take care of that . . . how to wash, how to take care, shouldn't be any infections, any epidemics, keep things actually clean. And this was my job.
>
> *Was it possible to do that?*
>
> As much as possible. But later I was switched. I worked in the housing . . . it was called Housing Department. So we took care of people who didn't have a house, and assigned rooms for them, assigned spaces for them. And this I did until I left the ghetto.
>
> *And who assigned these jobs to you?*
>
> The Jewish commander was Gens. He was the head of the ghetto.

Jacob Gens was not only instrumental in keeping the Ghetto as clean and as orderly as possible, but he helped shape the community's sense of threat, as well as their sense of the best way to respond to the threat. For this reason, he played a central role in the Ghetto's history—including the FPO's failure to achieve their goal of an armed uprising in the Ghetto.

Jacob Gens and the "Work to Live" Response

Born in 1903, Jacob Gens was a Lithuanian Jew who had an established military career before World War II, enlisting at the age of sixteen and eventually rising to the rank of Captain in the Lithuanian Army. Such a career was unusual for a Jew at the time, but Gens was accepted and respected by his fellow soldiers and officers. He married a non-Jewish Lithuanian woman, Elvyra Budreikaite, with whom he had a daughter, Ada, born in 1926; Gens later divorced his wife so that she and their daughter would not have to join him in the Ghetto.[13] Gens' ability to protect his family also set him apart from other Jews, and bespoke his privileged position; throughout Nazi-occupied Europe, spouses and children of Jews were subject to the racial Nuremberg laws, and were usually ghettoized along with their Jewish families (Gutman 1982; Shneidman 2002).

One might think that Gens' interfaith marriage and military career would render him somewhat disconnected from his Jewish identity. This was true, to a point; Gens socialized mostly with his officer colleagues in the military, none of whom were Jewish. Yet, while he was a committed Lithuanian patriot, he also had strong commitments to the Jewish nation. Notably, Gens was a member of the right-wing Revisionist Zionist movement; while he had no personal interest in moving to Palestine, he believed strongly in protecting and serving the Jewish people.[14] One of Gens' classmates at the Lithuanian military officer's school described how he sought to protect the rights of Jews in that institution:

> He had personal charm . . . he had leadership ability, he had personality and he had principles . . . The entire school was led to church services every Sunday morning . . . Gens argued that we must emphasize our Jewishness . . . He submitted a memorandum in which he explained that, as a Jew, he did not think himself bound to attend church services. As a result, an order was issued exempting Jews from the obligation of going to church. (quoted in Arad 1982: 285)

As Ghetto Chief, Gens saw it as his duty to protect as many people in the Ghetto as possible, for as long as possible. The way to do that, in his assessment, was to make sure that the Nazis saw Vilna Jews as a productive work force—even if that meant sacrificing those who could not work. Gens therefore called upon the Ghetto community to work for the Germans, whenever and wherever commanded to do so. He also directed the Jewish Police to assist in roundups to remove the non-productive workers when needed. As William T. put it,

> He believed that somehow the ghetto will survive. Not 20,000, 10,000, but some people will survive. If you don't obey, nobody will survive.

In his memoir, Israeli historian Yitzhak Arad (a Warsaw native who fled his home at the start of the war to live with relatives in Święciany [Švenčionys], a city eighty-five kilometers northeast of Vilna) described Gens' visit to the Święciany Ghetto, on the occasion of the announcement that Święciany's Jews would be transferred to the Vilna Ghetto:

> Hundreds (myself included) crowded into the synagogue to see and hear the man reputed to be the sole power in the Vilna ghetto and to wield influence with the German authorities. He came in with some members of our *Judenrat* and a few Vilna police. He was about forty years old, tall, broad-shouldered, with a round, pleasant face. He strode energetically through the crowd, which parted to permit him and his entourage to get to the platform. His military background was evident in his bearing. Word had it that Gens had been a captain in the Lithuanian army and had fought for Lithuanian independence. He and his men were wearing the distinctive caps marked with the Shield of David, of the Jewish police force in Vilna, and their dark blue uniforms bore insignia of rank. There was absolute silence in the synagogue as the crowd waited tensely to hear the message Gens had brought. He opened with the words: "My Jewish brothers!" . . . There were many places of work, he stated, in the Vilna ghetto, and manpower was needed . . . Gens called on the people not to succumb to despair, but to bear the persecutions with dignity and patience and hope for a better future. We must go on clinging to life in the faith that this period will pass and we will see better times. (1979: 93–94)

Firmly convinced of his "work to live" frame, Gens used his power and authority as Ghetto Chief to ensure the work productivity of the ghetto. He promoted this vision frequently in speeches and other proclamations; more broadly, he constantly assured the Ghetto community that, despite the hardships of Ghetto life, the Ghetto was temporary and survivable. On January 13, 1943, on the occasion of the one-year anniversary of the Ghetto theater, he said in a speech:

> These are dark and hard days. Our body is in the ghetto but our spirit has not been enslaved. Our body knows work and discipline today because this maintains the body. The spirit knows of tasks that are harder . . . We must be strong in spirit and in body . . . I am convinced that the Jewish [life] that is developing here and the Jewish [faith] that burns in our hearts will be our reward. I am certain that the day of the phrase "Why hast Thou deserted us?" will pass and we shall still live to see better days. I would like to

hope that those days will come soon and in our time. (quoted in Shneidman 2002: 122; additions in original)

Gens' assessment of threat in the Ghetto, then, was that it was applicable, but malleable, in Thomas Maher's and my (Einwohner and Maher 2011) terms. That is, he realized that Jews in the Vilna Ghetto were in danger, but he believed they could reduce that danger, and preserve their lives and community, by working. This conclusion, and its resonant response, made sense and was worth supporting in the eyes of many Ghetto residents. Echoing Gens' views, fifteen-year-old Yitskhok Rudashevski wrote the following in his diary on January 27, 1943, after a visit to a Nazi-run factory:

Here on Rudnitski 6 the ghetto industry is concentrated. Here our professionals work. This is the foundation of our existence. The ghetto has exerted its entire effort to create what we have seen here today. We go from department to department, workshops for locksmiths, mechanics, tinsmiths. The work sings to the accompaniment of the tools. There is knocking and clanging. Everything bears the stamp of serious work . . . As I left the workshops I carried away the impression of the power of the will to live which emanates from everything here. It seems that everything I have seen here was created solely by will . . . I think about the fate of our work. Wolves and dogs benefit from the products of our work. But our will to live that I have discerned today proclaims distinctly that the dark game will cease, that finally a specter such as the one named Murer [the Nazi official overseeing the ghetto] will disappear. (1973: 125–127)

Further, as Snow and Benford (1988) argue, one reason why frames resonate with their intended audiences is that they have empirical credibility. Gens' "work to live" frame was seen as credible, especially after April 1942. The community was told that their work passes would expire on March 31— a deadline that caused great consternation because people feared it would signal new roundups. However, they received new passes instead. Jews in the Ghetto could finally relax, it seemed; all those able-bodied workers who could demonstrate their worth through work would be allowed to stay in the Ghetto, and live on (Arad 1982: 275–283).

Not only was Gens' response to the threat credible in the eyes of the Ghetto community, but he used his authority to ensure compliance with his views. A community meeting in June 1942 provides just one illustration. In response to a group of Ghetto residents who complained to him about food distribution in the Ghetto, Gens said "I am the ghetto. I alone am responsible for the ghetto and what goes on in it. Whoever opposes me will be expelled from the ghetto" and refused to allow others to take the floor (Tushnet 1972: 172; see also Einwohner 2007).

To maintain order and keep people working in the Ghetto, Gens also had to hide the truth of the killing fields at Ponar and the liquidations of smaller ghettos in the area. Rubin L., who survived roundups and a harrowing escape from the ghetto in his hometown of Grodno, described what happened when he tried to tell his story to Gens upon his arrival in Vilna:

Okay, now we're already entering the gate in the Vilna ghetto . . . and we see like a . . . a different world. The Jewish police were in beautiful uniforms, head bands, marked Jewish police. So we say, we tell the guys we want to see the head of the Judenrat. His name was Mr. Gens. "Just take us away. We have reasons to see him." So he took us in. We knocked on the door and let us in, and his name was Gens. Said, "My Gens, Mr. Gens, we escaped from the Grodno ghetto and things are very bad there. They took all the Jews out, very few were left when we left. And we are afraid the same thing will happen here. So we want to let you know what's going on." So he says, "That's a different situation here. Here everybody works for the Germans. Everybody's a tradesman and they will not hurt us because they need us." "They need us," he said, see. "And meantime, if you guys want to stay here you will have to keep your mouth shut not to tell the people in the ghetto that you escaped from Grodno and create a panic." "I don't want it here," he said. "Because if you do it I will take you, hand it over to the Gestapo and that's the end of you. But if you will keep your mouth shut I will let you stay. I will give you a ration card. I will give you a place to live and a job to work and everything will be all right. But you must promise not to talk about your escape." So we accepted it, naturally, and we got into the ghetto.

Most importantly, Gens' assessment of the threat, and his preferred response, stood in direct opposition to that of the FPO. Whereas the FPO believed that the threat was lethal (Maher 2010) and not malleable, and that resistance was the only response—even if it would not save any lives— Gens firmly opposed resistance. In his view, resistance was the exact opposite of what Jews in the Ghetto should do: resistance would lead to a certain death, whereas "working to live" would likely save some portion of the Ghetto community. Again, this assessment is somewhat puzzling, because Gens himself was a member of a political movement (Betar), and therefore both understood and respected, in a way, resistance. In fact, despite the FPO's secrecy, Gens was well aware of their plans, and in fact indicated to them that he too would join them in battle if it was absolutely clear that there was no way to save any Jewish lives (Porat 2010: 104; Shneidman 2002: 127). Publicly, though, he did all that he could to encourage Ghetto residents to work to live, and, therefore, to prevent resistance. Ghetto resident Herman Kruk's diary entry of May 19, 1943, describing Gens' reaction to rumors that Jews in Ghetto were mobilizing arms for the purpose of resistance, read:

> "Watch out. Everyone should watch everyone else, denounce every case." He himself will make them responsible. He will take their families, the residents of the apartments, the whole block, etc. In short, an internal means of "ensuring" collective responsibility . . . To try to resist means to assume the fate of the entire ghetto. (2002: 544)

Gens was not the only person in the Ghetto whose framing of the situation stood in stark contrast to the resistance fighters. Zelik Kalmanovitch, a well-known scholar and intellectual in the ghetto who was a member of the YIVO board of directors, also knew of the resistance efforts. Like Gens, he opposed them fiercely, believing that resistance would only lead to the destruction of the ghetto (Porat 2010: 96–98). Kalmanovitch did not survive the war, but his diary did. One entry shows exactly what he thought of the resisters:

> Young boys . . . have defiled the name of God . . . [and] the attempt to equip themselves with weapons is the fruit of that defilement. It is the fruit of the exhaustion of all thought . . . and of the desire to live . . . [They are] cowards and confused thinkers . . . [and] bring shame on the tens of thousands who have died. (quoted in Porat 2010: 98; a slightly different excerpt and translation is quoted in Shneidman 2002: 67)

This alternate framing, which opposed resistance, was ultimately important to the fate of resistance in the Ghetto. However, there was another, third response to the threat that complicated matters further.

More Options for Action: A Third Response

While the FPO and Ghetto Chief Jacob Gens were at odds on the question of resistance, a third segment of the community offered yet another response to the threat of mass murder: fleeing the Ghetto to join the partisans operating in the nearby forest. Thus, place—here, the ghetto's proximity to the forest, and its partisan activity—shaped the possible responses to the threat. Although this is the option the FPO eventually took, it was originally the response preferred by other, non-affiliated individuals who believed that the conditions were so bad in the Ghetto that they could not be survived. Because the FPO was operating secretly and was largely unknown to the Ghetto community, these individuals reached their own decisions about action.

Beginning in the second half of 1942, many Jews knew, or at least had heard rumors, about anti-Nazi partisan units operating in the woods surrounding Vilna (Arad 1982: 250). Despite sharing the word "partisan" in their respective names, these groups were distinct from the FPO. Most of the partisan units in the forests were pro-Soviet, either comprised of Russian soldiers who had become separated during the German invasion or of local party members and civilians committed to resisting against the Nazis (see Slepyan 2000, 2006). There were also armed groups in the woods affiliated with two Polish national resistance organizations, the AK (*Armia Krajowa*, or Home Army) and the AL (*Armia Ludowa*, or People's Army), but many Jews did not want to join them, fearing ill treatment due to anti-Semitism.[15] Although anti-Semitism was certainly not limited to Polish forces, the "partisans," a term generally reserved for Russian units or Jewish groups fighting as part of the Russian units, were believed to be relatively safe for Jews—provided that Jews could demonstrate their soldiering abilities well enough to join them.

How did Jews in Vilna know about the partisans? Stories spread largely by word of mouth.

Ida K.:
We were always aware that there is some Jews being taken out of the ghetto to go to the partisans.
And did you know what happened to them when they were with the partisans?
Some of them were caught. And some managed to join the partisans.

Paula N.:

There was a youth organization, which I belonged to, which somebody said one day to me, you know, the usual when kids get together . . . What we talked about mostly is Zionism and getting out to the partisans . . . And, of course everybody lived with the hope of somehow getting out.

Some Jews in the Vilna Ghetto learned about the partisans more directly, through personal contacts. Ted S., for instance, learned about Ponar, as well as the partisans, when he was sent out of the Ghetto as part of a work brigade:

I was sent to cut wood, lumber, trees, outside Vilna, about 40 miles away from Vilna . . . And as I was working there . . . there was a farmer and the farmer happened to know my father . . . He was a very nice man . . . He was working for the . . . already for the underground . . . He was what we call a "contact man" . . . His name was Billich . . . and he says, "Listen, we have information that 10 miles away from here is Ponary . . . " "And I want you to know," he says, "that they take the Jewish people from the ghetto and they kill them there. They bring them in by train from all over around, open up the doors of the train and the Ukrainians and Lithuanian soldiers with machine guns are opening up fire and they drop them in the . . . in those big open holes," . . .

Did you believe him?

I believed him. Of course I believed him. I realized right away what this . . . And I turn around to him and I said to him, "Billich, why are you telling me all those things?" He said to me, "You know, Ted, there is a way out. We have to fight them back." He wasn't Polish, he was Russian.

And not a Jew.

No. No. A farmer. I says, "How can we fight them back?" I [sic] said, "There is an underground. There are partisans."

While the idea of joining the partisans was a reasonable response to the threat in the Ghetto, it was not at all easy to put that idea into practice. Joining the partisans meant finding a way to escape from the Ghetto, which was very risky; not only was it difficult to run away from work brigades, but workers' absences could lead to harm to their families or others left in the Ghetto. Those who aspired to join the partisans also needed weapons, which were hard to come by. Lucie C., for instance, wanted to join the partisans, but did not have a gun:

And I was ready to join and I couldn't buy a gun. If you were able to get a gun, then you were going in the partisans . . . you were going out in the woods. But you needed a gun. I had the money and I had no way to buy a gun to go out.

Rubin L. made plans, along with ten other people from his hometown of Grodno, to flee the Ghetto and fight as a partisan unit. They were successful: they left Vilna on June 20, 1943, and joined Markov's Brigade, a partisan brigade commanded by Fiodor Markov, a Belorussian and former teacher who was married to a Jewish woman (Levine 2009: 215):

So we were a group of ten, and we stuck together. And everybody in the ghetto knew after a while, there's the Grodno group, this is the . . . he is part of the Grodno group. We had a good reputation. And the partisans organization told us, "We will take you in but you have to bring some . . . some weapons. We cannot take in anybody without weapon." "Where are we going to get weapons?" "That's your problem," they said. "You're a group of ten, you want to stick together, you have to deliver at least three handguns or three hand grenades. Then we'll take you all in and you will be part of the armed resistance." Some of the fellows did have some gold coins and there was black market. You could trade gold for weapons in this ghetto, we found out, if you have the right contacts. So we finally got three revolvers and we were taken in officially. And we were the first on the list to go to the partisans.

To join the partisans, one also had to be willing to leave one's family behind— if one's family was still alive, that is—because the partisans would only take young, able-bodied adults. Michael M. knew this first hand:

[Y]ou knew only three or four people. In case they got you, you shouldn't be able to squeal on other people. So you only knew one or two people. Once in a while we meet . . . but I wasn't accepted by the end because they wanted to take only me, and I insisted of my father. And they said, "Your father's too old for us." So I stuck to my father.

Others who perhaps would have liked to join the partisans simply did not know how to find them. Finding a mobile unit of people engaging in anti-Nazi sabotage, and who therefore did not want to be found, was a daunting task. Benjamin A., when asked whether he considered escaping from the Ghetto, replied:

> We didn't know where to run. That's what I say, there was partisans just who didn't . . . first of all, to be a partisan you need a gun, they wouldn't take you in. To go, we didn't know where to go. The partisans was far away, it was in the forest. And a city . . . a city of people, they was lost. They didn't know where to go. Then we was sitting there and waiting for a miracle.

Despite the difficulties involved,[16] many people saw joining the partisans as the only way to survive. Those for whom this response resonated therefore attempted to obtain weapons and head to the forests. Some, like Alexander B., simply wandered around in the woods and were lucky enough to cross the partisans' paths:

> *Did you have any idea where you were going?*
> No, it was . . . we heard that's partisans all around but we didn't know where.
> *. . . Tell me how you met them. How did you meet the partisans?*
> In . . . in the woods. They were hiding there and there was time to go farther, walk by the border. But we heard a little noises. So we sneaked in and we heard talk in Russian. And in Polish. So went to find out, they are partisans, so they came over and they took us in.

Some Jews who joined the partisans were aided by individuals who went to the Vilna Ghetto to "take people out," or help them find safe passage out of the Ghetto and into the woods. Some Russian partisan units actually sent representatives to the Ghetto to recruit Jews. Colonel Markov himself sent a letter to the FPO asking them to send their members to the forest to join his unit, but the FPO refused (Arad 1982: 382; Porat 2010: 112; Shneidman 2002: 57). Some of the other partisans who came to the Ghetto to recruit people were Jews themselves. Ted S., whose connections to Billich, the "contact man," led him to the partisans, was introduced to a Jewish member of the unit:

> And one night I slept in his [Billich's] house, he asked me to sleep over in his house. He woke me up around one o'clock in the morning, took me outside, and I saw the first time five dressed military . . . And as I am standing and looking at them, all of a sudden a little fellow walks over, a short little fellow,

with a heavy machine gun . . . a Jewish boy. He says to me, "Mister Yid? Are you Jewish?" I said yes. He says, "What are you doing in the ghetto? What . . . what's the matter with you guys?" I said to him, "You know, there are families and this you can't just dump them, forget about it." He said, "Get out of here, because you'll all be killed. There's no question." . . . This was my first encounter with these people.

Boris K. also learned about the partisans and found a way to join them. Upon his arrival in the Vilna Ghetto, having survived the liquidation of the ghetto in his hometown of Michaliszki, he was lucky to get a job in a locksmith shop. Based on his previous experiences in the other ghetto, however, he knew about the threat facing Jews in Vilna:

I . . . I was fortunate to have a good job, but I knew that there's no way out. And . . . and when the first opportunity arised, they came from . . . then it was already in the . . . in the woods they were organizing already the partisan brigades. And there were some young Jewish boys in the partisans and they were sent by the commander of the brigade, Morkow [Markov]. They were sent to Vilna Ghetto to take out young Jews to join the partisans. . . I, through acquaintances, through friends, I found out that a certain night a group will go out.

Joining the partisans was therefore a third response to the threat facing Jews in the Vilna Ghetto. Importantly, though, those who desired to join the partisans had a fundamentally different approach from the FPO: partisans were fighting forces operating in the woods, while the FPO wanted to fight in the Ghetto, leading the community in battle at the moment of the final liquidation. Of course, the positions of the FPO and the partisans were both anathema to Gens, who wanted to promote the idea of the Ghetto as a functional, working place and therefore could not have able-bodied young people planning for resistance. Due to these conflicting views, Ted S. noted that resisters had to "worry about the inside and the outside":

And he [Gens] felt that if he has a chance to survive with a thousand Jews . . . the ghetto carried about 25,000 Jews in those days. He says it's worthwhile. In other words, any time when they ask people to deliver some people to the camps or anything, they would the pol—the Jewish police had to fulfill the orders. But he's thinking . . . he wanted to save as many as he can, but his thinking was wrong. It means the people who got involved to the partisans had to worry about the inside and the outside.

Porat (2010: 112–113) describes another example of aspiring partisans having to worry about the "inside," or the Ghetto administration. A young Jewish man, Moshe Shotan, who came to the Ghetto to recruit young people for the partisans, was caught by Ghetto police and addressed by Gens himself:

> Some of the ghetto youngsters decided to take the initiative [to go on their own to join partisans in the forests], and one of them, Moshe Shotan, was carrying a list of those who intended to go with him when the ghetto police arrested him. Gens gave him a dressing down and told him in no uncertain terms that if youngsters left the ghetto, only the children, the elderly, and the infirm would remain, and the Germans would execute them without delay ... However, Shotan recovered, accused Gens of fostering illusions and of interfering with the actions of those who could fight and perhaps survive, and threatened to tell Markov of his position. Because Gens was extremely interested in good relations with the Soviets, hoping they would arrive first, and because most of those on Shotan's list were refugees who in any case did not work for the Germans in the ghetto, Gens finally agreed to let them leave. (see also Shneidman 2002: 127–128)

Like the FPO activists, those who sought to join the partisans assessed the threat in the Ghetto correctly, reaching the conclusion that the Ghetto was unsurvivable and that everyone there would eventually be killed. Where they differed with the FPO was in their response to the threat. Like Gens, these individuals saw the threat as malleable, something that could be mitigated through action. Where they differed with Gens was in their belief as to which actions would best manage the threat. In their view, the way to survive was not to work for the Nazis, but to flee to the forests to fight with the partisans. Ted S. was one of those who adopted this "forest ideology" (Arad 1982: 267):

> I personally felt that our chances to survive in the ghetto is zero. The only chance what we have is to put up a fight is in the woods.

Bernard D. felt the same way:

> *And was there anything that you felt that you could do or did you feel that you*
> *wanted to help people in the ghetto to do, to get away?*

There was no way out . . . the only way out was Ponary, or to go to the woods.

Each response was, in its own way, intended to do what was best for the Jewish people as a whole—i.e., to save Jewish lives, or, in the case of the FPO, to resist until the end and achieve an honorable death. However, these incompatible conclusions and responses were on a collision course. They came to a head in July 1943, when the Gestapo targeted FPO Commander Yitzhak Wittenberg.

The Wittenberg Incident

As a coalition representing the range of political ideologies among Vilna's Jewish youth activists, FPO members knew each other's political identities. They knew, therefore, that Yitzhak Wittenberg was a Communist. What they did not know, at first, was that he was also a member of a Communist underground in the city of Vilna, beyond the Ghetto walls. Unfortunately, this association proved deadly. On July 9, 1943, a German agent who had infiltrated the city Communist group arrested one of its members: Waclaw Kozlowski, a non-Jewish Communist. Under torture, Kozlowski gave Wittenberg's name to the Gestapo. While he identified Wittenberg as a member of the Communist underground in Vilna, not as a member of the FPO, it was enough to doom Wittenberg (Porat 2010: 114–115; Shneidman 2002: 58–59). The Gestapo then demanded that Wittenberg turn himself in—or else. Wittenberg was arrested by the Jewish police in the Ghetto but his comrades in the FPO freed him, after which he went into hiding.

Fearing Nazi reprisal, the Ghetto administration was desperate to find Wittenberg. Aron K., the chimney sweep, was expected to join in the search. It was the first time he heard of the FPO:

> We became aware of the organizations, really became aware, when they arrested Itzik . . . All of a sudden we found out that the Germans are . . . gave an order to the Jewish police to arrest and bring out of the ghetto Wittenberg. And he was . . . he was hiding and that was the first time that, as I told you, we, the chimney sweeps, were also firemen, they engaged us, they gave us white bands with . . . with . . . with Stars of David, that we were . . . we should become police helpers to find Wittenberg.

So . . . so did you go around to look for him?

Well, I didn't. I didn't. I found a way not to go, and I didn't know what it was all about. I didn't know who Wittenberg was, but I was strictly against police and I was strictly against police work, so I and my brother didn't. But that's when we became aware . . . of the FPO.

Due to the secrecy of the FPO's operations, most people in the Ghetto, like Aron K., had no idea that a Jewish resistance organization was operating in their midst. Wittenberg's arrest therefore made the FPO public. Unfortunately, it also drew the ire of the Ghetto community. Afraid that the Germans would destroy the Ghetto, people took to the streets, demanding that Wittenberg be handed over to the authorities. They were in fact exhorted by Gens to do so.

At a public meeting on July 15, Gens called on the Ghetto community to find Wittenberg. The alternative, Gens promised, was the destruction of the Ghetto (Porat 2010: 117). Gens implored the community not to listen to the underground, "the runny-nosed kids with the sticks," (Porat 2010: 117).[17] Sol A. was present for Gens' speech:

So the next morning the ghetto was closed. And Gens said everybody in the ghetto has to come, there was a place where he would have speeches. There was room enough, like a plaza for maybe 6, 10,000 people. So everybody . . . the police . . . the ghetto police would go to every house and say, "You must go to that place. You must go to hear what Gens has to say." And everybody went to that place and Gens came out on a balcony, you know, a porch, and he started to tell the story about Kozlovski . . . He said, "A man by the name Kozlovski was arrested in the city and he said that a man by the name Wittenberg is running a organization against the Germans here in the ghetto. And we tried to arrest Wittenberg and he disappeared. We cannot find him anymore. And the Gestapo said if we don't deliver Wittenberg 'til two o'clock, they going to bombard the whole ghetto and kill everybody." He says, "And it's up to you people, do you all want to be killed because of one man?" I was there myself. I heard him saying it. He says, "I don't think that one man . . . because of one man everybody in the ghetto should be bombarded and killed. And it's up to you. You must go out and find Wittenberg and deliver him to me," he said, "and to the Gestapo."

Later that night, the crowd heeded Gens' words. Chanting "One or twenty thousand!," people took to the streets. Tensions were high; shouting matches and fist fights broke out. "The Jews looked at us as though we were their murderers," wrote Shmerke Kaczerginski, a Ghetto activist and poet. "Our members became street victims and our own mothers cursed us" (quoted in Porat 2010: 120). Michael M. also described the reactions in the Ghetto:

> And the people . . . start yelling, "Why should we give, because of one person, the life of everybody?" And the whole night the ghetto didn't sleep. There were arguments, and yelling, and fighting, and negotiating.

The FPO was caught between a rock and a hard place: give up their leader to the Nazis, or go against the wishes of the Jewish community, thereby driving a wedge between them and the very community they hoped to lead in battle. If they refused to turn over Wittenberg, the Nazis would attack the Ghetto, which in turn would prompt the uprising. However, the fighters were concerned that they would first have to fight their fellow Jews before engaging the enemy. Seemingly, all roads led to disaster.

Wittenberg alone made the decision to turn himself in.[18] On July 16, 1943, after an agonizing night, Wittenberg handed his pistol to Abba Kovner and declared Kovner the Commander of the FPO. Then, after pulling himself away from his tearful girlfriend[19]—who called everyone else in the room traitors— he walked by himself through the Ghetto streets to Gestapo headquarters. The assembled crowd, lining the streets, watched him silently as he walked to the gate. Members of the underground saluted, raised fists, and cried (Porat 2010: 125). Sol A., who witnessed Wittenberg's final walk through the Ghetto, said:

> He came out of his hiding place and walked towards the gate of the ghetto, you know, erect and saluting all of us, because he knew exactly we were staying on the sides and watching him the way he was walking out to the ghetto. So he was walking and saluting and saluted and the moment he went out there were . . . the Gestapo waiting for him and put handcuffs on him and took him into the Gestapo building.

Wittenberg's body was found at Gestapo headquarters the next day.[20]

Even though the Ghetto community had called for Wittenberg to turn himself in, his death was a sobering event, one that further illustrated the precarity of Jewish lives and the difficult choices people had to make in order to survive. Paula N. remembered,

> The Germans demanded his surrender, or they will destroy the ghetto. And that's another feeling that I can almost physically feel. You didn't want him to die. He was a very charismatic young man. You wanted him safe. And, at the same time, you wanted the ghetto to survive. Because the pervading feeling was we're not going to give up till the last minute. Another day, another day, liberation would come, the Allies will come. So everybody wanted to just push to survive a little longer. The . . . finally, he himself . . . he gave himself up.

Similarly, Abram Z. recalled:

> It was a terrible dilemma. From one side have been the Germans from the Lithuanians around the ghetto. Inside was the Jewish police. And Gens had the order, either you bring Wittenberg alive or we'll liquidate it, the ghetto. And Gens send out Jewish policemen to tell all the Jews, there is a question or . . . either we find Wittenberg and bring him alive to the Gestapo or all the ghetto will be liquidated. And of course nobody of the Jewish population wants to be killed for one person . . . And this was the terrible dilemma. You understand? After so long, staying alive, when the most important thing was to stay alive, because of one person, to annihilate all the ghetto.

A famous song about Wittenberg, written by the poet Shmerke Kaczerginski, illustrates this point as well:

> *Night faded, it tore us,*
> *As death stood before us,*
> *The ghetto in fever did pant.*
> *In turmoil the ghetto—*
> *Commands the Gestapo:*
> *It's death or it's your commandant.*
> *Then spoke up our Itsik*
> *As quick as a blink is*
> *"I must heed this edict, that's clear.*
> *I'll not forfeit your lives*
> *To the tyrants' cruel knives."*
> *To death he goes without fear.*[21]

The Wittenberg Incident shows how assessments of threat, as well as ideas about how best to respond to threat, changed over time in the Vilna Ghetto. In fact, the stories of resistance in both the Vilna and Warsaw ghettos rest on central turning points that illustrate each community's critical conclusions and resonant responses. Like the onset of the Great Deportation in Warsaw, the Wittenberg Incident was an important turning point in Vilna with respect to decisions about resistance. Yet whereas the Great Deportation facilitated a ghetto uprising, the Wittenberg Incident hampered it. Further, this event demonstrates that assessments of threat are dynamic, and can vary within a community. The loss of Wittenberg, a seasoned activist and strong, decisive leader, was damaging to the FPO. Worse, the circumstances surrounding his death intensified debates within the organization about the real goal of resistance—i.e., whether it was better to stay and fight in the Ghetto, as Wittenberg and Kovner maintained, or to flee to the forests and fight as partisans. FPO Deputy Commander Josef Glazman actually split from the FPO as a result of these debates, and on July 24, 1943, he led a group of fighters toward the forests. Calling themselves the "Leon Group"—in homage to Wittenberg, whose underground name was "Leon"—they were ambushed by German troops along the way. Glazman survived this fight and was able to join a Jewish partisan unit, but later died in another battle in the forest (Porat 2010: 133; Shneidman 2002: 65).

The circumstances of Wittenberg's capture and death, and the reactions of the Ghetto community, weighed heavily on the young members of the FPO. They eventually reached the difficult decision to abandon their fellow Jews in the Ghetto and relocate to the nearby forests, where they formed partisan units and carried out sabotage and other acts of resistance for the rest of the war. That decision, along with other events, signaled the end of the Vilna Ghetto.

The End

The end of the Vilna Ghetto came a few months after the Wittenberg Incident. Roundups began again in August 1943, as German soldiers resumed the forcible removal of people from the Ghetto. On September 1, 1943—almost exactly two years after the Vilna Ghetto was established—German soldiers again entered the Ghetto. It was the beginning of the final liquidation, the moment that the FPO had long determined would be the point when they would begin their armed uprising. In fact, on September 1, Abba Kovner sounded the "Liza is calling" alarm, and activists went to their agreed-upon battle positions. At noon that same day he put out the following statement, which was distributed throughout the Ghetto:

> Jews! Defend yourselves with weapons! Do not believe the murderers' false promises! Anyone who leaves by the ghetto gate has only one road to travel and it leads to Ponar. Ponar means death! Jews! We have nothing to lose because no matter what happens we will die! Neither flight nor cowardice will save our lives! The only thing that can save our lives and honor is armed resistance. Brothers! It is better to fall in battle in the ghetto than to be led like sheep to Ponar! Know this: within the ghetto walls there is an organized Jewish force which will rise up with weapons. Join us in revolt! . . . Long live liberty! Long live armed resistance! Death to the murderers! (quoted in Porat 2010: 138)

Yet, the final battle that the FPO hoped for never took place. A Jew working as a Nazi informant betrayed one FPO battalion, whose members were rounded up and taken away (Porat 2010: 138). Other units were in place and ready to fight, but for some reason never received the command to begin shooting: given the FPO's small arsenal, units were told to wait until the command to begin shooting, so as to use ammunition as efficiently as possible. While some shots were fired in the Ghetto that day, they were not initiated by the FPO; instead, they came from a separate fighting group, led by Yechiel (Ilya) Scheinbaum and known as the Second Group, or Second Struggle Group (Shneidman 2002). This group was known to the FPO, and in fact the two organizations had discussed joining forces, but deep disagreements about the structure and nature of the resistance prevented a true merger. Scheinbaum and his fighters insisted that the only real response to the Nazi threat was to flee to the woods, where individual Jews might have some chance at survival; they did not believe that a mass uprising in the Ghetto was possible, and felt that any attempts toward that end would lead to the certain deaths of all involved. Still, they were committed to armed resistance against the Nazis (albeit not in the form of a sustained ghetto uprising). On September 1, 1943, while positioned with his fighters at 12 Strasshulu (Strashun) street, Scheinbaum fired at advancing Nazi soldiers; they then returned the fire, striking Scheinbaum in the throat and killing him instantly. Simon T. was with Scheinbaum and saw him fall:

> September 1st, and the ghetto was closed. That's when my father, my uncle were taken away also to Estonia. At that point the ghetto was closed, we were mobilized by this resistance organization and we were positioned in the ghetto. The street was called Strasshulu. It was a narrow street that we were supposed to defend it. And I wound up in the forward position of Strasshulu number 12, which was an entrance into the street. And when the Germans were trying to round up people for the transport, they demanded 5,000 people and people were hiding in hiding places. So, at one point they reached this street and our men in charge gave a command to shoot and they started to shoot, with a hand gun of course, we had nothing but hand guns. Then the Germans sprayed us with submachine gun fire and this man got hit by a bullet in his throat. He was next to me. I really remember propping him up in my arm from falling. He was killed immediately. Then the Germans withdrew, but about ten minutes later we heard a cry that they are laying dynamite under the building, so we decided to run. And we jumped out of the second story window into the backyard and we regrouped at the other end of the street, the Strasshulu 6. And the building was demolished by . . . exploded. And some of our boys were caught in the explosion . . . And there we sat for a couple of days until this action was finished. They made them, the ghetto police and administration were leading the . . . the Germans away from the spot where we were so they shouldn't come to another clash. So when after this action was over, we were given the red [sic] light to go to the woods.

Abram Z. was an FPO fighter who was also in position to fight, down the street from Scheinbaum's group. He, too, saw what happened:

> 'Til about five, six o'clock in the evening, the Germans didn't come to this street. And on this street was only one side for another street to come in. We put up our people in the front of the street, where there was one group. I was with another group on the other side. And we had the only machine gun. And we waited . . . the Germans to come. The Germans come over. We still didn't have an order to shoot. Now, on the other position, opposite them, Yehiel Scheinbaum was the commander of this group. And he start shooting the Germans. The Germans withdrew. Then, after a while,

154 HOPE AND HONOR

we come over, put some mines, and throw up all these building. And there Scheinbaum was shot and another friend of mi—a school friend of mine . . . have been killed. And the Germans, instead of attacking us, withdrew . . . And then it come, about three weeks, where the Germans didn't attack us. And we didn't attack the Germans. And every day a couple of thousands of Jews have been sent to Estonia. In the meantime, two of our groups went out to the forest.

After their skirmish with the Scheinbaum group, the German soldiers did withdraw; apparently, as a result of a deal cut by Gens, by which German and Estonian forces would leave the Ghetto and allow the Jewish police to continue the roundup and deportations themselves. The role of the Jewish police did not go unnoticed, and was not forgotten by those who were later in a position to do something about it, such as FPO member Vitka Kempner. Porat (2010: 139) writes:

Thus in effect Gens began a civil war within the ghetto, in which police and informers searched for Jews hiding in melinas and brought them out by force, while the Jews hid in every conceivable corner. During those last days of the ghetto hatred for the informers and police and for those who betrayed other Jews reached its height and was later manifested in the forest: "I was running around in the ghetto and saw Lotek Zaltzwasser accompanied by police officers open a melina full of crying children and screaming mothers, and drag the men out," recounted [Vitka] Kempner. "I caught him by the arm and yelled, 'Lotek, in the name of God, what are you doing, have you gone mad!' He had once been my brother's friend and even a member of the underground. And he betrayed and abandoned us and went over to Gens. After we went into the forest I returned, found him in hiding and brought him back with me so he might be executed, and I am proud of having done it."

More importantly, Scheinbaum's death, coupled with the German retreat and the strong belief that the Ghetto populace would not join them in battle, convinced the FPO to leave for the forests.

Sol A.:
And we saw that even when the time comes that we could fight the ghetto to some extent, we were not going to have the support of the people in the

ghetto. And we decided at that point to get out of the ghetto and go for the forest. And that's where we did go. So we went out in little groups. And, again, the women helped us going out, because many of the women lived already in secret apartments in the city and when a man would go out of the ghetto they would join the man, take him under the arm, lead him . . . because we had to go about seven or eight miles on the outskirts of the city and from there, go to the partisans.

Some FPO members fled the city through the sewers; once they got beyond the Ghetto walls, they were met and assisted by fellow activists, such as Vitka Kempner. Abba Kovner used this route, and was among the last fighters to leave the Ghetto.

Over the next few weeks, the Ghetto was slowly emptied. For all Jacob Gens' efforts to save the Ghetto community, he was shot by the Gestapo on September 14, 1943. Until the end, though, some Ghetto residents did not know that the final deportations would lead to their deaths. Because her father was friends with Jacob Gens, Zofja L.'s family learned about the impending liquidation and were able to flee:

> *Did you know what was going to be the fate of the Jews in the ghetto left behind?*
> Well, we knew that they were going to liquidate it the next day.
> *So it was a common knowledge that they would be killed.*
> Um, some people still believe that . . . that being in the ghetto and didn't quite believe that everybody will be killed. I think people still believed that they'll be taken to kind of labor camps, concentration camps. And some people did. But I think that . . . that mostly people would know, but what could they do? You know, one person with a gun is much stronger than . . . than hundreds just with their bare hands.

Actually, a lucky few were not killed in the final liquidation but were sent instead to work camps in Estonia. That was how Michael M., who was among the last of the Jews rounded up from the Ghetto, survived:

> [T]he whole ghetto started to move through the gate, my father, my mother, [crying] my three sisters, me, and my brother-in-law, my oldest sister['s] husband . . . we were walking all together. And we saw . . . is being a selection, the men separate, and the women separate. And my mother walked

over to me and she had . . . a thermos bottle. And she said to me, "Listen, give this to your father. He will need it more than me. I don't think I'll need it." And she walked over to my father and she talked to him. And I will never forget what she told him. She called him Judah. His name was Yehudah in Yiddish. "I thank you for a beautiful life. And God will be good to you. And God should forgive me if I did something, what was not acceptable to you." And she kissed him, and this was the last time I saw my mother. She went . . . my sister voluntarily went with her. And my father, and my brother, and my brother-in-law, and me, and my uncle, and his son, we went all together. We marched. And on the sidewalks, again, the non-Jewish neighbors, they were yelling, and spitting, and insulting, and, "Good for you," the whole thing again and again. They brought us a couple kilometers out of Vilna . . . They kept us there overnight, and it was raining. It was September, the 23rd of September, and it was raining. Then, the next day, they took us to a train. They put us in those wagons, you know, the cattle wagons.

The Vilna Ghetto, the remnant of the "Jerusalem of Lithuania," was emptied on September 24, 1943.

Conclusions

Whereas war with Germany came earlier to Warsaw than to Vilna, the mass killings of Jews started in Vilna. It was the "birthplace of everything"— the initial region in Eastern Europe to experience genocide, and the place where young Jewish activists first assessed that threat accurately. In fact, if it were not for the critical conclusions and resonant responses of the activists in Vilna, the Warsaw Ghetto Uprising might not have happened. But there *was* a sustained armed uprising in Warsaw—so why wasn't there one in Vilna?

Young Jewish activists from Vilna *did* participate in armed resistance[22] against the Nazis. Famously, after fleeing the Ghetto, Abba Kovner, Vitka Kempner (who later became Abba's wife), and Ruzka Korczak formed a Jewish partisan unit called HaNokmim ("The Avengers") and carried out acts of sabotage for the rest of the war; they also helped the Red Army liberate Vilna on July 13, 1944 (Cohen 2000). This evidence helps refute the persistent myth of Jewish passivity during the Holocaust. Yet while these Vilna youth resisted, it was not in the manner they wished; they never achieved their goal of a sustained armed uprising in the Vilna Ghetto. Why not?

The trajectories of the two ghettos were similar in many ways, but the timing of important events was different. In Warsaw, after a period of relative calm, the onset of mass deportations gave the community undeniable evidence of the Nazis' genocidal plans. The reverse was true in Vilna: *aktionen* began immediately after Nazi occupation and were followed by relative normalcy, giving Jews the false impression that the Ghetto was survivable. Vilna Jews who evaded the roundups in the latter half of 1941 had done so either by hiding, or by gaining the necessary work permits. These survivors knew that others had been taken away, but believed that productive workers (and those lucky enough to be included on their permits) could stay in the Ghetto and work. The question remained as to what happened to those who were no longer in the Ghetto. How did Vilna's Jews understand this situation? What was their assessment of threat—i.e., the answer to "what will happen to us if we fail to act?"

The case of the Vilna Ghetto illustrates three different ways that Jews assessed the threats facing them, arriving at distinct sets of conclusions and responses. One segment of the community believed that at least some proportion of the Ghetto population was likely to survive. For them, work was the key to life. This conclusion (that the Ghetto was survivable) and response ("work to live") was actively promoted by Ghetto Chief Jacob Gens. Another segment of the population, the youth activists, received information about what happened to the deportees—and, importantly, they believed it. This information led to their conclusion that the Ghetto was not survivable, and that all European Jews would eventually be targeted for death. They therefore came together to form a fighting organization—the FPO—for the express purpose of an armed uprising in the Ghetto. Yet, there was an alternate option for resistance, one that was shaped by place. Vilna's proximity to the forests, where partisan units were active, gave resistance fighters an option that did not exist in Warsaw. A third response to the threat, promoted by some unaffiliated youth, was the "forest ideology," or heading to the woods to join the partisans. These individuals agreed with the FPO that the Ghetto was unsurvivable, but rather than fight to a certain, albeit honorable, death in the Ghetto, they hoped to survive in the forests with the partisans.

These competing assessments precluded a single, resonant response to the threat, and worked against the possibility of a sustained armed uprising in the Vilna Ghetto. The lack of resonance of the resistance frame stemmed from multiple local, lived experiences and interpretations among the community. Some had seeming evidence that work saved lives, and others placed their trust in their abilities to flee and fight in the woods. The FPO disagreed with both responses but, due to the necessary secrecy of their work, could not advertise their own vision for resistance broadly. The fighters' views were revealed to the Ghetto community as a result of another important event: the Wittenberg Incident. However, Wittenberg's death also showed the FPO that their plans for resistance did not enjoy broad support. When the time came to fight, then, the FPO reluctantly left the Ghetto to fight in the forests.

Both hope and honor played an important role in these assessments and decisions about action. But unlike in Warsaw, where the notion of hopelessness was adopted broadly after the Great Deportation, the different assessments in Vilna meant that some people had hope that they could survive, and therefore did not support resistance in the Ghetto. More broadly, in both Warsaw and Vilna, critical conclusions and resonant responses shaped the decision to resist. When all hope was lost, resistance in the Ghetto made sense, but if there was a way to survive—either through work, or by fleeing to the forests to fight with the partisans—resistance was a less viable option. Honor shaped these assessments as well, as the three sets of responses reflected different ideas about how to act honorably. The FPO sought to avenge the Jewish nation by dying honorably, while Gens believed that he was acting honorably by saving as many Jews as possible. Finally, the partisans wished to both resist and save their lives at the same time, as Bernard D. explained:

> So we weren't asleep in the ghetto. But we had one problem. We had to get organized and go out to the woods. And Abba Kovner was against us, okay. He says, "We have to fight inside the ghetto for honor." I said, "A dead Jew has no honor. Only alive Jew has to have honor," okay? If he survives Hitler, he's got a lot of honor, okay?

It was the Wittenberg Incident that brought these three, seemingly reasonable yet incompatible sets of conclusions and responses to light, forcing the Ghetto population to choose from among them. The community's decision to support Gens decreased support for the FPO and ultimately led to the fighters' decision to call off their plans for a Ghetto uprising, turning to resistance in the forests instead. As FPO member Anna D. explained:

And the Germans demanded his [Wittenberg's] ouster. So we tried not to do it, but the people from the ghetto were against us. They were afraid that because of Wittenberg, they're going to liquidate the ghetto. And they forced us . . . they wanted to attack us all. They knew that we are hiding, Wittenberg was in hiding. So we made a decision. And he agreed to give himself up. So since then we saw that our aim to fight in the ghetto is not realistic because the people didn't want to join us.

A comparison of Warsaw and Vilna demonstrates that critical conclusions and resonant responses can either facilitate or hamper resistance. In both ghettos, those who planned armed uprisings did so because they believed that the ghettos were unsurvivable and that resistance was honorable. However, whereas there was support for such resistance in Warsaw, competing assessments of threat, and different resonant responses, precluded a ghetto-based uprising in Vilna.

The story of the Vilna Ghetto gives further support to my argument that a critical conclusion of genocide was not enough to produce a ghetto uprising; the idea of armed resistance in the ghetto as a proper response to the threat also had to resonate with enough people to put plans for such resistance into action. But was this conclusion truly critical—that is, a necessary factor in the emergence of an armed ghetto uprising? I answer that question by turning to my third case, the Łódź Ghetto, where an armed uprising never emerged.

5

Hope and Hunger in the Łódź Ghetto

What can I tell you about Łódź Ghetto? This was a ... a disaster over there. No food. Nothing. People are dying. People were committing suicide. People jumped from the windows. Torture; they tortured the people, they cripple. Took away the children. And, uh ... there's a lot of things, a thousand things.

—Survivor Zalman S.

It was just a day to day survival. It was just hunger and fear.

—Survivor Eva S.

The Łódź Ghetto is still hermetically sealed. In spite of our repeated attempts to make contact with the Jews in Łódź we have not suc- ceeded ... [It] is an island severed from the rest of the world.
—From a secret report sent to London by the Jewish National Committee, operating in hiding on the Aryan side of Warsaw, May 24, 1944 (quoted in Trunk 1981: 333, fn 5)

In early August 1944, Dora G. was one month shy of her twenty-eighth birthday. A shoemaker's daughter, she was the only member of her family left in the Łódź Ghetto when German soldiers came to her door. They came to send her to Auschwitz:

This was this ... you know, this was the last thing, what they did, when they start, you know, get all the Jews out to Auschwitz. Then they start coming to the doors where we lived. And we have to open it. If not, we're going to get killed ... I remember, there was one German ... Biebow [Hans Biebow, chief German administrator of the Łódź Ghetto] was his name. And he said that we have to pack whatever we have. "And wherever you're going to go

Hope and Honor. Rachel L. Einwohner, Oxford University Press. © Oxford University Press 2022.
DOI: 10.1093/oso/9780190079437.003.0005

it's going to be all right." We're going to have food and everything. And this was Auschwitz.

Twenty-seven-year-old Morris A. was also deported to Auschwitz in August 1944, along with his mother and several siblings. Like Dora G., he recalled Biebow's announcement that it was time to leave the Ghetto:

> [T]he . . . main man from the Łódź Ghetto, maybe you hear about him. His name is Biebow. He came, he make an appeal, on a big market and everybody has to come out, "Everybody should get dressed up and take all the best stuff, the dishes, the silverware, with the children . . . You're going to have better than here. And take it. Don't be afraid. You're going to have good," and he . . . he lied to us.
> *But you . . . but people believed him?*
> Everybody thought it's telling the truth.

Hans Biebow, a former businessman from Bremen with short, blond, slicked back hair and a youthful appearance, did not have much experience with the Nazi Party when he arrived in Łódź in May 1940 at age thirty-seven to serve as a Ghetto administrator (Horwitz 2008: 64). Nonetheless, he enjoyed great success. Under his helm, the Łódź Ghetto turned enormous profits for the Reich, both in terms of valuables confiscated from Jewish deportees and goods produced by Jews who worked as laborers in ghetto factories. Yet in August 1944, with the Red Army advancing into Poland, orders came to liquidate the Łódź Ghetto. Although he knew he was literally killing his profits, ever the patriot, Biebow facilitated the deportations, telling Jews that they were being sent to other work camps in Germany where they would have food and would be paid in German Reichmarks.[1] On August 7, 1944, for instance, in a speech made before a group of Jewish tailors who were told to report for relocation, Biebow said:

> The shifting of the ghetto should be carried out in calm, order, and quality . . . I give you the assurance that all of us will take pains to continue to do the best and through the shifting of the ghetto to maintain your life . . . There is enough space in the train wagons. Sufficient equipment is being transferred. Come with your families and bring pots, drinking vessels, and eating utensils . . . I assure you again that you will be taken care of. Pack and present yourselves. (quoted in Trunk 2006: 290–291)

By the time Biebow was making these speeches in August 1944, the Vilna Ghetto had stood empty for nearly a year, and the Warsaw Ghetto—or the pile of rubble that remained after its destruction—had been silent even longer. In contrast, the Łódź Ghetto was never fully liquidated, even after the deportations in August 1944 and a subsequent roundup that sent Łódź Jews to other camps in October 1944. At least several hundred, and possibly as many as 1500, Jews remained in the Łódź Ghetto, and some portion lived to see the city's liberation by the Red Army on January 19, 1945 (Crago 2012: 81; Trunk 2006: 269).[2] Łódź was, in fact, the longest-lived of the Jewish ghettos, from its establishment a few months after Germany's invasion of Poland until its liberation few months before Germany's surrender.

Part of the reason that the Łódź Ghetto was never destroyed, or even completely emptied, is that Jews there did not stage a mass armed uprising against the Nazis. In a sense, the lack of armed resistance in Łódź is not problematic. It fits the persistent, albeit inaccurate, belief that European Jews were "sheep-like," passive victims of the Holocaust. Theories of social movement emergence are not troubled by the lack of armed resistance in Łódź, either—in fact, these theories would predict that such resistance could not take place in a Jewish ghetto under Nazi occupation. The absence of armed resistance in the Łódź Ghetto is still worth exploring, however. By explaining why armed resistance did not happen in Łódź, this chapter further supports my argument about why it did happen in Warsaw. It shows that in Łódź, Jews' assessment of the threats facing them, and the responses to those threats that were most resonant, combined to prevent armed resistance from happening. It also reiterates just how remarkable sustained armed resistance in Warsaw was.

From Manchester to Litzmannstadt

On the eve of World War II, the manufacturing city of Łódź was the second largest city in Poland. Its Jewish population, approximately 233,000, represented more than one-third of the city's residents, making Łódź the second largest Jewish community in Europe (Crago 2012: 75; Miron 2009: 403). It was also one of the biggest textile manufacturing centers in Europe, surpassed only by the English city of Manchester. Łódź thus became known as the "Manchester of Poland."

Most of Łódź's sizable Jewish population made their living in some way that was related to the textile industry. Wealthier families were the factory owners and large distributors, while the middle class ran the smaller shops. Łódź, and its signature industry, supported a variety of jobs: while some Jews worked in large factories, others did hand-sewn finishing work in their homes. Bałuty, a bustling, crowded neighborhood home to the city's Jewish working poor, was the center of the garment district, as historian Gordon J. Horwitz (2008: 6) writes:

> To walk the streets was to be aware of the textile work in all its variety . . . Manufacture, visible to passersby through nearby windows, spilled from homes and workshops into the streets. Carts filled with pyramided bales of cloth crisscrossed the narrow thoroughfares; on market squares stalls were set up; hawkers called out to potential customers to come and examine their wares; boys marched past with baskets filled with warm bagels and pretzels to sell.

The textile industry, and all those it attracted, made for a vibrant Jewish community. Samuel P., who was born in Łódź in 1920, recalled:

> It was a wonderful life for Jewish people in Łódź. Łódź was a second largest city in Poland. It was an industrial center, primarily in textiles. It wasn't a pretty city because of its industries. Very rarely did you see in the city tree-lined streets. There were only a few of them, but it had some very nice parks with young people used to gather and meet, you know, boys and girls. And it had some nice streets where they had beautiful stores . . . And we used to gather, we used to meet . . . of course we didn't have the conveniences and the entertainment that is available to young people today, but we used to . . . we weren't bored [laughs] . . . the building that I lived had a large courtyard, and it . . . was the gathering point of youngsters from the entire building. We used to stay up at night and joke around and . . . and meet and talk and plan and dream and just like other . . . any other children, young people in the rest of the world, I guess.

Just like in Warsaw, however, things changed drastically, for children and all residents, in September 1939.

The German Invasion

German forces occupied Łódź on September 8, 1939, a mere week after the beginning of World War II. Because Łódź was in the region of Poland that was ceded to Germany in accordance with Hitler's pre-war pact with Stalin, it became part of the Reich,[3] and German officials quickly embarked upon the Germanification of the city. Łódź's main artery, Piotrkowska Street, was renamed Adolf Hitler Straße, while other streets were renamed for additional, notable German cultural and historical figures such as Haydn, Handel, and Wagner.[4] Officials also began using a Germanified spelling, Lodsch, for the city's name. Soon, the city's name was changed altogether: on April 11, 1940, it became Litzmannstadt, in honor of the World War I German war hero General Karl Litzmann, who defeated Russian forces at the Battle of Łódź in 1914.[5] This renaming served the broader goal of remaking Łódź entirely, transforming it from an industrial town to a beautiful, cultured city worthy of the Reich. To that end, plans were made to rebuild the city, including improved infrastructure and the creation of new parks. The ethnic German *Volksdeutche* would be resettled from elsewhere in Poland to Łódź, thereby "beautifying" the city's demographics as well (Horwitz 2008).

The Germanification of the city included efforts, big and small, to rid the city of non-Aryan influences, such as Jews. Just as in other cities, Nazi soldiers harassed and abused Jews in Łódź from the beginning of the occupation, looting Jewish stores and beating and humiliating Jews in the streets. Adek F., one of six brothers, was from a family of merchants who owned a spice shop:

[T]hey came in in September of 1939 and the first months was . . . a Nazi used to come up with a girlfriend to our store and just picked up anything he wanted . . . and this continues, not only to our store, but to any Jewish owned store, to any Jewish organization. They used to take typewriters and . . . they used to come in with a girlfriends and just pick up what you like.

Similarly, Eva B. testified:

We couldn't go out in the street. We didn't go out in the city, because whoever walked the street they catch him to work, to take to work. They were beating . . . if they got an Orthodox Jew, forget it. They would cut his beard, they would hit him, they would . . . especial people like . . . like my brother

and my father they would . . . they would hit them. They probably wouldn't
come back at all.

New edicts also formally restricted Jews' rights and freedoms. Even before
the Łódź Ghetto was established, Jews had to turn in radios, currency, and
other valuables, could not walk in certain places, and were required to show
deference to Nazi soldiers.

> Josef Z.:
> I can't remember exactly the . . . the date. But it was in September, October.
> And then they got a order, well, the Jews don't supposed to walk on the side-
> walk. They only have to walk . . . when they see a German, they have to walk
> on the street, not on the sidewalk.

Lucia M. described how German soldiers humiliated her parents when
forcing them to turn in their radio:

> A German truck will come to each courtyard of the houses were there, and
> they would come to each apartment and . . . take the radio. They didn't take
> it, they made us take it down to the truck. And my father wanted to take it
> because the radios were big clumsy . . . kind of like a piece of furniture. But
> they said, "No," my mother had to carry it down . . .
> *Why was that?*
> Why? Just to . . . to make more humiliation for everybody.

As 1939 neared its end, restrictions against Jews intensified. Jews were no
longer allowed to go to public parks or ride trolley cars. They had to wear arm
bands with Jewish stars on them; later, they were forced to purchase Jewish
stars to sew into their coats, both front and back. These markers were different than the white armband with the blue star worn by Jews in the Warsaw
Ghetto. In Łódź, city of the Reich, Jews wore yellow stars:

> Eva S.:
> It was a yellow . . . like a *Magen David*, like a Jewish star. And inside there
> was written in black *Jude*, what means "Jew."
> *And were these stars supplied to you?*
> Yeah. You bought them. Yes.
> *You had to buy them.*
> Yeah.

New edicts were announced daily, as Sam N. explained:

> Every time something else . . . One day we have to take off the hats if we see
> a German. One time we . . . we have to go . . . if we see a German we have to
> go on the street, not on the sidewalk. Every day something new and it was
> hectic. Then they came out that we have to leave this part of the city and we
> go to another . . . this will be a ghetto.

Like Jews in Warsaw and Vilna, Łódź Jews were eventually forced into a
confined ghetto, and ultimately deported to death camps. Yet, while the
story of the Łódź Ghetto is similar to the other ghettos in many respects,
some characteristics of its location and circumstance set it apart. In particular, I show in this chapter that distinct, place-based features of the
Łódź Ghetto shaped residents' assessment of the threats facing them, and
help explain why Łódź Jews never organized for armed resistance against
the Nazis.

The Łódź Ghetto

Earmarked to become a symbol of superiority of German culture, the
transformation of Łódź into Litzmannstadt could not be realized with a
large Jewish population, a people deemed by Nazi racist ideology to be
physically and morally inferior, in its midst. Accordingly, the city was
to be *Judenrein*: cleansed or free of Jews. Yet rather than concentrating
Łódź Jews into a ghetto, German officials initially sought the complete removal of the Jewish population from the city. This goal was to be
achieved by deporting Łódź Jews to the General Government, that region
of the former Poland (including Warsaw) that was occupied by Germany
but not officially part of the country. Such deportations began as early
as December 1939, but quickly ended in response to the complaints of
Hans Frank, the governor of the General Government. Plans were then
made for a ghetto in Łódź, which would house Jews from Łódź and surrounding towns as well as Jews deported from western regions elsewhere
in the Reich (e.g., Vienna and Prague) (Crago 2012). The Łódź Ghetto was
the first large ghetto in Nazi-occupied Europe, and it became the second
largest ghetto in Poland—smaller only than Warsaw—with an estimated
163,000–170,000 residents.[6]

The Ghetto itself occupied about four square kilometers, or 1.6 square miles, spanning the Bałuty, Stare Maesto, and Marysin neighborhoods in the northern part of the city. Bałuty and Stare Maesto were some of the city's oldest neighborhoods, with narrow streets and dilapidated buildings, while Marysin had better housing and more open, green spaces than elsewhere in the Ghetto. Marysin was set aside for schools, an old age home, and an orphanage, as well as (eventually) premier housing for members of the Ghetto administration, while most Ghetto residents were forced to live in the older neighborhoods of Bałuty and Stare Maesto (Old Town), in a 0.9 square mile area where there were 2300 homes.[7] The Ghetto was officially decreed on February 8, 1940 and sealed on May 1, 1940 (Crago 2012: 76; Horwitz 2008; Miron 2009: 404–406).

If Nazi officials could not remove all the Jews from Łódź immediately, they set out to create a ghetto that would effectively keep the Jews as isolated from the Aryan population as possible. Barbed wire, electrified in places, surrounded every parcel of land open to Jewish foot traffic, although some sections of barbed wire were later replaced with wooden fences. Every fifty to one hundred meters stood a guard, armed with a machine gun and orders to shoot anyone who approached the fence from within the Ghetto. Harry S. described people getting shot near the fence:

It was a guard, uh, standing around the ghetto, uh, watch—uh . . . uh, guarding the . . . the people will not go out or whatever. And from time to time they were shooting. And once . . . I didn't see the shooting but I saw taking away the corpse of a . . . a woman. And the son . . . He was running after, uh . . . with a horse and wagon, running and yelling, "Mother! Mother! Mother!" That . . . that is unbelievable that . . . terrible. And she was killed. And I would like to mention also, that was one place on Lutomierska, in one corner, that whenever a Jew went by . . . that was a lot of shooting there . . . And I remember one of the days, I went there, and I passed by. And I can feel it today, that nobody . . . nobody was on the street in the middle of the day. I . . . was just me. And the guard on the other side of the fence, very close. The pass—passage was very close to the fence. And I took off my hat and I said, "Good morning," to the guard. And I walked. And he was behind me. And every time I was feeling, I . . . I am going to get shot. And I said what will . . . my mother will never forgive me, what I did, because I went by myself there. He didn't do anything to me, and I am still cold now. I'm shivering. That . . . that was a terrible feeling.

From within the Ghetto, Jews of course knew that they were confined; the barbed wire, and guards shooting at those who approached the Ghetto borders, made this painfully clear. Even beyond those well marked barriers lay a "no-man's land" of sorts, an empty perimeter, vacant except for striped guard houses and electric lights, that separated the Ghetto from the rest of "Litzmannstadt" further. German authorities moved Poles out of the area and even burned down vacant buildings to create the neutral zone (Crago 2012; Horwitz 2008). Ostensibly, this empty zone was created as a fire barrier; it was also justified as a means of preventing the spread of disease. Yet, if it served the purpose of preventing fire or disease from spreading to the rest of the city, it also served to prevent Jews from leaving the Ghetto and ruining Litzmannstadt's Aryan aesthetic. Morris C., who arrived in the Łódź Ghetto in 1942 with two of his sisters, described the "no man's land":

> There we was . . . when the Germans coming in, the like a neutral place. And in and out was just for the Germans to come in and out, wherever they want to go, for Jews there was only one side. And every ten feet you had a soldier and it was all wired with electrical wires. And, you know, it was 200,000 Jews wired in.

Interestingly, despite all these efforts to separate the Jewish population from the rest of the city, the Ghetto's Zgierska Street and Limanowskiego Street remained open to through traffic—that is, open to Gentiles, not Jews. These streets, which crosscut the southwestern part of the Ghetto, were technically not part of the Ghetto; they were fenced on both sides, allowing trucks and trolley cars to pass through the Ghetto while still keeping Jews confined. Three wooden footbridges, two over Zgierska Street and one over Limanowskiego Street, allowed Jews to move from one side of the Ghetto to the other. This design meant that passengers in vehicles traveling along these thoroughfares could see into the Ghetto, and they could also see the Jewish foot traffic on the bridges above (see Figure 5.1). Harry S. had another memorable experience there:

> The ghetto was with fences on both side. And the street car was passing through the street. They had to connect one side of the street to the other side. And a woman was standing on the . . . on a very open place, on the street car. And I passed by. I was going to the . . . to work, as a child. I was maybe fifteen, fifteen and a half. And she put down . . . uh, sticked out the

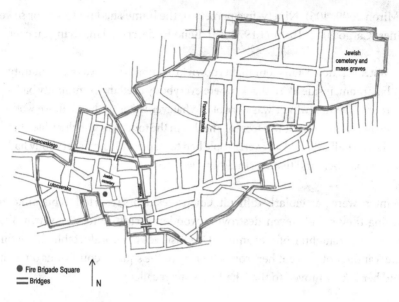

Figure 5.1 Map of the Łódź Ghetto.
Credit: Elle Rochford

tongue on me. And I was so hurt, 'til today . . . I will never forget her, this. You know, why? What did I do? . . . couldn't understand, why a person would . . . not knowing me, and just child, why she put out the tongue on me, you know, in a mean way. You know, and my question was always why, in the ghetto. I couldn't understand. I didn't see that the Jews are different, or worse than somebody else. And when all those things happened, like putting out the tongue, it was a insult. It was worse than somebody would slap you on the face . . . I feel it today. I see her, today, staying on the . . . on the streetcar, and . . . and putting out the . . . I would most probably recognize her [chuckles] after sixty years maybe, or fifty something years. I was very insulted.

Life in the Ghetto

The condition of the housing in the Bałuty and Stare Maesto neighborhoods that became the Łódź Ghetto was quite poor, in terms of construction as well as infrastructure. Most dwellings lacked running water and connections to gas lines, creating problems of sanitation and heating during the winter

(Miron 2009: 406). Ninety-five percent of the homes had no toilets or sewer lines (Cargo 2012: Tushnet 1972: 15). Beno H. described his living quarters:

> Water was downstairs four flights down in a pump. There was a community bathroom, inside like a shack, where everybody used the community bathroom. The first winter was horrible. Whatever water we had left, we woke up in the morning, it was frozen. The dirt in the toilet was unbelievable, that the feces all over and all over. People had to step over it, and everybody had bed chambers and that's . . . that's how we lived.

Winters were particularly difficult. Ghetto residents resorted to burning anything they could—even destroying wooden furniture to stay warm. Elsa R. was the daughter of a prominent dentist, yet her comfortable life before the war did not prevent her from suffering in the squalid conditions once she and her family moved to the Ghetto. As she recalled:

> The winters were terrible. The water froze. And there were even ice on the walls at night.
> *Did you have any heat?*
> No! Not at all! Except that we had a lot of blankets and pillows, so we could go under maybe six layers of blankets and pillows to keep warm. But we . . . we had to . . . it was very difficult with the frozen water and stuff like that. And then we had to constantly fight with bedbugs and lice. This was another scourge of the ghetto. I remember I had a metal bed, so my father was able to burn it up . . . he took the bed upside down once a week and he was burning the bedbugs alive. They were falling like anything. But then they came back anyway [laughs].

Wolf D., an only child who was fourteen when the war started, lived in one room in the Ghetto with his father and mother:

> Yeah. It was one room. It had . . . it had a double bed, the pre-war bed. It had a wardrobe, a double wardrobe, a table, two or three chairs, I can't remember, and a sort of a bench on one side on which we had the bucket for water. Because there was no running water and no sewerage. So there was . . . water had to be pumped from a pump in the yard and carried upstairs in pails. And there was another bucket for . . . for dishwasher, for dirty water, for washing up water. And that was about that.

A dense population living in facilities without plumbing meant that authorities had to address a growing sewage problem in the Łódź Ghetto. They solved it with Jewish labor. Ghetto sanitation workers loaded human waste into large canisters that they transported by wagon and then dumped in a corner of the ghetto (see Horwitz 2008: 87–82). Humans, not horses, pulled the wagons. Charles H. recalled seeing people perform this difficult work:

> The living in ghetto were terrible . . . People were . . . they cleaning up the toilets is where a place, so people cleaned this up and there people work by this, they clean it up and they were putting two men in the front or two women in the front, and they carried this, like a horse, and two or three pushed this in the back. And they put it in someplace else, in another field to fill it out and clean out the toilets. The filth . . . And these people, you see it, when they were working, pushing the wagon, they had such a swollen feet. Women, men.

Work

Sanitation work was not the only job open to Jews in the Łódź Ghetto. In fact, there were some 100 factories in the Ghetto, all employing Jewish workers. Most created goods to support the German war effort, but some factories, or workshops (known as *Arbeitressorts*, or simply *ressorts*) created merchandise to be sold in German department stores. In the workshops, Jewish laborers manufactured clothing (including soldiers' uniforms), shoes, boots and straw overshoes for soldiers, furniture, and even toys. Over ninety percent of the Ghetto population was employed in 1943 and 1944 (Crago 2012: 78; Hilberg 1979; Miron 2009: 407; Unger 2002). Rose M., a middle-class grocery store owner's daughter, described the jobs she and her family had:

> Every one of us got . . . had to go to work. My mother worked by . . . by straw . . . like you make a braid, a braid [out of] straw. And from that she sew like boots for the . . . for the German soldiers. I worked by the ladies hats. And I don't remember what my sister did, truthfully. My mother . . . my father worked by transport, that means they have some horses. So he work by them, to take care of him, nearby, not far. And everyone . . . was a very hard life.

Sam N. started working in the Ghetto at age 14, in 1941. His job was in a leather factory:

> Always there we worked for the . . . for the German soldiers. We made different kind of things, you know, all . . . belts, buckles . . . knapsacks, hats for the pilots. Different things. Whatever . . . whatever to do with leather we did it in the Ghetto.

Charles H., a tailor's son who was sent to Łódź from a smaller ghetto in the nearby town of Brzeziny, had a job cleaning and delousing German soldiers' uniforms:

> [F]rom the eastern front when the Russians were . . . where they were fighting with the Russians, were soldiers over there they were wearing the fur. And the fur were ripped up with blood, with everything. And they took it over there . . . we have over there a machine in Łódź, in the ghetto what they cleaned it out, the . . . all this . . . the dirt with chemicals to clean it out . . . the fur, we cleaned it out. And then the fur . . . Fur to clean is hard. This were cleaned by fire, you know, for lice . . . That's we are working. They took in the fur over there were millions of lice . . . We put in fire. And the fire . . . and this were running all around. And the fur were inside. And the heat killed the lice.

Though clearly useful to the German war effort, these were not jobs in which workers were paid a fair wage or had any rights. Instead, Jews worked long hours (often ten- to twelve-hour shifts) and were paid a pittance. Working conditions were also harsh: factories and workshops were usually crowded and unsanitary, just like the workers' homes. Workers who complained could lose their all-important daily meal, and the penalties for working slowly or stealing supplies were even harsher. Abe L. described what happened to a man who took a small piece of leather home from his job at a shoe factory:

> This man was in the shoemaking factory. He was a shoemaker. So he got soles, leather for soles . . . for the wintertime, high boots . . . boots, you know, leather boots. That's a specialty for the Germans. They like always shiny boots to wear them, because with this they're going . . . they're going to clap on one another and make a noise. So they catched him as he took home a little piece of leather. And they . . . he, right away been sentenced

to die. And where will he die? They put a hanging thing in the middle of a big place in the ghetto and they ordered all the Jewish people, all the people in the ghetto, not to go to work today, they have to come in this place and this man was hanged. Because they found a little leather. They're supposed to be a . . . a . . . to learn when you will steal something from the factory, it's just not yours, you will be hanged or killed. And I been seeing all what's happened. And we been living in the Ghetto in so many awful situations that nobody can believe it.

As difficult the working conditions and as distasteful as some of the jobs were in the Ghetto, working was much better than the alternative. Ghetto residents understood the importance of work. Indeed, they were constantly reminded of the need to work, and to prove useful to the Germans, by the Jewish head of the Ghetto, Chaim Rumkowski—the "Eldest of the Jews."

The Eldest of the Jews

Mordechai Chaim Rumkowski was the Nazi-appointed Jewish leader of the Łódź Ghetto. He was actually named to this position in October 1939, well before the Ghetto was established: even before the Ghetto, German officials wanted a local *Judenrat* (known, in Łódź and other cities annexed to the Reich, as the *Ältestenrat*, or Council of Elders) that they could use to ensure that their ever-growing list of edicts would be carried out. On October 13, 1939, Rumkowski was appointed and immediately directed to create a governing council for the Jewish community (Crago 2012: 77; Horwitz 2008: 15; Trunk 2006: 33).

Bespectacled, and with a shock of white hair, Rumkowski was easily recognizable—both for his looks and for his antics. Born in rural Belorussia in 1877 to a family of modest means, and with a limited formal education, he was a self-made person who used his confidence and energies to succeed in a number of businesses, including textiles and insurance. He lost his fortunes in the aftermath of World War I and the Russian Revolution, but relocated to Łódź and, by 1939, had rebounded with a career noted by social services administrative work, largely as a director of orphanages.[8] He was equally well known for his self-promotion. Historian Gordon J. Horwitz describes Rumkowski as a man who "craved authority, saw no reason to abandon it, and, it was said, reveled in his moments in the limelight" (2008: 14). There are different versions of the story of how Rumkowski, at age sixty-two, was chosen as the "eldest" of the Jews in Łódź (*Judenältester*). Some say that he sought the position himself, while others say that the Germans chose him because his white hair made him look like the oldest person in the room.[9] As Noah H. explained:

> There's another story, that we had another leader, whom the Germans asked, "Who is the oldest man here?" In Germany, if it's the oldest, it means he is the leader, he calls. So they asked a man who was a member of the Jewish community but he wasn't up to be a leader. So who is the oldest? And he [Rumkowski] had gray hair. And he was old, so he said, "I am the oldest." "So you will be the leader of the ghetto." And he stayed there too. Rumkowski . . . That's how he became the leader of the ghetto.

Whether due to his ambition or appearance, Rumkowski got the job. It was one that he embraced. Emmanuel Ringelblum, the Ghetto historian in Warsaw, described "King Chaim," as "an old man of seventy, extraordinarily ambitious and pretty nutty . . . He considers himself God's anointed."[10] Rumkowski became known for driving around the Ghetto in a horse-drawn carriage, befitting (he believed) a man of his stature, and making frequent public speeches to the community, to whom he referred as "my Jews" (see Figure 5.2). The *Chronicle of the Łódź Ghetto,*[11] a daily bulletin created under Rumkowski's administration, referred to him with capitalized pronouns. A short-lived series of postage stamps bore his image, and the Ghetto currency, officially called *Mark-Quittungen* (mark receipts), was known popularly as "*rumkes*" or "*chaimkes*" (Dobroszycki 1984: xxvi; Gutman 2006: xxxii; Trunk 2006: 317).

Self-aggrandizement aside, Rumkowski was an effective leader in some ways. Confined to the Ghetto, Jews had great need for social services. Rumkowski developed a welfare system for non-workers and saw to it that schools, orphanages, soup kitchens, and homes for the elderly were built and operational in the Ghetto, at least in its early years. He formed a Ghetto Health Department that oversaw hospitals, created public baths, and vaccinated children. He also supported cultural and religious institutions in the Ghetto, which helped maintain community life. As Elsa R., the dentist's daughter, explained:

> They tried to maintain a little bit culture, you know. I remember there was one concert that my father took me to, that the people in ghetto organized

Figure 5.2 Chaim Rumkowski delivering a speech in Fire Brigade Square in the Łódź Ghetto, 1941 or 1942.

Credit: The original uploader was Danny at English Wikipedia. Transferred from en.wikipedia to Commons by Sfan00_IMG using CommonsHelper. Public Domain, https://commons.wikimedia. org/w/index.php?curid=6625948

a concert, playing Beethoven and violin concerto. My father was a . . . he played violin. A matter of fact, he was supporting himself when he was studying dentistry by giving lessons, violin lessons. So he played violin very nicely. So we were very music conscious. He was playing a lot of violin during the ghetto too, until they came and they took it away from him.

And Samuel P. confirmed:

There were Shabbat services in certain places. There were . . . holidays were celebrated. I used to go to holiday services, just to . . . my heart wasn't in praying [laughs], to tell you the truth at this time. But still, I wanted it to be different from . . . from every day. I knew it was a holiday and I knew it was important to be with people at the . . . in a house of prayer. And there was . . . there was life otherwise in the ghetto. They had a theater at one time. They were composing plays and they had a . . . they had an orchestra that played in the ghetto for a little while in the beginning. They tried to . . . to resume life as normal as people possibly can, but the . . . the feeling of hunger, the feeling of being deprived of your freedom and of your . . . of your goods that you were used to, was so strong that you really didn't have any . . . you didn't do anything wholeheartedly, like you did . . . you couldn't enjoy things like you did before. But, yet, people tried and they put on the best they could to make an appearance of . . . of dignity and of . . . of . . . of a normal life.

Importantly, Rumkowski was also the person who sold German officials on the utility of Jewish labor. In an April 5, 1940 letter to the Mayor of Łódź he successfully pitched a plan to create factories that would employ the skilled tailors, seamstresses, leatherworkers, and other craftspeople in the Ghetto to create goods for the Reich. In Rumkowski's view, this arrangement protected Jews from being grabbed off the streets for forced labor and other abuses; for their part, German officials were happy to profit from Jewish labor (see Trunk 2006: 53, 83).

As the undisputed head of the Ghetto, Rumkowski set policy, and ran the Jewish police force and other Ghetto agencies. He even performed weddings in the Ghetto,[12] such as Morris C.'s marriage to his first wife:

And the marriage was performed by the big man Rumkowski. He signed the certificate.
Not . . . not by a rabbi.
No. He was the rabbi, he was the god, he was everything.

However, not everyone in the Ghetto was impressed, nor were they pleased to be under the thumb of a powerful, centralized leader. When German officials made demands, it was up to Rumkowski to meet them—whether that involved carefully rationing food or finding Jewish workers for German factories, or, later, facilitating deportations from the Ghetto (via the Jewish Police, who were part of his administration). Not surprisingly, many in the Ghetto resented Rumkowski and directed their ire against him. Gusta B. said he was "worse than a Nazi":

What could you tell me about the Judenrat of the Łódź Ghetto?
The *Judenrat* was Rumkowski.
He was the head of it?
He was the head of the ghetto and he was worse than a Nazi.
Why?

He could report somebody right away to the . . . to the Gestapo for no reason whatsoever. If somebody opened a mouth or whatever it was, or somebody didn't do the job right . . . He lived like a king. He had everything . . .

Still, as Eva B. said, the Ghetto needed a Jewish leader as a go-between with the German officials:

How I feel about Rumkowski? We all hated him, but we were afraid to say it. We . . . we didn't know what to do. We needed somebody to talk to us. The German didn't talk to us at that point. They let everything run by the Jewish people. He was like the representative of them.

Food Rationing

Food rationing was one of the most prominent, and most controversial, features of Rumkowski's job. Again, because the German officials only begrudgingly agreed to the Ghetto—much preferring to remove all Jews from Litzmannstadt so that the Aryanization of the city would be complete—they had little interest in supplying adequate food to those trapped within the Ghetto fences. The food that was provided had to be rationed, a task whose implementation fell to Rumkowski's Provisioning Department. Ghetto residents received ration cards for purchasing food and fuel. Food was sold at distribution points, where Ghetto residents stood in long lines to receive their allotted shares. Eva B., the daughter of a tailor and clothing manufacturer who was fifteen when she went to the Ghetto, recalled:

You spend a lot of time staying in line because we didn't have of what to cook. So they had like gas . . . they had gas that people were staying in line to get a chance to cook something. So sometimes you have to stay in the line two hours, three hours until you got a chance. Some people would . . . fainted.

Staples such as bread and potatoes were in small supply; beef and eggs were unheard of. Meat, when available, was usually horsemeat. In June 1941, the official weekly rations included 2.25 kilograms of bread and 200 grams of horsemeat for workers, and less for the unemployed. However, these were only rations on paper; in practice, people never received that much, due to an uneven supply (see Trunk 2006: 108–109). Root vegetables were usually more plentiful, although not necessarily desirable, as Elsa R. noted:

> We got a lot of turnips from the Germans. It was a horrible food. When I think of turnips, I would never touch them anymore in my life, because there were turnips all the time. And, you know, and this is not a very versatile food, like potatoes. Turnips are just turnips. You can't do much with them. Very watery, very blowing up, you know. Miserable thing.
> *Did you have any meat?*
> Once in a . . . once in a while we got a portion of horse meat. Very seldom. So it was . . . to us it was tasting very good, because, you know, it was still meat.
> *Chicken?*
> No! No! This was the only thing. Once in a blue moon there was a little portion of horse meat, like a can of sardines it looked. I mean if . . . you know, very small. No, we didn't have any vegetables. We didn't have any . . . I mean, besides turnips and potatoes. There was, I think, radishes, maybe sometimes too. Otherwise, no sugar, no fruit, nothing . . . nothing . . .
> *Any dairy products?*
> No. No.
> *Cheese?*
> No. Nothing like that. And very little bread.

The quality of food was poor as well. Vegetables were sometimes frozen or rotten, making for meals that were unpleasant at best (see Figure 5.3). In fact, in January 1941, the *Chronicle* reported an effort by Ghetto resident Henryk Wosk, "a known inventor and holder of a number of patents," to create a Department of Ideas that would collect good ideas for solutions to problems of Ghetto life, including ideas for "the utilization of frozen or spoiled potatoes" (quoted in Dobroszycki 1984: 7–8).

> Nathan G.:
> Have you ever boiled a frozen potato? . . . you see, until today my wife wonders, I don't eat any vegetables because they used to give it. White radishes. Do you know what white radishes are? Did you ever try to boil white radishes or turnips? One potato, four turnips, three radishes, you boil, make mash out of it. You know when you boil this thing you've got to walk

Figure 5.3 Child eating soup in the Łódź Ghetto.
Credit: Yad Vashem Photo Archive, Jerusalem. 7317/811

out of the room because it smells awful. And to eat this . . . And the radish is one of the best, they were rotten. It was really very bad.

German officials were unhappy with the food system as well, but for a different reason. In September 1941, a year and a half after the creation of the Ghetto, officials complained that the cost of supplying food to the Ghetto was higher than the revenue produced by the Ghetto, claiming that food cost 1.3–1.7 million Reichmarks a month, while revenue from factories and the sale of confiscated valuables was only 205,000 Reichmarks per month (see Trunk 2006: 107). Given the quantity and quality of the provisions, however, this claim seems dubious at best.

Hunger

Without enough money to buy food, and without enough food to purchase in the first place, hunger was rampant among Jews in the Ghetto. Further, any attempts at food smuggling were thwarted by the armed guards, who could easily police the empty perimeter beyond the Ghetto fence. And even if that perimeter could be safely breached, the *rumkes* only had value in the Ghetto and were useless for buying food on the outside. Jews in the Łódź Ghetto therefore had to rely on the official rations. However, because people received rations meant to last a week or a month, they had to carefully portion out their food on a daily basis. Desperately hungry people often ate their rations well before the next allotment was available and had to suffer until the next distribution. Those without jobs had to rely on public soup kitchens. Workers fared a little better, earning meager wages as well as extra food at work, but the available meal—usually a bowl of watery soup during the workday—provided few calories. As a result, deaths from starvation were widespread. Hunger was the prime cause of death in the first years of the Ghetto's existence, more so than diseases caused by high-density, unsanitary living conditions (e.g., dysentery and typhus). Deaths from hunger skyrocketed in 1941, from 1.8 percent of deaths in the Ghetto in 1940 to 18.6 percent of deaths in 1941; the rate was even higher in 1942, with hunger accounting for more than one-quarter of deaths in the Ghetto between January and June. According to historian Isaiah Trunk, hunger was "the angel of death of the Łódź Ghetto."[13]

In Fall 1941, Jews deported from elsewhere in Nazi-occupied Western Europe (e.g., Berlin, Prague, and Vienna) began to arrive in Łódź (Crago 2012: 77). These new arrivals, especially those who were from the upper class, had a particularly difficult time adjusting to Ghetto life, and many perished quickly.

Adek F.:
In the Ghetto Łódź, in addition to our 60,000 Jews from different parts of Łódź, we got . . . they sent in, they forced people . . . Jews from Luxembourg were sent in to the Łódź Ghetto. Jews from Hungary, from Romania were sent in to Łódź Ghetto. Those people came in and they were told that they are going to a health spa, that they are not . . . you know, those people were so wealthy and they were with fur, with jewelry . . . jewelry, with the nicest dresses, completely like outside world. And they came to Łódź Ghetto and they . . . when they saw the conditions, when they witnessed the condition, a lot committed suicide. They couldn't take it.

But everyone was suffering. Henry R., who survived both the Łódź Ghetto and, later, Auschwitz, said that he actually had more food in Auschwitz:

Auschwitz was . . . you get it a little better food in Auschwitz than . . . than in Łódź. Yeah, I got it . . . I feel I got a little better food. The work was worse.

In the Łódź Ghetto, people resorted to eating anything they could get their hands on: vegetable peelings, coffee grounds, even dirt. George S. described a typical day:

> We used to get up early in the morning. In the summertime it wasn't too bad. I used to wash my face, have some coffee, try to eat some bread. And sometimes I didn't have any bread to eat. Because I was so hungry, that I eat the bread . . . when I used to get it, I used to eat my portion. And then I had . . . by the time the seven days got around, I didn't have any. So my mother made pancakes, black pancakes out of coffee grinds. And these were not regular coffee but it was coffee made out of grai—uh, some kind of a barley maybe, that kind of a . . . a coffee, ersatz coffee. And, ah, if we had potato peels we were lucky. Then she would put in potato peels. And I . . . so I had something to put into my stomach. There was no nutrition in it. So I ate that and went off to work, and wait 'til I would get the soup, do some work, whatever it was required of me to do, under the assignment that I have. And then during lunchtime I get that soup with . . . made of a small piece of potato and turnips, mostly, at the time. The coffee, I mentioned, was made out of grain. The soup didn't hold me much, mostly was water. And everything we did, we had to stay in line. So we had to stay in line for the soup too. And you only had an hour . . . Well, anyhow, and then I came home from work and waited for my mother to make some soup, to eat some soup. If we had beets, she cooked beets. Sometimes we had horse meat, if we're lucky. And if we run out of fuel, we cut up some of the furniture, to cook with.

Rose M., whose Ghetto job was in a factory making hats, described making a bitter cake out of coffee grounds, but she was very happy to be able to eat it:

> I remember, we had, uh, from the coffee, you know, what do you call it, this . . . the grounds. I would take it and apart, and put some flour, and I guess . . . we used to get brown sugar, some kind. And I would take it to . . . with me to work, if I worked during the night, because there were shifts. Sometimes I work in the morning and sometimes at night. So I would take this. But we had, in the factory there, like gas burners because we need

the steam for the hats, for stretching and making forms. And I would take that pot with me, and put it in a pot of water, and cook it overnight. This was our cake . . . and it was bitter, like . . . whatever, but this what we . . . we were happy we could do that. It was a very hard, tough life.

Aron L., a tailor's son, was nineteen years old when the Ghetto was created. After both his parents died, leaving him to care for his seven siblings, he found work and did his best to support his family:

> We tried every way to obtain food, to survive. People were grabbing from the trucks. People went on the street looking for food, just . . . whoever couldn't organize, they just died from hunger, that's it. You can go up in the morning, you go out in the street, you see people just dead, laying there. They was dying, that's it. Some people, they had food, who were involved any kind of food business. You know, they had more to eat than the average person. I used to bring home some extra soups, some extra potatoes. Because I was working in daytime in the shop. In the nighttime I was watching . . . they used to call it the nightw—just . . . I did some extra work to get some food. That's the way how we tried to survive. But little by little everybody . . . most of the people are dying from hunger. There was nothing to eat.

People who were lucky enough to work in bakeries or soup kitchens could eat a few morsels of food on the job; sometimes, this meant the difference between life and death. For a while, there were agricultural plots in Marysin, the region in the northeast section of the Ghetto that had more open, green space, that were run by Rumkowski's administration. People who worked there, like Samuel P., could also get a little more food:

> I used to walk around, if I had enough time during the day, walk around to places where they used to grow potatoes and see in the dirt if I could find some potatoes that were left by the people who were gathering them. And if I found a few of them, that was a good day for me. I went home and cooked it. I was lucky that in my job I had the freedom of part of the day of doing those things. Most people spent their times in the shops and they couldn't get away, they were working for 10, 12 hours.

Beno H.'s father got even more creative to bring a tiny bit of food home from his Ghetto workplace:

> My father finally got a job as delivering flour to bakeries. So what he did, he robbed the flour which fell on the ground, he used to put it in his pocket and he used to tie his shoes . . . the pants with a piece of rubber . . . laces or something, used the shove the flour which fell on the ground, so we had a little bit flour, so my mother used to make flour soup out of it. She mixed flour and water, couldn't . . . because we couldn't cook too much, because we didn't have enough fuel anyways, and this is how we sustained them.

One of the most devastating aspects of the food rationing was the way it affected families. Driven to desperation, family members sometimes stole food from each other. The diary of Dawid Sierakowiak, a teenager whose daily journal entries describe his life from the summer before the war began until a few months before his death in the Ghetto from tuberculosis and starvation in fall 1943, repeatedly describe how his father ate his own rations quickly and then stole food from Dawid and his younger sister, Nadzia (Adelson 1996). Gusta B. described a similar scenario:

> *Tell me about the rations. What . . . how . . . what amount of food did you get at that time?*
> And we got very . . . what should I say? Not too much bread. We got . . . I don't remember how many grams or whatever to be . . . our bread was rationed, our food was rationed. Once a week we got a piece of bread. Once a week we got a piece of bread. My . . . the husband of my cousin . . . it was . . . one didn't trust the other. He used to take his bread, his ration, and put it in a pot and hid it for his wife. He tied it around. He was afraid that his wife could take a bite from his bread. It . . . it was terrible.

But there was heroism as well, as families tried to protect each other with the little food they had available. During his testimony, Henry R. wept when remembering how his sister gave her own food to him in the Ghetto to keep him alive:

> [T]hey took away my sister. [weeps] I thank her I'm alive. She give her food, she give it to me. I should survive. She knows I like to eat a little more and

she ... she cut down her food to give it to me. And we didn't have no food anyway. And so then they took her away in May.

By mid-1942, the official rations were around 600 calories a day; 18,000 people died in the Łódź Ghetto in that year alone (Crago 2012: 78). Hunger was so bad that some families did not bury their deceased loved ones right away, in order to keep their precious bread cards for a few more days and provide extra food for the surviving family members. Given the Jewish tradition of burying the dead within twenty-four hours, these delays showed just how desperate living conditions had become.

Abe L.:
[W]hen somebody died in a family, and you went and made ... and registered that this man died, they cut off right away the portion, they didn't give the place, this piece of bread for the portion. But when you didn't say nothing, the dead man get a portion. So people have not rushing until the dead body fall apart. And that time they call that they have to come and take them out.

Nathan G.:
I recall, one instant I walked into a friend of mine, his house. And I turned to him, I said, "Hey, Mack ... " His name was Mack, I'm just giving ... "What's smelly? Something is smelly. I cannot stand it." He said, "Sshh, the grandfather died." In the meantime, here's a few days here because we're getting the rationing. Before we spilled the beans, in the meantime we're getting rationing. But after a few days, the body's so bad we have to throw him out ... how people live, how bad it was. It was unbelievable.

As bad as things were in the Łódź Ghetto, they were about to get even worse. Against the backdrop of this extreme suffering, the deportations began, bringing another level of anguish to the Ghetto entirely.

Deportations

Like Ghetto Chief Jacob Gens in Vilna, Rumkowski believed that establishing Jews' work potential would convince the authorities of their worth, thereby protecting the Łódź Ghetto from destruction. Accordingly, he exhorted the Ghetto community to work, under whatever conditions were present. In truth, Jews' utility was only temporary, from the point of view of the Nazi regime: ultimately, all Jews in Łódź were targeted for death, the "Final Solution" that superseded any local officials' profit margins. Unbeknownst to those in the Ghetto, by December 8, 1941, a death camp at Chelmno—fifty kilometers north of Łódź—was operational. Lacking this key piece of information, the number of factories producing goods for the German war effort seemed, on its face, a positive indicator, and Rumkowski held fast to the belief that the Ghetto could be preserved as long as able-bodied workers contributed to its productivity. He made this position clear, and frequently, both in public speeches and official announcements. For example, in a speech made on November 1, 1941, before a group of newly arrived residents who had been deported from elsewhere in Western Europe, Rumkowski proclaimed:

> On the 6th of April, 1940, I moved into the ghetto. I then notified the city's President that I was going to the ghetto because there is a gold mine there. To the astonished questions, I replied briefly:
> "IN THE GHETTO I HAVE FORTY THOUSAND WORKING HANDS. THIS IS MY GOLD MINE!"
> As I organized work here, the authorities began to confer with me and to take me more and more into account . . . The highest representatives of the authorities often visited these factories. The inspectors were full of admiration. More than once they said to me that until now they knew only the figure of the Jew-merchant or broker, but they did not known that Jews could work productively . . . By doing good work, the ghetto demonstrates that despite being an impoverished residential quarter, it does not ask for beggar's bread for itself. Work became the ghetto's advertising; created trust for the ghetto; multi-million credits are eloquent evidence of this trust . . .
> At first, it was difficult getting orders for the ghetto. With the passage of time, when the authorities and private clients became acquainted with the level of ghetto production—orders began to pour in to us from different lines of business. Today, the ghetto is not only a center of work, but also a city of production . . . In the ghetto one does not work with watch in hand. The effects are great: The more we are esteemed, the more we are consulted. (quoted in Trunk 2006: 369–370, emphasis in original).

No one needed to sell the Ghetto community on the idea of work; it was the best, and really only, way to receive extra food. Tragically, however, the "work to live" frame had a corollary: those who could not work—the elderly and sick, for instance—could no longer stay in the Ghetto. This was the framing Rumkowski used when he was put in the unbearable position of having to facilitate deportations from the Ghetto, as ordered by Nazi officials, beginning in January 1942.

In truth, it seems Rumkowski did all that he could to manage the pace of deportations and the number of people that were being sent away. In December 1941, the first deportations from the ghettos were announced: 20,000 Jews would be "resettled" elsewhere in January 1942. As the "Eldest of the Jews," it fell to Rumkowski to select the deportees. His pleas to the German officials reduced that number to 10,000, giving Rumkowski the false impression that he held some sway. Unfortunately, it still meant that 10,000 people would be forced to leave the Ghetto. Henry R. recalled Rumkowski's speeches at the time:

> Sure. I see him speaks. He speaks a lot of . . . a few times I saw him and he was speaking to us . . . that we should work and we should . . . he wants that we should be in the ghetto and we shouldn't liquidate the ghetto. That's his job and he is going to . . . and when we . . . and when if the sick people what in the hospital have to give it away, they can't work, they can't be in the ghetto and we have to arrange that everything . . . and we should listen what the German tell him and we should listen to him so we're going to be alive.

Wolf D. echoed Henry's point:

> We saw him from time to time because he used to give . . . make speeches and . . . he was in very invidious position because he believed that by carrying out the orders that he was given by the Germans, he at least . . . while he was sacrificing many tens of thousands of people, at least he will be able to preserve and save thousands of others.

As did Eva B.:

> He [w]as making speeches about how much he work hard not to deport all the people. But he has to deport some. Like he was fighting with them, instead of . . . let's say, of 25,000 people he would only send out, to give you an example, 20,000 people. He said he has to save the population, so that why he has to send out the . . . the German need the people to work in Germany. We didn't know where we're going. We didn't know what was happening.

Deportations from the Ghetto began in January 1942. "Criminal elements" and welfare recipients who refused to work were taken first, followed by sick and elderly "nonproductives." From January 16, 1942 to May 15, 1942, nearly 55,000 people[14] were deported to Chelmno from Łódź (Dobroszycki 1984: xx).

The sustained demands for deportees could not be met by sacrificing the sick and elderly alone, however. The next vulnerable population was the Ghetto's children.

"Give Me Your Children!"

Miriam M. was twelve when she came to the Ghetto from Zelów, a small town fifty-four kilometers south of Łódź, where she lived with her grandparents. Upon her arrival, she was immediately told to pretend that she was seventeen in order to work—and survive:

When I came to ghetto, I must have been twelve-and-a-half, going on thirteen. And what happened is suddenly you hear, you can't be, if you want to survive, you have to play a role as an adult. You are not twelve. You're seventeen. And it was instilled in you: You're not twelve, you're seventeen. If anybody asks you how old you are, you say you're seventeen. And the first encounter was, we came in one day, two days later was a selection. And the selection was in old part of the ghetto, and we all stood outside. And I decided on my own to go in the end and stood on my tiptoes, that nobody will see that I am small or something. And somebody said, "Well, I have some beets, why don't you put some rouge on your cheeks so they are red" . . . somehow I was fortunate. They took out so . . . so many people that, um, that took out mostly, they took out elderly people. And youngsters, very small children.

Deportations from the Ghetto abated in May 1942 but began again in early September. On September 1, 1942, 2000 patients were deported from hospitals (Tushnet 1972: 51). Immediately after that, Rumkowski received another order from the German command, demanding that an additional 20,000 people be deported, including all children under ten (with exemptions for the children of Ghetto administrative personnel, such as the Jewish police). In a now infamous speech, delivered on September 4 in a public square behind the offices of the Fire Brigade on Lutomierska Street, Rumkowski exhorted the Ghetto community to "give me your children":

> The ghetto has received a hard blow. They ask of us the best we have—children and old people. I never had the luck to have a child of my own and so I gave up the best years of my life to children . . . In my old age I must stretch out my hands and beg, "Brothers and sisters, give them to me! Father and mothers, give me your children! . . . Yesterday I received an order to send some 21,000 Jews out of the ghetto. "If you don't do it, we will." And the question arose, "Should we do it or leave it to others?" Even more important is the question of not how many will we lose but of how many can we save? We all, myself and my closest associates, have come to the conclusion that despite the horrible responsibility, we have to accept the evil order. I have to perform this bloody operation myself; I have to cut off limbs to save the body! I have to take away the children, because otherwise others will also be taken, God forbid! . . . I stand before you a broken-down Jew. Don't envy me. This is the worst task I've ever undertaken. I stretch out my weak, trembling hands to you, and I plead—give me those victims to forestall their demand for more victims, to save a hundred thousand Jews. (quoted in Tushnet 1972: 52–53)

Rumkowski's speech was met with weeping, cries, and pleas, but the deportations continued. Some parents hid their children, and others went with them voluntarily. A mother threw herself under a wagon taking away her child and was crushed to death; another was shot after refusing to give up her child (Trunk 2006: 245–247). By mid-September, over 15,000 children, elderly people, and sick people were deported to Chelmno, and nearly 600 were shot in the streets (Crago 2012: 80; Dobroszycki 1984: xxi; Tushnet 1972: 54). Henry R. recalled the *aktions*:

> I was right there it was Germans, it was like a selection. They come down and they said everybody has to go up on the . . . on the . . . in like in a courtyard from the house, in the building. Everybody has to go down. We all . . . that was during the day. No work. That time he said, "Nobody goes to work. Everybody has to be home. It's going to be selections. We have to resettle some people." So they took all this old people and young people and kids. They took them all in the . . . took them all away to this . . . the children they throw it on a wagon, like packages. They throw . . . I saw myself and I saw where they took away my . . . my brother's baby [weeps] they throw

him like . . . such a beautiful baby, such a nice baby. So they throw him away and they took him away . . . This was in '42, in September.

Abraham L. also described the scene:

No, this was terrible . . . he call a conference, you know, a meeting to Rumkowski from the SS, give up the children, so and so . . . and it was tragic. They were throwing . . . throwing the children . . . people from the . . . from the third, fourth floor on the trucks. When . . . from the hospital . . .

. . . so you saw this happening, you saw them throwing people out of the hospital windows onto the trucks. And this was the same deportation as when they took the children.

Yeah . . .

. . . And what were the parents told? Why did the . . . why were they told they have to give up their children?

Why? They says they need people to work.

Noah H. recalled the intense pain of losing his nephew:

He was six years old . . . And that was a time was they took children on the train, because after ten they could do some work for them . . . I was helpless, powerless. I couldn't do anything to save any . . . Well, they came. We did everything to hide him. Then they discovered, and they come . . . they took the child. And I went down with my sister. They put it on a little carriage. And he wasn't the only one; was a full truck with him. And the cries and the screams, and the children . . . now just imagine, you take a six-year-old boy who doesn't understand. He . . . he didn't cry. He looked at our face, so frightened. How can a . . . a baby like that, a little boy like that survive? How . . . how did he feel? And that has been haunting me all my life [cries]. I cannot forget that picture [cries] . . . And I had a friend there, was . . . you see, it was such a deport—a . . . a action of deportation, especially with children. They mobilized the police, all the police. All the people who went worked in the fire brigade, and the post office, used to know those people, they wanted, in case they need help. So he was waiting at that station . . . He told me months after that, that night, when my sister cried after her baby, the whole police station cried with her. It was so heartbreak—I mean, it haunts me all my life, you know. I can never forget that.

The deportations of the children were devastating, but the Ghetto went on, with its remaining population continuing to report to work and attempting, as best as possible, to survive. Deportations to Chelmno continued throughout 1943. By the end of that year, only 75,000–80,000 people remained in the Ghetto, roughly half of its original population; eighty-five percent of those who remained were employed in some fashion, working for the German war effort (Crago 2012: 80; Tushnet 1972: 57). In February 1944 deportations started up again, but now it was workers who were being sent away, after being told that they were being "resettled" for work elsewhere. Adding to the deception, some of these deportees sent postcards back to the Ghetto, telling family and friends that they were well and were working, but these were written under duress, likely right before their authors were put to death. The deportations continued sporadically until the summer of 1944. Throughout August of that year, Chaim Rumkowski used speeches and notices to appeal to what remained of the Ghetto community, calling for Jews to assemble for deportations when summoned to do so. The "eldest" himself was on one of the last transports out of the Ghetto on August 30, 1944; this one was bound for Auschwitz, as Chelmno was no longer in operation by that time.[15]

By the end of August 1944, most of the Łódź Ghetto had been emptied, without any armed resistance. Five hundred additional Jews were sent to Ravensbrück and Königs Wusterhausen on October 21, 1944. Several months later, on January 19, 1945, Łódź was liberated by the Red Army, at which point some 850–1000 Jews remained (Corni 2002: 1; Crago 2012: 81; Dobroszycki 1984: lxvi; Hilberg 1979: 329).

The story of the Łódź Ghetto is, in many ways, similar to that of the ghettos of Warsaw and Vilna: once established, each ghetto suffered abuses and hardships, followed by mass deportations and, ultimately, liquidation. Yet, Jews in the Łódź Ghetto did not stage armed resistance. The reason is that armed resistance was not a resonant response to the situation, as Łódź Ghetto residents understood it. Notably, Jews in the Łódź Ghetto did not reach the conclusion of genocide. As I demonstrate in this chapter, the case of the Łódź Ghetto demonstrates further that assessing the threat facing Jews as genocide—targeted annihilation that could not be mitigated or survived— was critical to the call for armed resistance.

The Importance of Time and Place

One notable difference in Łódź's trajectory, as compared to Warsaw and Vilna, is that there were no distinct events that served as turning points in the community's assessment of the threats they faced. Unlike in Warsaw, where the onset of mass deportations changed people's perceptions of their situation, allowing those who survived the roundup to reach the critical conclusion of genocide, deportations in Łódź did not signal the same thing. In other words, while the deportations were heartbreaking, they did not usher in a new understanding of the dangers of life in the Ghetto.

I have argued that to understand armed resistance, or the lack thereof, in the ghettos of Warsaw, Vilna, and Łódź, it is important to pay attention to time and its effect on critical conclusions and reasonable responses. Sequences of events—and community reactions to those events—illustrate how, over time, Jews in the ghettos came to certain conclusions about the threats facing them and made decisions about how best to respond. Yet, those assessments and decisions were made in particular *places*. In the Vilna Ghetto, proximity to partisan units in the surrounding forest shaped how some members of the community assessed their chances for survival and their ideas about appropriate action. This chapter also shows that both time and place shaped the Łódź Ghetto residents' assessment of the threats facing them, and how best to respond.

All human activity is emplaced, in that it happens in, and is shaped by, a place. Collective resistance is no different. Sociologists studying a variety of cases of mass protest, from the Paris commune to anti-nuclear activism in Boston to student protest in China, have established the role of place in movement dynamics, showing how features of the built environment in which actors live, work, and dream facilitate collective action (Gould 1995; Kelly-Thompson 2020; Miller 2000; Tilly 2000). For instance, because place shapes how and where people live, it affects where they are likely to hear about potentially protest-worthy issues: on college campuses, posters placed near dormitories and along central routes can easily spread the word about collective action (Zhao 2009). The story of the Łódź Ghetto illustrates the role of place by showing the opposite: rather than facilitating mobilization, place *hampered* it. Importantly, Łódź was a place characterized by its isolation. Although all Nazi-created ghettos were isolated, by definition—indeed, the whole point was to separate the Jewish population from the rest of society—distinct features of the Łódź Ghetto rendered it cut off completely from all other ghettos, in a way that was not the case for Warsaw and Vilna. The extreme isolation of the "hermetically sealed" Łódź Ghetto had notable effects.

An Isolated Place

Łódź is only eighty-five miles from Warsaw, but that distance was understandably difficult to traverse during war-time—especially for Jews. Yet Warsaw might as well have been ten times as far, given the virtual impossibility for Jews to get out of the Łódź Ghetto. It was equally difficult for anything, and anyone, to get in. The boundaries of the Ghetto, with its guarded fence surrounded by an empty perimeter, were essentially impenetrable; the penalties for attempting to escape were unmistakable. As Elsa R. explained:

> And we were not like Warsaw Ghetto. We were completely isolated.
> *You were walled.*
> Yeah . . . no, we didn't . . . I don't know walled. We were isolated and we couldn't have anywhere . . . there were guards and there were I guess gates, because in Warsaw they had contact with the out—with the Poles, with the outside, through the sewers, through the canals, but not Łódź Ghetto. We were completely isolated. And one person tried to get away, the Germans made a whole spectacle. They hanged . . . hung him in the middle of the ghetto and everybody had to get out of the house and witness it. Everybody was forced to go and witness the hanging. So we were really closed in.

Similarly, Abraham L. testified:

> The ghetto was closed up from the whole world. Who was trying to smuggle in they got killed, or they smuggle out they got shot. Cut . . . with one word, was cut off from the whole world.

The voices of these survivors describe not only the physical structures of the Ghetto but also what the place meant: a place that was cut off from the rest of society. That the concept of a "hermetical seal" could apply to a ghetto that literally had an open street running through it, traversed by people who could potentially help Jews suffering on the other side of the fence, shows how formidable the barriers between the Ghetto and the rest of the city were. When asked about the possibility of escaping the Ghetto, Charles H. explained:

> You couldn't run in the Łódź Ghetto. You couldn't go no place. From the ghetto you went around . . . where could you run? You couldn't run. Soon you go out on the street they recognize you who you are. Everybody were

undernourished . . . You have to wear a Jewish star. You cannot go without a Jewish star. If you could . . . even if you could take off the star you could not run away from the ghetto. You have no place to go. Where you gonna go? Nobody would take you in.

Why not?

They wouldn't. You ran away? They want to take you in? They risk their whole life . . .

You said there was a bridge that went over the streets.

Yeah, where you gonna jump? You cannot jump off from the bridge, because underneath were the railroad. Under the bridge were railroad and over there was street, people were working. Are you going to jump down to the street? You get killed, you jump down.[16]

In this sealed, isolated place, Łódź Jews did not know what was happening outside their ghetto. Nazi edicts contributed to the isolation. Radios that could have been used to maintain contact with the outside were expressly illegal, on penalty of death. Jews in the Ghetto were also forbidden to read the *Litzmannstadt Zeitung*, the city's daily newspaper. While residents of the Warsaw and Vilna Ghettos faced similar restrictions, the geographies of the ghettos varied somewhat. In both Warsaw and Vilna, where the ghettos were constructed literally by building walls around existing city neighborhoods, movement in and out of the ghetto was risky, but possible; therefore, food and supplies could be smuggled into the ghetto and couriers could transmit messages (Arad 1982; Batalion 2021; Gutman 1982, 1994). However, the "no man's land," policed by armed guards, that surrounded the Łódź Ghetto made moving in and out of the ghetto virtually impossible. Further, unlike in the ghettos of Warsaw and Vilna, if a resident of the Łódź Ghetto did manage to get across the fence, there was no bustling city scene to fade into and, likely, no passersby who might be hired or begged to provide shelter and assistance (Dobroszycki 1984). The Ghetto's location in the infrastructure-poor Bałuty neighborhood, whose homes had no sewer lines, also contributed to the isolation, for there was no sewer system that could have facilitated (albeit at great difficulty) movement in and out of the ghetto (Adelson 1996: 123, fn). The structure of work contributed to the isolation as well: unlike many other ghettos, Łódź Jews were not sent out of the ghetto for factory work or manual labor, but instead worked exclusively inside the ghetto (Dobroszycki 1984).

Information was not only hard to get from the outside, but it was difficult to share. The built environment of the Ghetto, with its empty perimeter and armed guards aimed the fence, facilitated external surveillance, according to Zalman S.:

> [C]an you make a guess, how big the ghetto was?
> Oh, maybe fifteen streets, fifteen or twelve streets, exactly. You see, the . . . the . . . the trick is, from the people, you didn't know what's going on in the . . . in the next street. This guy doesn't know what's going on in the next street. Sometimes we got communication, what's going on over there, whatever. However, most of the times, uh . . . you know, we got a little information, a little, only not too much.
> You couldn't walk from one street to the next?
> We could walk. However, they watch you from all direction. You know, this is . . . it's like in a camp, like in a tower. They just have a big thing, and they watch you, and . . . It was hard.

Of course, if no information was getting into the Ghetto, no information was getting out, either. Without news from Łódź, people in Warsaw thought it had been liquidated (Tushnet 1972: 44). Importantly, the Ghetto's "seal" meant that activists from other ghettos could not communicate with Łódź and share their assessments and plans for resistance. Recall that news from Vilna was crucial in developing Warsaw activists' sense of threat and their own calls for resistance. Łódź, by contrast, received no messages from activists in Vilna, or anywhere else. Referring to the crucial role of women couriers in Jewish resistance, Zivia Lubetkin, the ŻOB fighter from Warsaw, said that these couriers helped keep ghettos in contact with each other (see also Batalion 2021). She noted, however, that couriers could get everywhere except Łódź:

> One cannot possibly describe this work of organizing the Jewish resistance, or the uprising itself, without mentioning the role of these valiant women. One of the major thrusts of our work was maintaining the contact made by our women liaisons with various ghettos. The Germans had cut us off from the outside world. They had carved Polish Jewry into impoverished and isolated segments. Each ghetto was a separate entity completely isolated from the rest of Poland's shattered Jewry. Our women liaisons took it upon themselves to frustrate this strategy and did so with some success. In their persons and actions they tried to unite the isolated and demoralized Polish Jewry imprisoned in the ghettos. For them, the walls of the ghettos

and the closed-off frontiers were not insurmountable obstacles, and they paid no attention to the restrictions imposed on Jewish travel. There was not a remote corner in all of occupied Poland (*save for Łódź*) they did not penetrate. (1981: 75–76; emphasis added)

The isolation of the Łódź Ghetto persisted, long after the Warsaw and Vilna Ghettos were liquidated. Given the place they were in, and without information from other ghettos, Łódź Jews had to reach their own conclusions about what was happening, and fashion their own response to the threat.

Assessing Threat in the Łódź Ghetto

Another distinguishing feature of the Łódź Ghetto is that it was a *long-lasting* place—in fact, the longest-lived of the major ghettos in Nazi-occupied Eastern Europe. Thus, time also shaped the meaning of this place. The Ghetto's continued existence, *despite* the deportations, affected the remaining Jews' assessment of their situation. They reasoned: If the Ghetto still existed, then its workers were of value to the Germans and could not be wiped out entirely. This assessment was, in some ways, not far from the truth. Even though Łódź, or Litzmannstadt, had become part of the Reich and therefore was supposed to be *Judenrein*, there was no denying that its Jews constituted a profitable work force. Jewish labor was so valuable, in fact, that interventions from ghetto and regional administrators Arthur Greiser and Hans Biebow staved off SS plans to liquidate the Ghetto early on (Miron 2009: 410). This reality contributed to Jews' assessment of their situation, leading them to believe that the Ghetto could indeed be saved, through work. Deportations were understood in terms of the Ghetto's productivity: those who did not or could not work could not stay.

Yet whereas it made a certain amount of sense, given such assessments, that "non-productive" Jews had to leave the Ghetto, it was not clear where those Jews were going. Without much information from the outside, most Łódź Jews did not know where the deportees were being sent, nor did they know what would happen to them. This was true not only of the deportation of children and other non-workers in 1942, but throughout the life of the Ghetto. When Rose M. was sent away from the Ghetto in 1944 with her parents and sister, they were told they were going away to work: "And they told us that we're going to work, to another place, to take us to work . . . We never knew there's a Birkenau. We never knew about, where they're taking us." Similarly, when Miriam M. was sent to Auschwitz in 1944, she had one final piece of bread in the Ghetto before being forced into large open trucks with other deportees:

> My last piece of bread. We . . . We didn't know we going to Auschwitz. We didn't know where we were going. But what can be worse than the ghetto? I'm sure we're going to go to a better place. This what they told us.

Thanks to Nazi misinformation, in the form of propaganda as well as flat-out lies, most deportees believed that they were being relocated to other places—other ghettos, labor camps, or possibly other German cities—where they would find work. Jews leaving the Ghetto were allowed to exchange their worthless *rumkes* for German marks, facilitating the ruse that they were being sent to work in Germany. Some even took tools and materials with them, such as sewing machines, expecting that they would be working wherever they went. As Beno H. said:

> [A]t the end of [the Ghetto] transport was going one another the other. One after another transports were going and people said, "You bring your sewing machine, bring whatever you have." It seems like it's you're going to a labor camp, because must have been very good because nobody came back. We never knew it. We never knew what happened.

Others believed that the deportees had been sent to live on some kind of reservation, similar to the treatment of Native Americans in the United States (Tushnet 1972: 57). Still others, such as Dora G., had only a vague sense that something bad was happening:

> *Were you aware of the existence of the concentration camps, of what was going on there?*
> A little bit, not much. A tiny little bit because it wasn't no way of knowing. We imagine. But knowing . . . but mostly there they didn't know but tell me no more. So it was nobody tell but . . . we imagine. In other words, like they took my mother and brother too. So I knew I'm not going to see them anymore.

But many people, like Victor B., simply did not know what was happening:

But, uh, everybody want to go with your family. They said, "Oh . . . " They came and said, "Need . . . need workers." The . . . the Germans, they . . . from the Gestapo, he came from the area, they were, he said, "We need workers. You will all be transport from one place to the 'nother one. And the factory will be worked in another . . . deeper in Germany." "Oh." Well, everybody said, "Oh, what's . . . the Germans . . . we will be in barracks but we will have food at least. The Germans will give us food. And we will work. There will be . . . " Nobody dream about this. And then when they put us in the trains . . . the trains came. In the ghetto was a special place where the trains came. And they put us in these trains. Everybody went . . .
Willingly.
. . . willingly. They . . . they rushed. Everybody want . . . want be first. Everybody want to go before you. Nobody knew.

Even if they had heard something about the fate of the deportees, some Jews did not, or could not, believe that Jews were being put to death. Instead, they preferred to believe that the deportees were merely being relocated to places where there was more food and better working conditions. Miriam M., who worked in a factory sewing buttons on clothing, survived the deportations and began to hear what was happening at a place called Chelmno:

> *Did you speak among yourselves about what might be happening to the people taken?*
> Yeah. We already . . . because in the same building when we were with people from Belgium, ah, from all over Europe, and we heard already a lot what was going on, and where the people . . . and that time, while we were in ghetto already, we knew that exist a place called Chelmno, and this is where we had a little bit of . . . we heard stories, but we didn't want to believe it, what really happened. We heard what the Germans did with the people . . . but we didn't want to believe that . . . We thought maybe somehow, some way they went somewhere else . . . We knew that this could be our parents, our grandparents, our families, but we didn't want to believe.

In fact, Harry S. explained that his mother did not allow the family to talk about rumors of death camps, even after he heard about notes left behind in train cars warning others of the reality of deportation:

Yes, I heard about, eh, Chelmno, I think. That is a . . . and people . . . there were rumors, they . . . they are gassed, and they're making, rh . . . soup out of the fat of the people. But who could comprehend it? Who could believe it? And like I mentioned before, my mother never let . . . talk about it at home. But I . . . I remember hearing it, that somebody was telling that people were going in the . . . in the wagons. When they were taken off from the wagons, they left little notes in the . . . in the train. And people were finding the notes and . . . and they did know. But I don't believe that somebody believed in it even. Even they . . . people vanished. People . . . nobody came back from . . . from the concentration camp.

The isolation of the Łódź Ghetto—a function of place—facilitated these des-perately hopeful beliefs. With precious little information trickling in from the outside, Łódź Jews had at best a vague sense of the threat, which could allow some to hope that the bad news simply was not true. This hope prevailed even after the tragedy of the deportation of the children, as Samuel P. noted:

> I saw him [Rumkowski] give the infamous speech, "Give me your children," when he asked the people of the ghetto to give up their children. This was the time when they sent away the orphanage . . .
> . . . *And what did you think then?*
> I . . . you know, you try to push those thoughts away from you, in a way, because if you . . . if you started thinking, the thoughts became so unbear-able that you were ready to give up, and you didn't want to give up. So you pushed thoughts like this away from you. You listened to rumors and what-ever it was the truth you believed it. There was nothing we could have done about it . . . You were just happy that everybody left you alone and that you could survive the day . . . from day to day, just . . . just by getting enough to eat and getting enough sleep and getting enough rest.

Hunger and Decision-Making

A lack of information, coupled with an inability to believe snippets of dev-astating information, led Łódź Jews to conclude that Ghetto life, while pre-carious, was still survivable. This conclusion went hand-in-hand with the suffering that Łódź Jews had already endured since the arrival of German soldiers. Beaten down, hungry, and exhausted from working long hours with inadequate food, Łódź Jews could focus on little other than the daily grind of survival. When asked about her reactions to deportations and beatings, for instance, Lucia M. said:

> I think . . . I think we were . . . we were so much . . . I think that our reaction was . . . were dulled, that we didn't react normally. I think the main objective was to survive the day, not . . . we didn't think very much about what is going to happen tomorrow . . . Somehow . . . that's how I recall, just . . . just to go on.

Thus, the misery of daily Ghetto life, with its all-consuming focus on finding enough food to survive until the next ration, took over all other considerations.

These assessments show that Jews recognized the threat of deportation, but did not—or could not—know exactly what that threat entailed. The resonant response to the threat, as they understood it, was to try to survive in the Ghetto for as long as possible. More importantly, while deportations were certainly threatening, it was *hunger* that was seen as the main threat in the Ghetto. Tellingly, when asked what people in the Ghetto talked about, Dora G. responded simply, "About food." As Samuel P. put it:

> Life in the ghetto was a struggle, a daily struggle for . . . for . . . to find food, to get your soup, to get your stomach full. It was the biggest . . . the most important thing in . . . in . . . in everybody's . . . everybody's existence at the time.

Because the "hermetical seal" surrounding the Łódź Ghetto precluded food smuggling, the problem of hunger was especially dire—even worse than in other ghettos. Threat assessment in Łódź—and, ultimately, decisions about resistance—must therefore be understood in the context of the debilitating, and life-threatening, hunger in the Ghetto. As Miriam M. explained:

> And every day, hunger did . . . does many things to human beings. And Germans really won with hunger, because they dehumanized the people. There was no . . . no food, no medication. Well, how can you survive? Very little.

George S. further described the impact of hunger:

> But hunger confuses people. It changed their outlook of life. It changed
> their structure. It's . . . you don't think with your head; you think with your
> stomach. Ah, that's all we could think of, is bread.

Concerns about hunger overtook all other matters: people had to find
food before they could do anything else. Yet without the ability to smuggle
food into the isolated Ghetto, residents' hunger also kept them compliant,
in the sense that they continued working in the factories, even after the
deportations, in order to receive whatever meager amounts of food they
could get. Ironically, the factory-heavy Ghetto, with a Ghetto leader who
continued to exhort Jews to demonstrate their usefulness through work,
gave the community some hope that they could survive—that is, if they
could only get enough food to survive until the end of the war. As George
S. continued:

> And the biggest problem in the ghetto was food, bread in particular. I used
> to dream about bread. All I was dreaming is that maybe someday I will sat-
> isfy myself, my stomach. And my . . . and I . . . I felt like I had a tiger in
> me, was taking me . . . and I used to succumb to the . . . collapsed from
> hunger, completely. Sometimes I couldn't even get up in the morning.
> I was so hungry. And I was so skinny, you could see my ribs from about ten
> feet away, every rib in my chest. And . . . but my father keeps pushing me,
> go . . . to go on, "Come on, the war isn't going to last forever. Keep going."
> So I did.

Abe L. confirmed:

> Now there was no meat, there was no . . . no butter, no bread, no sugar, no
> salts. They been . . . people growing up three years, children which didn't see
> how an egg looks, because there were no eggs. It was just a dream. How we
> living over there nobody can even imagine.
> *What made you go on?*
> It . . . make us go on only one thing. Tomorrow will be another day. And
> maybe we will still be alive, because people have been falling like fly.

Resonant Responses

Like the other ghettos, the conditions in the Łódź Ghetto were life-threatening. So why didn't resistance emerge as a resonant response to the suffering? Again, place is important here. The "hermetical seal" that cut off the
Łódź Ghetto from the rest of the world kept information out, and therefore
kept residents from learning about the mass murder of Jews, precluding the
conclusion of genocide that was critical for armed resistance to emerge. That
genocide was critical to the decision to resist is illustrated by Victor B., whose
parents taught him to be tough in the face of anti-Semitism (as he explained
it, "how more the anti-Semitism is, the . . . tougher will you be"). He said that
if he had known about the death camps, he would have fought back with his
bare hands:

> Nobody knew that there's a Auschwitz, or a Treblinka, or a Mauthausen, or
> there's something, they're burning Jews. No one from us may . . . will be go,
> from the youth especially. With . . . not . . . with bare hand we will fight.

Yet it was not simply a lack of knowledge of genocide that precluded armed
resistance in the Łódź Ghetto. As the stories of the ghettos of Warsaw and
Vilna show, an assessment of threat alone does not lead to resistance; for
resistance to emerge, it needs to be seen as the appropriate response to the
threat. Thus, even with a critical conclusion of genocide, one might not have a
corresponding resistance frame. Malka F., who lost her parents in December
1939 and survived in the Łódź Ghetto until August 1944, at which point she
was sent to Auschwitz, provides an illustration. Like Victor B., she was a survivor who, in retrospect, indicated that if she had known about the genocide,
she might have taken some action. However, she explained that her response
would have been suicide rather than armed resistance:

> *Did you know anybody who had a radio even in secret?*
> No, we would be afraid to keep a radio.
> *Did any of the people that you knew get any mail from outside the ghetto?*
> I don't know of any. I wish we got and we knew about it.
> *Did you have any idea about what was going on in the war or in the outside*
> *world at the time that you were there?*

That's why I said I wish we knew about . . . maybe we handle differents. Maybe we wouldn't go to Auschwitz, maybe we will do something to kill ourselves, because this was worse than killing.

Elsa R., the dentist's daughter, said that her father did manage to learn about the camps; on the basis of this knowledge, she and her family contemplated suicide, and had a plan in place. However, her mother's hope for Elsa's survival made them change their minds:

> My father . . . my father found out about Auschwitz from one of his patients. I think there were a few radios in the ghetto, you know, hidden . . . And that's how they knew a little bit what was going on outside. Not much, but a little bit. So he knew about Auschwitz, but he never told my mother and me. But he did take us, the two of us, once . . . it was toward the end, and he said to us, "You know, we . . . I feel that we should commit suicide, because it's . . . it's not good. The situation is not good for us." So he brought out pills, three white pills, and he said, "If you want to, we're going to commit suicide." So I agreed. I was the first one to agree. I didn't want to stay without them, and I had a feeling that, you know, they are older than I and I had no chance to survive. But my mother said, "She's young and she may survive. I don't want her to . . . I don't want to do it." So my father listened to my mother.

While people like Elsa and her family were unusual in the Łódź Ghetto, in that they learned about the death camps, it is still notable that they did not respond to this assessment of lethal threat with armed resistance. As Malka F. explained, suicide seemed to be a more reasonable response.

Placed and Misplaced Resistance

Yet while there was no armed uprising in the Łódź Ghetto, it is inaccurate to say that there was no resistance in that ghetto at all. Łódź Jews did fight back—but not with weapons, and often against the wrong foe. Their decisions about resistance, including the form of resistance they chose and whom it targeted, reflected their assessment of the threats facing them and the responses to those threats that made the most sense. Following Gieryn (2000) and other scholars who theorize the role of place in human social action, I argue that these assessments and decisions were "placed," in that they were shaped by place-specific assessments—which, in Łódź, reflected the built environment of the Ghetto and its corresponding isolation. At the same time, because these placed assessments and decisions also led to unarmed acts of resistance that were directed not at the broader Nazi genocidal regime but at Ghetto leader Chaim Rumkowski and his immediate control of the Jewish community, I also refer to some of the resistance in the Łódź Ghetto as "misplaced." The lack of armed resistance in the Łódź Ghetto, and the placed and misplaced resistance that did occur, resulted from an assessment of threat and a resonant response to that threat, as Łódź Jews understood it.

Like the ghettos of Warsaw and Vilna, there were a number of individuals living in the Łódź Ghetto who were active members of pre-war movements and political organizations. The presence of these movements is not surprising, given the size of the Ghetto population; again; Łódź was among the largest ghettos in Poland, second in size only to Warsaw. In fact, there may have been as many as 5000 youth activists in the Ghetto, hailing from the same movements that spawned resistance in Warsaw (e.g., HaShomer HaTzair and Betar) (Tushnet 1972: 66). These movements were active, especially in the Ghetto's early years; members met routinely for political discussions, and served the community as best they could. Notably, Rumkowski initially assigned land plots to some youth activist groups in the Marysin section of the Ghetto, where they formed collectives and grew food. As Noah H. described:

The movements were organized, that we got some ground, you know. And outside, in the ghetto, there was still some places which were not inhabited. And there were big yards, big fields, you know, ground. And they . . . each group, each Zionist movement group, you know, the Shomer HaTzair, [HaNoar] Hazioni, B'nai Akiva, Agudat Israel, all those people . . . they all got, Betar, pla—you know, some places, you know, some ground. And they used to grow . . . started to grow things, like a community, like a kibbutz. We used to stay there. It was a . . . sort of a kibbutz life. We grew vegetables there. And we got some supplies from there, because each one had a . . . a ration, you know, a card, so that . . . a coup—coupon. And the coupons, they got food for us. While I was in the kibbutz, I was sent . . . there were schools which were colonized there. They gave them special . . . from little children, orphans, and people were . . . who wanted to have a bit more food, they thought they will get more food, they sent them there. And they were guarded by the teachers. And I was an instructor. I was helping. That was part of my job there. That's also a job which I can never forget. Most enjoyable because I had to do with small children, seven, eight, nine, ten. And they adored me and I adored them.

While Rumkowski disbanded the youth collectives in March 1941 (Trunk 2006: 332), he supported them initially. However, he was far less supportive of other political activity in the Ghetto. Rumkowski was especially vexed by strike activity—clearly, a type of resistance—staged by Ghetto factory workers in response to food shortages (Adelson and Lapides 1989; Trunk 2006; Tushnet 1972; Zelkowicz 2002). Such protests began in the summer of 1940, soon after Rumkowski first developed the system for rationing food, and occurred regularly over the next year and a half until mass deportations began in early 1942 (Adelson and Lapides 1989; Tushnet 1972: 24–25). Rumkowski used his bully pulpit to restore order, speaking out against the unrest in various proclamations and public speeches. In the summer of 1940, after a number of strikes by furniture workers, textile workers, and shoe workers, he implored:

> Jews!
> What happened here recently is due to irresponsible elements who want to bring disorder into our lives. Those people have their own plans and they do not include constructive social help for the people.
> Stay quiet. Don't let yourselves be misled by irresponsible people who want to interfere with our present work and the plans for our future. (quoted in Tushnet 1972: 25)

Rumkowski also countered some of these protests with force, as applied by the Ghetto's Jewish police, a unit which fell under his administration. For instance, in October 1940, a crowd broke into and looted a potato store; police killed two in the crowd in the ensuing melee, and injured four others (Trunk 2006: 109). Repression was not always violent, however. Strikers were often jailed, but Rumkowski's speeches warned of even greater repression from the Nazis if factory work was disrupted. In a speech at the conclusion of another workers' strike in January 1942, he said:

> Had the strike attempts that recently took place here come to the attention of the authorities, the snow would have been red with blood . . . I am certain

that if the ghetto does its work in earnest and does it well, the authorities will not take repressive steps. (quoted in Adelson and Lapides 1989: 201)

These repressive tactics were effective. Dora G. was arrested after participating in a strike:

> And that time was a strike, you know, like for the ones that make hats. It was like [a] meeting. They didn't give them food and no pay. So I happened to be there. Throughout on that time I was older and . . . organized, you know. But it happens that somebody, you know, squeal on that meeting. And they came up and they arrest all of us to . . . in the jail. And naturally, it was no good to be arrested. And that time [voice cracking] . . . but somehow there were people, you know, in which they told me, "He's [Rumkowski] not going to let us go . . . [crying] There were a few people, which they were in contact with him and he let us go. And we were eight days there.

These strikes illustrate Ghetto residents' resistance as a response to what they perceived as a threat: food shortages and poor treatment of Ghetto workers. Yet, while the strikes may have been a response to the overall suffering of Ghetto Jews, which was ultimately caused by the Nazi occupation, these actions were not directed primarily at German officials. Importantly, they were not a response to the deportations. In this sense, such resistance was misplaced.

Beyond the misplaced strike activity, there were some examples of organized, but not armed, acts of defiance directed more explicitly against Nazi officials, ranging from illegal radio-listening to sabotage of equipment in the Ghetto factories. All these are examples of "placed resistance." While all human action is emplaced, as Gieryn notes, I use this term to reiterate the role of place in Łódź Jews' choices about resistance. When they did resist, they did so in ways that reflected how they understood what was happening in the Ghetto, and what they felt was their most appropriate response.

One example of "placed resistance" was listening to the radio—a resistant act, since the possession of a radio in the Ghetto was strictly forbidden. Even with the clear dangers of doing so, some people had managed to hold on to their pre-war radios, or were able to build new ones. These resisters could share precious, inspirational news of war developments that helped give the remaining Ghetto residents hope that the war would soon end.[17] As George S. explained:

I was told that there was a radio some place in the ghetto. And I think that there was a radio in the ghetto. I never seen it. And some people, who had contact with the outside of the ghetto, used to bring in certain news. And yes, we did know about the . . . the Germans are going to be defeated, yes. And we did know when the United States came to war with Germany.

Abraham L. was involved in resistance work with the radio; while he did not listen to the radio himself, he distributed the radio news, in the form of written bulletins. In contrast, Adek F. actually did listen to a radio, to which he had access as a member of Betar, the right-wing Zionist youth group in the Ghetto:

> *Where would you go to listen to the radio?*
> In a secret places. We usually . . . this area where they were assigned, now I can say it. Remember I mentioned that the agriculture area? And this was isolated places over there, because they actually evacuated Polish people from this area to give the Jews this agriculture piece of land and do it. So we used to go over there at night, when it was a good quiet . . . no traffic was . . . and we were . . . and we used over there . . . and then we buried the radios in the certain areas, put some papers around . . . we didn't have plastic. So we grease some papers and buried and hooked it up with power . . . there was some power. And we could . . . and it was . . . we had some amplifiers, because sometimes it wasn't as clear, depending on the fog. And we had a person that taught us the atmospheric condition when the radio waves are better or worse. If it's a rain, we didn't have a good reception. If it's a fog we didn't have. If it was snowing we didn't . . . so he taught us when and what to do it. So we were more or less prepared for this.
> *How long did you do this for?*
> I did this, I would say, probably around a year, a good year.

Such resistance was placed, in that it was appropriate for the place where it happened: in the isolated Ghetto, without access to information from the outside, Jews resisted by doing what they could to rectify that situation, i.e., by listening to the radio even though it was expressly prohibited. Clandestine radio-listening can also be thought of as "everyday resistance," political scientist James Scott's (1985) term for acts of resistance that are often hidden or otherwise intended to go unobserved by those in power. Scott includes work slowdowns and workplace sabotage as additional examples of everyday resistance, and Jews in the Łódź Ghetto engaged in these acts as well. Work slowdowns in the Ghetto factories were common, especially in 1942, and the term "p.p." (*Pracuj powoli*, or work slowly) was used widely (Trunk 2006: 161). There were also acts of sabotage in the factories. For example, Wolf D., who was part of a small Communist cell led by a pre-war school friend, engaged in risky acts of sabotage in the leather goods factory where he worked:

> There was also, at one stage, again, in . . . up until about 194 . . . end of '42, '43, our group from school had another brilliant fellow called Niutek Radzyner, who . . . whose father became the manager of the metal work-shop. Now Niutek Radzyner[18] was a brilliant orator, even at that stage, and a brilliant chess player. And he organized in the school a section of the, I sup-pose Communist Party. It was like a resistance group in the ghetto. But we used to have meetings and we used to try to . . . he used to get news from the radio so we had some information. . . And he even organized a strike in the ghetto, which was punishable by death, in his father's factory. We tried to . . . to sabotage some of the work, but we had to be very careful because the Germans only knew one punishment and one law: you get killed or sent out of the ghetto to a . . . to a extermination camp. But I remember one of the things we used to do, we used to work with two needles, special needles, one in each hand. So we used to try and break . . .
> *Needles for the leather?*
> For sewing leather. Yes . . . So we used to break the needles, but . . .
> *As a resistance.*
> Yeah, trying to . . . well, eventually maybe they will run out of needles, you know.

Why No Armed Resistance in this Place?

James Scott's concept of everyday resistance is distinct from full-blown uprisings, the latter of which are difficult to achieve and, therefore, rare (1985: xvi). That does not mean that everyday resistance is disorganized. In the Łódź Ghetto, the small meetings, radio-listening, and work slowdowns were all organized, and at least some of these activities were planned by ac-tivist youth. This organizational capacity should, in theory, lead to armed resistance (Finkel 2017). So why didn't these activities translate into the emergence of a larger armed uprising, as in Warsaw (or what was planned, but not achieved, in Vilna)? Again, place plays a role here. As the survivor testimonies indicate, the built environment of the Ghetto, with its formidable barriers to the outside world, precluded the large-scale smuggling of weapons and other materials that would have been needed for armed resistance.

Amazingly, the survivor testimonies show that a precious few people were actually able to smuggle things into the Ghetto, at least in its early days. Maurice S., who was nineteen at the start of the Nazi occupation, had the looks and language skills to pass as a Gentile. Thanks to his job in a hat factory that was located near one of the open streets that ran through the Ghetto, he was able to make contact with and purchase butter from Polish street cleaners whose own jobs required them to come near the Ghetto fence. Maurice began his food smuggling activity initially to try to help his ailing sister, but then briefly helped members of the Bund smuggle packages into the Ghetto before he was arrested and eventually sent to Auschwitz:

> 1940, May, they closed the ghetto. And it must have been a few months later when we start the factory. And that was, like I mentioned before, on the same street where the middle of the street was non-ghetto. And we were right next to the wires. I used to wear a star and a band that I'm an official, I could walk there. And on the middle of the street are [street] cleaners. And I organized through the cleaners to get into the ghetto butter . . . my sister got sick. And on the . . . on the chest she had something wrong with her lungs. And doctor said, "What can I give him [sic]? She needs butter. She needs good food to overcome it." And you can't get anything from the ghetto. So I start getting this through the Poles . . . That was very dangerous. I could get shot . . . and I talked to them. From behind the gate, I talked to the man who cleans it. I said, "Could you organize some butter. I pay as much as you like. Could you organize this?" And I . . . and I did it. He threw it over, and I threw back the money. And I used to get it through the wire. They call it smuggling . . . I did it because I want to save the family . . . then the Bund, like . . . he said to me, "We need some more. If you've got contact with them, we need some information." He was in the underground. The Bund organized under—I don't . . . they wanted to . . . in the ghetto you're not allowed to have radio and papers, or whatever. So we used to get from them the papers and communications. I don't know where he got it from but he gives different underground

work. And I use to provide them with all the things they asked for . . . And I got caught . . . and they arrested me.

Beno H. was another person who was, miraculously, able to make contact with people beyond the Ghetto fences. With his flawless German language skills and non-Jewish appearance, he could pass as a German. While working at an agricultural plot at Marysin in the Ghetto's early days, he was contacted by people who recruited him for a network of anti-Nazi resistance activities:

[O]utside of the [Ghetto] limit where nobody lives there was a big empty plot. There was a border between the ghetto and outside. And it was experimental farming . . . I joined the underground and they said they need me and so I . . . because I spoke German . . . so they smuggled me out of the ghetto and they sent me to a city by the name of Częstochowa . . . And over there I met a woman by the name of Renya . . . She was a French nationalist, but she worked for the British CIC. This woman, if you looked at her, she had the most angelic face you ever saw, and was the most ruthless killer you ever met. [laughs] But . . . and under her . . . under her tutelage, I became an expert in train demolitions. And she got me a job, this Reyna . . . by then I was a German. I was a German. I got a job in . . . a big, big building, big, big, big building where they used to take the uniforms from the soldiers which . . . on the front, which were filthy, which were with blood stains, which had to be sewn, which were ripped and everything else. . . They used to fix them. They used to clean them and later send them back wherever they're supposed to be. My job was to . . . remember the patches of the numbers, where they comes from. Because, you know, it's the second division, then we know the second panzer division is in *Ostfront* [Eastern front]. The third panzer division is on the west front. So this is the reason I used to keep a count, one, two . . . two, three . . . two, three, one. So I kept accounts and later I give that to Renya and she give it to . . . to somebody else . . . The only thing is, to make it more legitimate, we . . . so every few weeks I used to go back, they used to take me back to Łódź, as a German, and I used to smuggle myself in by the border where the so-called potato farm was, so nobody missed me. If they asked me where was I, I told them I was on a potato farm.[19]

These testimonies challenge the typical portrayal of the Łódź Ghetto as "hermetically" sealed; they show that some bits of information did trickle in. Still,

Łódź was much more isolated than the ghettos of Warsaw and Vilna, and its walls were much less permeable.

Moreover, while the testimonies show that a few Łódź residents were able to breach the Ghetto's formidable barriers, their efforts could not mobilize more broadly or become sustained. Some people, like Maurice S., were caught and arrested. Others could not even engage in such work, partly because of the built environment (the wall, the surrounding "no man's" land, and so on), but also because of the hunger that was a result of that environment. Wolf D. explained:

> Until about 1943 the hunger the devastation and . . . and . . . that pervaded in the ghetto . . . pervaded the ghetto was . . . we were . . . we just lost interest in everything. There was only one thought in everybody's mind: how to avoid deportations and how to get an extra slice of bread or rotten potato peels or anything. And, as the song, the ghetto song goes, there was only one thought, and one idea in everybody's mind, and that was food.

Hunger, which was ultimately a function of the Ghetto's isolated place, also shaped people's responses to the threats of the ghetto and their decisions about how to act. They simply *had* to find food before they could do anything else—resistance included. Survival, rather than resistance, was the resonant response to the perceived threats of the Ghetto. As Morris C. explained during his testimony:

> *Okay. Were . . . at the time were people fearful or did they think this would be over soon and they would get out? What was the mood?*
> Well, everybody was afraid to talk, that the police, you know, don't arrest you, or somebody don't say that you try something. There really was not organized, nothing what I know, if there was, not to my knowledge.
> *Did you ever try to escape?*
> Not from the ghetto. No.
> *Did other people? Were you aware of people trying to escape?*
> There was a few, but they got shot . . .
> *. . . How about resistance? Were there resistance groups that . . . ?*
> No, not in the Łódź ghetto. Not that I know. It was not organized . . .
> *. . . So, as . . . as far as you were concerned, people just worked? Tried to . . . tried to survive.*
> Mind your business, go home and survive.

Aron L. corroborated Morris C.'s point of view:

Did you ever think about trying to escape, trying to get out of the ghetto?
Was no way to escape. Was no way. Even you thought about it, was no way. First of all, you are too weak. You were fighting the daily life to have a piece of bread, to survive. There was no way to escape. Was always soldiers around. You know, the ghetto was closed up. And your . . . your mind was working to survive with that piece of bread, not to escape. We didn't even know where to escape to. Some people did get out, but very few. Few.
Was there any Jewish resistance in the ghetto, that you knew of?
Not that I know about it, not in the Łódź ghetto.

Emplaced Hope

Hope itself was also a resonant response to the threats of the Ghetto. Despite the horrific conditions, people sought to inspire each other and to maintain hope as a means of survival. For instance, Adek F.'s activism with Betar, which included illegal radio-listening, was intended to maintain hope:

Okay, I belonged to a movement that was actually trying to spare . . . to do anything that wasn't legal, let's put it this way. First of all, to teach ourselves Hebrew, and this was illegal. Discussing political situations, illegal. To see if we can resist in any way, to do it, that was illegal. To bring up the morale of Jews by dispensing news from the BBC. We could not hear Voice of America, but we got good broadcast from the BBC in English. And then, where I came in, and any person that spoke English or came in too, and we were spreading verbally at meetings what the latest news are. And those people who were present at this, their function was to go again and spread it the same. Not saying where they heard it, but the rumors are that such a thing happens, that the Nazis lost so-and-so . . . that Bismarck was sunk, that other ships were sunk, that, you know . . . and we . . . and this was our job, my job was to build up the morale of the population.

Spreading information was not foolproof, however. When some people heard scraps of news from beyond the Ghetto, they did not know what to believe. Simon H. described his work in an electronics factory, where he sometimes heard news about what was happening outside the Ghetto:

We were rewinding . . . we were repairing electrical things. And I learned a little bit there about electronics and things like that. And of course there was a lot of people there, discussions . . . but a lot of it was just exaggerated, you know. We just didn't know which is true and which is not, because officially nobody was allowed to have a radio. But it was just going around, rumors, and . . . and you just carried on as . . . as you could.

Perhaps more devastatingly, some in the Ghetto believed that information had to be withheld in order to maintain hope and morale. In a telling quote, Sam N., a youth activist who began to suspect genocide after the deportation of the children from Łódź in September 1942, admitted that his organization struggled as to whether or not to spread the word about their suspicions:

[A]fter that, you know, we had a dilemma in the ghetto. We didn't know how to solve it. We had meetings and all this . . . for instance, a question was what should we do?
Regarding which issue?
To tell them . . . tell them what happened to the kids, because we were, in that time, almost . . . we didn't believe it, I mean, but all we're sure for the kids were cremated. And . . .
How did you know that?
Through different, through different little . . . little what comes around. And then they mention a name Chelmno, and Chelmno not was from far away, you know, that they . . . the cars came back too early, you know. So we start to know. And then was a dilemma, what we do now? Tell the people or don't tell the people. We were divided. One . . . one says, "How can you take away the only hope from the mother what think, you know, that that kid is still alive?" . . . one says the kids are going to be spread out between the German women with they don't have any children, you know, they will adopt the children. Other says they will go to new homes . . . special homes for different . . . different versions. And I saw . . . when I saw when they took away the children, it's un—impossible to describe what over there. I think that in mine eyes the German want maybe ten . . . in my eyes, for ten minutes they won the war. When I saw, you know, when the mother and father stood outside and they said . . . saw the kids . . . four or five years old, they took down the kid and throw it in the wagon. And the mother says, "It's your fault. I want to hide the kids." And the father says, "No, we . . . we all will be killed." And when those . . . this . . . that's this fighting what went on with a husband

and wife. I think this was the German's purpose, we should fight each other instead . . . instead to put in the guilt on the Germans they're putting the guilt on their husbands and vice versa. And then we started . . . as I told you, we start . . . what to do . . . we want to decide what to do . . . So, by us, we let it hang. We couldn't . . . we didn't say yes and wouldn't say no. And this was hanging . . . I'd say we did the right thing or no. But the main purpose was, and I think I was thinking the same thing, not to take away the hope from the mother what still hopes that her kid is alive, her father is alive and ulti- mately we let it hang.

Yet by keeping up morale, such efforts only reinforced Jews' determination to survive, if at all possible. This response to the conditions in the Ghetto therefore worked against the idea of armed resistance. The fact that some organized activist groups busied themselves with place-based resistance (e.g., keeping clandestine radios) rather than attempting armed resistance supports this claim.

Still, place is crucially important here. The structure of the Łódź Ghetto— with its factories, and the fact that some people could work until the end— prevented most people from reaching that critical conclusion of genocide. Rumkowski also contributed to these perceptions, by reinforcing the "work to live" frame. In his testimony, Noah H. blamed Rumkowski for the lack of armed resistance in the Ghetto:

And that Rumkowski, I can't forgive it of him. I mean, I . . . I . . . I'm not the only one. He did everything, he had in the opinion, if he could save some . . . if he'd give away the children, he'd give away the older people, he will save the young people. He will save something. But that was wrong. If he wouldn't have sended us and he wouldn't have talked to us like that, if he would have made . . . I mean, he put our mind like that. Because we . . . we wanted believe the best. So we wouldn't have voluntarily went to . . . for the deportations. Because the end would have been the same. They would have killed us . . . they killed us in Auschwitz. At least we would have had that . . . when . . . that feeling that we have done something to fight against them. There was no one German killed in Łódź Ghetto, you know that? That's . . . I blame him for that.

Finally, while place is important, so is hope. Adek F. considered suicide on several occasions, such as when he first realized how much his father was suffering from starvation. He contemplated touching the electric wire that surrounded the ghetto, but decided not to, because he found the hope for survival:

> *What kept you from going to the wire that day?*
> It kept me that the hope. And some news. This was getting closer. We were taking . . . we're talking about 1944 . . . When I heard over the radio that the Russian front is closing on and I said, "Maybe, maybe, maybe it'll end." . . . in 1944, the Soviet Union soldiers were close to Warsaw and could . . . and Warsaw from Łódź was 120 miles, approximately. So when they were standing on the other side of Vistuła, of the river, we thought they'll be in Łódź very close . . . I thought that, you know, it's the Soviet Union is close to Warsaw, it's 120 miles from Łódź. Why not . . . we'll wait till they come through.

Hope for survival kept Adek F. going, despite the dire conditions in the Ghetto. With such hope, certain responses to those conditions outweighed others: Adek chose to try to survive, instead of taking his own life. Notably, he did not consider armed resistance as a resonant response—even though he was a member of an activist group.

Eva B.'s testimony provides a different view, one that is particularly useful because she was one of the few Łódź survivors in my sample who said that they knew about resistance efforts in other ghettos. Even though she knew other Jews were fighting back, that response did not resonate with her, given her understanding and assessment of the threats facing her in Łódź:

> Some people they were listening to radio. They were making their own radios during the night, they knew how to do it. They were listening to news, and in the morning they would take them apart, because it was death penalty. So we knew that the Warsaw Ghetto was fighting. We knew what that is already they're fighting there.
> *How did you feel when you heard that?*
> I gave up on myself. I said to myself, "Why should I fight? Why . . . whatever happened to me is gonna happen. Why should I be better than them?" And anyway, nobody's gonna survive anyway. We didn't . . . at that point we knew we are not going to survive. So, but we are like living animals, like you do the best to eat, to survive.

This response is completely different than that of resistance fighters in Warsaw and Vilna. Unlike the fighters in those ghettos, whose hopelessness made resistance possible, Eva's hopelessness did not translate into resistance: instead, she felt defeated, such that she could not fight and could only try to survive. Thus, Eva's testimony also illustrates the importance of the development of the insurgent frame (and how it does not necessarily follow from an assessment of unsurvivability). Some people who did have access to clandestine radios did actually end up hearing about the Warsaw Ghetto Uprising. But as Eva's words reiterate, decisions about resistance are based on both an assessment of threat and the identification of the response that resonates best with that assessment. Again, though, Eva was an outlier among Łódź survivors, most of whom never heard about resistance in Vilna or Warsaw. For those who did hear about it, like Eva, it was too late for that new information to change anything.

Conclusions

The story of the Łódź Ghetto provides bookends of a sort to the history of the Jewish ghettos in World War II. It was the first major ghetto created in Nazi-occupied Europe, and was also the last one standing. As a "negative" case, or one in which there was no armed resistance, this ghetto also helps support my overall argument about the emergence of such resistance. Throughout this book I have argued that resistance depends on actors' assessment of threat and how best to respond to it. This chapter supports those claims: Łódź Jews' conclusions about threat, and their responses to it, explain why there was *not* a mass armed uprising in the Łódź Ghetto.

Whereas the histories of the Warsaw and Vilna ghettos point to pivotal events that shaped people's assessment of threat, in ways that either facilitated or hampered resistance, there was no such turning point in the Łódź Ghetto. Rather than a transformative event, the story of this ghetto is better understood in terms of place—that is, geographical and other place-based aspects of the Ghetto itself, which distinguished it from Warsaw and Vilna. I argue that structural and geographical features of the Łódź Ghetto contributed to the critical conclusions—or lack thereof—and resonant responses that can account for the absence of an armed uprising in the ghetto.

Łódź was a place that was severely isolated, even for a ghetto. Surrounded by electrified barbed wire fences abutting a "no man's land" that was near

impossible to breach, it was incredibly difficult for Łódź Jews to make contact with people outside of the Ghetto. Without access to newspapers, radios,
or word of mouth passed along by people who were able to sneak out of—or
into—the Ghetto, most residents did not know about the genocide enacted
against Jews and other peoples throughout Nazi-occupied Europe. Even
activists in the Ghetto did not know about mass killings elsewhere, it appears,
because fellow activists in Warsaw and Vilna could not reach them to share
the news. The Łódź Ghetto's isolation precluded both an emergent sense
of the genocide and the receipt of credible information from activists elsewhere. The built environment of the Łódź Ghetto prevented armed resistance in another way as well, for even if Łódź Jews had reached the conclusion
of genocide, the physical nature of the Ghetto made it virtually impossible to
smuggle in weapons and other supplies for resistance. The Ghetto itself hampered Jews' knowledge of genocide on a mass scale, and prevented people
from thinking they could do anything about their situation. Thus, the idea of
armed resistance did not emerge, much less resonate with the Ghetto population as a whole.

Łódź Jews assessed the threats facing them in a different way, which
also reflected the place in which they lived. The isolation created extreme
hunger in the ghetto, as Jews were unable to bring in food to supplement
their official starvation rations. While deportation was a very real threat,
hunger was seen as much more threatening. As I have argued with my colleague Thomas Maher (Einwohner and Maher 2011), there are different
dimensions of threat, each of which are assessed separately by activists.
One of these is the immediacy of the threat (see also Maher 2010). In
the Łódź Ghetto, hunger was the immediate, clear threat that had to be
addressed. The resonant response to that threat was to try to find food.
Jews therefore put all their efforts into securing employment in Ghetto
factories (which made people eligible for food cards) rather than planning
for armed resistance against the Nazis. Simply put, starving, weary Ghetto
residents had little energy for armed resistance. In a telling quote, Dawid
Sierakowiak, a member of a youth Communist cell in the Łódź Ghetto,
wrote in his diary on May 7, 1942, "we are in such a state of exhaustion
that now I understand what it means not even to have enough strength
to complain, let alone protest" (Adelson 1996: 164). This response was
made even more resonant by the actions of the "Eldest of the Jews," Chaim
Rumkowski. Like Ghetto Chief Jacob Gens in Vilna, Rumkowski advo-
cated a "work to live" strategy, publicly exhorting Jews to demonstrate

their utility and worth to the Germans by working in Ghetto factories (Corni 2002; Hilberg 1979; Tushnet 1972).

Yet despite their suffering, Łódź Jews remained hopeful that they could survive long enough for the war, and therefore the Nazi occupation, to end. This assessment also worked against armed resistance. As the stories of both the Warsaw and Vilna Ghettos corroborate, as long as Jews believed that they could survive, armed resistance—which would lead to a certain death—was not a reasonable response to their situation. Łódź Jews did resist, however, engaging in both placed and misplaced resistance. In the earlier days of the Ghetto, Łódź Jews did actually protest their poor treatment, but their actions were directed against controversial Ghetto leader Chaim Rumkowski, who controlled the food distribution, rather than the Nazi oppressors. Other acts of resistance included clandestine radio-listening and workplace sabotage. This "placed" resistance was possible because of Jews' pre-existing organizations and capacity for resistance, which, as Finkel's (2017) outstanding study of Jewish resistance finds, helps explain when and where Jews resisted. Yet, my argument both complements and goes beyond his. Łódź Jews had preexisting organizations and seeming capacity for resistance, so they did resist. The form of their resistance, however, depended on the critical conclusions and resonant responses that were shaped by place, and ended up as unarmed, placed and misplaced resistance.

The story of the Łódź Ghetto adds important considerations to our understanding of the emergence of collective action, especially under repressive conditions. In Warsaw and Vilna, transformative events drove people's assessment of threat and decision making. In Łódź, however, what could have been similar events (i.e., the deportations) did not have such effects. As social movement scholar Suzanne Staggenborg (1993: 332) claims, critical events can change perceptions of threat and shape mobilization, tactics, and outcomes; she argues further that threatening events spur mobilization more than positive events. Yet her use of the term "critical" to describe events implies that some events can be "non-critical," suggesting that it is the *interpretation* of an event as threatening that is key to its transformative power. The Łódź Ghetto brings this point into clear focus.

Paying attention to place also helps illuminate Jews' assessments and decision-making with respect to resistance in the Łódź Ghetto. The location, materiality, and meaning of the Ghetto all shaped Łódź Jews' critical conclusions (or lack thereof) and resonant responses to their situation. Łódź's location in what had become the Reich, and the meanings attached to that; the material form of the ghetto, with its barbed wire fences and empty perimeter; and the very meaning of the ghetto itself (was it a miserable, war-time factory town, or a stopping point along the way to the death camps?), are all relevant to the absence of armed resistance. Yet we can see the role of place in Warsaw and Vilna as well. As stated earlier, Vilna's proximity to the forests, where partisan units operated, gave resistant-minded Jews another option for action and contributed to the FPO's inability to unite the ghetto in a single fighting force. Warsaw's ghetto walls separated the Ghetto from the Aryan side, but if one could breach that wall safely, one was immediately in the rest of the city of Warsaw, where limited resources existed (albeit at great risk).

Even without armed resistance, the case of the Łódź Ghetto illustrates the mobilizing force of threat. It shows that threat can mobilize in different ways, depending on how it is assessed. Jews in the Łódź Ghetto did not assess the threats facing them in a way that led to the critical conclusion of genocide and the unsurvivability of the ghetto. In addition, their resonant response to their threat was shaped by the unbearable hunger, which was much more of a threat than deportation. These assessments were made in a particular place, and reflect the way that place—both the built environment and its effects on people's lives—shapes collective action. Yet while my argument about the lack of armed resistance in Łódź refers to place, it ultimately gets back to hope. As long as there was hope for survival, the idea of armed resist-ance against the Nazis could not emerge and gain support among the Ghetto population.

Thus, the absence of armed resistance in Łódź makes sense. But it was not because Jews in the ghetto were meek and submissive. Instead, I argue that the absence of armed resistance stemmed from the way they assessed the threat. The Ghetto was an all-encompassing place: the daily threat to exist-ence, coupled with a lack of information from the outside that could confirm the existential threat to all Jews, guided Jews in prioritizing survival at all costs. Without information from beyond the Ghetto, it was near impossible to imagine the worst. These perceptions prevented the critical conclusion of genocide that was needed for the development of insurgent consciousness that was necessary for armed resistance against the Nazis. Threat, and re-sistance, are cultured; they reflect the meanings that people associate with their circumstances. They are also placed—that is, features of the place where actors operate can affect what people know, or think they know, about what

Figure 6.1 Daffodil-covered memorial marker on the Path of Remembrance,
April 19, 2019.
Credit: Charles P. Golbert

that day, but people in other neighborhoods could be seen wearing them
as well. Finally, with or without daffodils, people on the streets stopped and
observed a moment of silence at noon, when air raid sirens rang and church
bells tolled, all in tribute to the Ghetto fighters.

The memorials to the Warsaw Ghetto Uprising, the flowers that
visitors leave upon them, and the moments of silence all serve as
reminders, both of the bravery of the Ghetto fighters and of the tragedy

Figure 6.2 Mural of Marek Edelman, Warsaw, April 2019.
Credit: Charles P. Golbert

of the Holocaust as whole. This book serves those same ends. However, they are not its primary goal. My main interest in the study of the Warsaw Ghetto Uprising, and in Jewish resistance in general, is to ask why it happened. Asking "Why did they resist?" does not detract from the fighters' bravery, nor does it diminish the pain of the Holocaust. On the contrary, this question was originally, for me, one of wonderment: how could Jews interned in the Warsaw Ghetto engage in a sustained armed uprising against a much more powerful foe? And what does the answer to this question teach us about protest and resistance more broadly? In this concluding chapter I outline what scholars of social movements can learn from armed resistance in the Jewish ghettos during World War II. I then draw implications of these findings for other cases of collective resistance in the context of extreme repression, such as rebellions by enslaved people, prison riots, and other insurgencies. Yet there are implications for politics and protest in less repressive settings as well. I end with a broader discussion about hate, and hope, in contemporary politics.

Theoretical Implications

The study of Nazism, and of fascism in general, was one of the original motivations for the development of what has been referred to as the "classical" model of social movements in the years following World War II. Early theorists, confounded by Nazism, sought to understand the social conditions that could give rise to authoritarian-led mass movements; their work led to theorizing about the role of mass alienation and relative deprivation in social movements (see Luft 2015b). By arguing that social movement scholars can continue to gain theoretical insights from the study of the Holocaust, this book brings that point full circle. Rather than studying the rise of fascism, however, I suggest that the study of anti-fascist resistance is theoretically useful. I base this claim on the observation that currently prominent theories of social movement emergence, which emphasize the importance of resources, opportunity, and actors' efficacy, *cannot* explain Jewish resistance during the Holocaust. Whereas one can reasonably argue that Jewish resistance during the Holocaust lies beyond the limits of what extant theories were originally intended to explain (i.e., largely peaceful protests in democratic settings), I maintain that asking "why did the Jews resist?" helps clarify scope conditions for our current theories and opens the door for further theoretical development.

Understanding Jewish resistance during the Holocaust requires the examination of another, different mobilizing factor: threat. While some social movement scholars have recognized the mobilizing power of threat, most studies examine cases with some amount of opportunity, which can make it hard to disentangle the separate effects of threat. This is true for research on protest in democracies (Johnson and Frickel 2011; McVeigh 2009; Reese et al. 2005) as well as authoritarian settings (Almeida 2003). By showing that threat can mobilize collective action even in the absence of opportunity, however, the study of Jewish resistance during the Holocaust extends the discussion by suggesting that it is threat, not opportunity, which matters most to the emergence of collective action.

Importantly, though, this analysis does not simply show that threat matters. It also illustrates *how* threat compels action—that is, how movement actors use motivational framing to convince people to act in the face of grave threats. Jews faced the same threat of extermination across all the ghettos in Nazi-occupied Europe, but only rose up in armed resistance in some places.[2] Why? My comparison of the ghettos of Warsaw, Vilna, and Łódź points to the role of critical conclusions and resonant responses in explaining sustained armed resistance. The Warsaw Ghetto Uprising stemmed from a resonant frame of honor, in conjunction with a critical conclusion of genocide and a belief in certain death. The notion of fighting to the death—because there was no option for life—was a reasonable response to the existential threat of the Ghetto. In the Vilna Ghetto, a portion of the community reached that same critical conclusion and adopted that same resonant frame. However, not everyone in that ghetto had that same threat assessment and response, which ultimately hurt plans for a ghetto uprising; as a result, the would-be ghetto fighters fled for the forests and fought as partisans. Whereas circumstances in the Warsaw Ghetto led the majority of Jews left there to reach the same critical conclusion and resonant response, the Vilna Ghetto illustrates a community grappling with their assessment of threat and the best response to that threat—the "what should we do?" that follows from the "what will happen to us if we do not do anything?" That case, in particular, demonstrates that assessments of threat are dynamic, and can vary over time and place—and even within a community. It also shows that a full understanding of the emergence of collective action cannot rest simply on threat assessments of activists themselves. It must also take into account the assessments of community leaders as well as non-activists. Finally, the place-based isolation of the Łódź Ghetto prevented Jews from reaching the conclusion that they would all be put to death. That, coupled with the extreme hunger—which was also a function of place—precluded the idea of armed resistance from emerging and being seen as a resonant response to the threats of ghetto life. In Łódź, it was not so much that the Jews were passive—protests against the "Eldest of the Jews," Chaim Rumkowski, suggest otherwise—but that they lacked information about the true nature of the threats facing them, and protested against what they believed to be the source of their problems. In all three ghettos, assessments of threat, and responses that made sense given those assessments, help explain why sustained armed resistance happened in some places but not others.

Although my argument is based on three war-time Jewish ghettos that existed in a particular time and place, it is reasonable to expect that similar dynamics may operate in other cases of collective action in situations of extreme repression and powerlessness, such as rebellions of enslaved people, prison revolts, and uprisings in refugee camps (although see Goldstone and Useem 1999 for an application of opportunity-based explanations to prison riots). Armed resistance in those settings is understandably rare, but it does happen. A focus on threat assessment may help explain why, for instance, rebellions of enslaved people happened at some times and places but not others. Marcus Rediker's (2013) work on the Amistad Rebellion, an 1839 armed revolt on board a ship that was taking captured Africans from Sierra Leone to a plantation in Cuba, suggests that this may be the case. The enslaved people rebelled on their second journey, after a layover in Havana during which they were sold to two Spaniards and placed on a ship called La Amistad. While on the Amistad, the resisters, who did not know where they were being taken, came to believe that they would be killed, dismembered, and eaten upon their arrival at their destination. They received this false but nonetheless consequential information from the ship's cook, himself enslaved to the ship's captain. Deciding that fighting their captors would be better than being murdered, the enslaved people rebelled, killing the captain and the aforementioned cook and taking control of the ship and setting sail for Sierra Leone.[3] This case provides another example of resistance under extreme repression, in which actors' threat assessment led them to rebel, even though they knew they might not succeed. Cases such as the Warsaw Ghetto Uprising and the Amistad Rebellion not only show that collective action can take place in extremely repressive settings, but that there may be no upper limit to the effect of repression on action. Extreme levels of repression might not quell action, but instead may inspire it. In another application, Bert Useem's (1985) analysis of the 1980 New Mexico Prison Riot shows that increased repression, coupled with other structural constraints such as the discontinuation of programming for people who were incarcerated, contributed to a situation that some rioters found unsustainable, prompting collective action, despite the risks. In the words of one incarcerated person, "The men that's here doing life and more you'd have to give them something for an incentive or you can't hold 'em. You're going to have to kill 'em or let 'em hit the fence" (1985: 683). Thus, unlike what some other research suggests, the relationship between repression and collective action may not be curvilinear, but exponential.

The Need to Know

The story of resistance in the ghettos of Warsaw, Vilna, and Łódź also teaches us that resistance rests on what people know, or think they know, about their social and political environments—and what they believe those settings imply, for their present as well as their future. Such perceptions are forged from the cues that people get from their surroundings, whether in the form of official statements, empirical observation, or news and rumors spread through networks. This general insight is similar to arguments made by McCammon (2012), whose study of the U.S. Women's Jury Movement stresses the importance of activists' read of the "signals" in their political environment before planning action, and Park (2019), who documents Korean democracy activists' evaluation processes between 1979 and 1983 as they assessed their previous actions (and the state's response) and planned new strategies. Tellingly, in my 120 survivor testimonies, the word "know" was the single word that came up most frequently. In fact, this word was uttered more often than other commonly occurring words such as "Jewish," "Germans," "people," or "ghetto." As this simple word count suggests, and as the preceding chapters make clear, Jews in the ghettos attempting to make decisions about action under unbearable circumstances had to figure out what they knew, what could be counted on, what risks they were willing to take, and what outcomes they were willing to accept (see also Einwohner 2009).

Yet, knowing something about one's environment is not necessarily a straightforward process. Actors' assessment of the perils and possibilities in a given setting, as well as their subsequent decisions about action, is shaped in part by their knowledge of the past and what they have done previously. As social movement scholar Kathleen Blee's 2012 study of the emergence of grassroots activist groups in Pittsburgh finds, when groups form initially there can be a broad sense of goals and possibilities for achieving them, but over time, the sense of what is possible tends to become narrower. As she explains, activists' decision-making over time is "path-dependent," as actors look to the past for insights and information about how to strategize in the present. Importantly, while new directions are possible, they require novel ways of thinking that depart from what has become the accepted way of doing things:

> How activist groups decide what to do is a path-dependent process. So are their shared interpretations. Options tend to narrow when prior actions and understandings solidify as the taken-for-granted character of the group . . . [but] trajectories are not fixed; they can shift at turning points along a sequence. In activist groups, turning points are those extraordinary times when people consider "options that were previously dismissed as unthinkable" or "moments of madness" that propel new actions . . . At turning

points, groups adopt new interpretations and see new kinds of actions as possible. (2012: 39–40)

Work on culture and cognition also identifies limits on actors' assessment of their situation and abilities to arrive at new strategies that depart from previous responses to environmental cues. If people can only make decisions based on what they have known in the past, it is hard to know how to act in the face of new circumstances—especially if they are confusing and dangerous. As sociologist Karen Cerulo (2006) has shown, imagining a future that goes well beyond what people have experienced in the past is difficult, both cognitively and culturally. An "optimism bias" predisposes most people to hope for the best, even in the face of daunting circumstances such as stage four cancer and other devastating medical diagnoses; it may also help explain why so few people in the United States have wills (see Cerulo 2014).

Allowing oneself to accept a previously unimagined reality, and undertaking risky actions in response, certainly qualifies as "extraordinary" in Blee's terms. It is this rare leap of faith that allowed Jews in the Warsaw Ghetto (and some Jews in the Vilna Ghetto) to realize that they were all being targeted for death, a critical conclusion that made armed Jewish resistance during the Holocaust possible. The extraordinary steps people had to take to reach that conclusion underscores just how remarkable such resistance was.

Lessons for Contemporary Politics

Insights from the study of Jewish resistance during the Holocaust are also applicable to politics today. Most people living in stable democracies enjoy the freedom to resist that was not bestowed upon Jews in the ghettos, or enslaved people in the Americas, or other confined, powerless people. They also, in general, can afford to wait through periods of diminished opportunities and heightened repression—what social movement scholars Verta Taylor and Leila Rupp refer to as going into "abeyance"—until conditions improve and visible, physical acts of protest are more feasible (Rupp and Taylor 1987; Taylor 1989). However, by demonstrating the mobilizing power of threat, the story of Jewish resistance in the ghettos of Warsaw, Vilna, and Łódź helps inform resistance in democracies as well. As I noted in Chapter 2, looming dangers, perceived as the answer to "what will happen if we don't act?," inspired the 2017 Women's March and other mobilizations in response to the threats of the Trump presidency in the United States (Fisher 2019). Protests also erupted after the police murders of George Floyd, Breonna Taylor, and countless other African Americans in the summer of 2020. These mobilizations were a resurgence of the broader Black Lives Matter movement that emerged in 2013 as a reaction to the ongoing threats to the lives and wellbeing of people of color (Kahn-Cullors and bandele 2018). Threat mobilizes on the right side of the political spectrum as well. As sociologists Rory McVeigh and Kevin Estep (2019) argue, Donald Trump's 2016 election resulted from his support from disaffected white voters who felt that they were losing their societal position vis-à-vis women and immigrants, a state of "power devaluation" that was similar to the economic and political circumstances that fomented the rise of the Ku Klux Klan in the United States decades earlier.

Not only does threat inspire action, but when the threat is perceived to be extreme and unavoidable—or lethal and imminent, as Thomas Maher's (2010) work argues—it can lead to collective action *in the absence of opportunity*. Put another way, resistance is most likely when actors believe that there is no other way out, as Jeff Goodwin's (2001) analysis of revolutions shows. Along with these scholars' work, this book shows that states and authorities wishing to contain certain populations should realize that repression has its limits. Walls do not keep people in, or out, of a given area. Such barriers may prevent movement for some, but people will find a way to breach walls, whether literally or figuratively—especially if they are desperate. I wish to be clear that I am not advocating armed resistance in the face of threat. My point is simply that perceived threat can mobilize people to resist collectively, even if collective action is risky or seemingly impossible. The lessons of Jewish resistance, and similar mobilizations, are that if people are pushed to the limit—if everything is taken from them, including their right to live—they will fight back, no matter their foe's strength or their own lack of resources.

Contemporary Hate

I was lucky enough to be in Warsaw on April 19, 2019. Seeing the visitors flocking to the Muranów District, and the mounds of flowers they left behind, was quite moving. My visit to Warsaw coincided with the start of Passover, the same holiday that marked the beginning of the Warsaw Ghetto Uprising seventy-six years earlier.[4] In fact, my husband and I attended a

Passover Seder, led by Chabad of Warsaw and attended by Jews from all over the world. Unlike the circumstances during the war, it felt safe to be a Jew in Warsaw, and it especially thrilling to be able to share the Passover ritual with fellow descendants of those who had been targeted for extermination in Hitler's Europe. Yet, the end of that Passover holiday was marked by sadness. We were back in the United States on April 27, 2019, the last day of Passover, and the day a nineteen-year-old gunman burst into the Chabad Center of Poway, California, killing one person and wounding three others (including an eight-year old girl). Three weeks after the Poway shooting, on May 19, 2019, there was an attempted arson at a synagogue in our Chicago neighborhood. Exactly six months before the Poway synagogue shooting, on October 27, 2018, a forty-six-year-old, heavily armed man burst into the Tree of Life synagogue in Pittsburgh's Squirrel Hill neighborhood on a Shabbat morning and murdered eleven Jews, while yelling "All Jews must die." In a still-sobering twist of fate, we were supposed to be at a family celebration at that very synagogue that morning. While our event had been rescheduled months before, had things been different, the words that I am typing now would never be written (at least not by me).

When I originally conceived this book in 1993, I never thought that I would be writing its final chapter in the midst of an upsurge in anti-Semitic attacks in the United States. The Anti-Defamation League reports that in 2019, anti-Semitic incidents rose twelve percent over the previous year and were at their highest recorded level (Anti-Defamation League 2019), and hate crime statistics collected by the FBI in 2019 indicate that the majority (60.2 percent) of anti-religious hate crimes were motivated by anti-Jewish bias (FBI 2019). Yet, increases in hate crimes are not limited to anti-Semitism. The gunman who attacked Jews in Poway, CA was also believed to be responsible for an attempted arson at a nearby mosque some weeks before. His attack on the synagogue was one week after series of bombs killed over 300 worshipers in Sri Lanka on Easter Sunday, an act which itself was a retaliation for a March 2019 attack on Muslims in two mosques in Christchurch, New Zealand, in which fifty people were shot to death. The Pittsburgh killings came on the heels of the murder of two African Americans in Jeffersontown, Kentucky on October 24, 2018; the gunman attempted to enter an African American church, but because its doors were locked, he headed to a nearby grocery store where he found his victims. More recently, in response to the COVID-19 pandemic—referred to as the "Chinese flu" by Trump and his supporters—violence against Asian Americans is increasing (Yancey-Bragg

2021). Sadly, the list of people lost to hate-based violence is seemingly endless, with examples in Charlottesville, VA, Charlotte, NC, Orlando FL, and many other places.

These events are painful reminders that anti-Semitism, and racist and homophobic violence in general, is very much alive in the world—both in the United States and globally. While one message of this book is that the events of the past can help us understand protest and resistance more broadly, another is that we simply must never forget the events of the past. At the same time, we must also acknowledge, and condemn, the perils of the present. Anti-Semitism is real. Racism is a scourge. So are Islamophobia, homophobia, anti-immigrant xenophobia, and violence against transgender and gender non-conforming people. Hate has consequences, not simply for the victims of mass shootings, but also for those harmed by policies and practices that divide families and communities, foment violence, and deny people basic human rights. And as the chilling events of January 6, 2021 made clear—during which a murderous mob populated by white supremacists stormed the U.S. Capitol—no country, no matter how seemingly democratic, is immune to organized hate.

I ask whoever is reading this book to stand up against hate, in all forms. Many Holocaust survivors owed their lives to those who gave them assistance that allowed them either to flee or to hold on long enough to survive the ghettos, camps, death marches, and all their after-effects. Do what you can to provide support for those who are targeted by hate, and for organizations that assist them. Tell your elected representatives that hate is unacceptable—and if they do not listen, vote them out of office. Confront this threat, safely, in your communities (both online and offline). The cost of inaction is too great not to act.

The Politics of Hope

While my goal in this book has been to explain resistance in three Jewish ghettos under Nazi occupation, that explanation points to the broader role of hope in politics and political action. Hope is a positive emotion, a future-oriented construct (Wlodarczyk et al. 2017). By definition, hope implies a belief that the future can be improved upon the present, even if the chances of that positive outcome are small. Hope is powerful. With hope, people can do extraordinary things: force disease into remission, restore ruined buildings to their former glory, bring endangered animal populations back from the brink of extinction, and win championships as underdogs. Hope is powerful in protest and politics as well. For instance, survey research conducted among anti-austerity protesters in Spain (Wlodarczyk et al. 2017) found that hope for the future was a mediating factor that translated the protesters' anger about perceived injustices of austerity measures into collective action. Similarly, Roscigno and Danaher (2001) show that radio broadcasts of Franklin Roosevelt's "fireside chats," along with protest-inflected folk music, helped mobilize southern textile workers during a time of repression by giving them a strong sense of solidarity and hope. And in a path-breaking speech at the 2004 Democratic National Convention, which some say opened the door for his presidency, then Illinois State Senator Barack Obama extolled the "audacity" of hope, saying:

> I'm not talking about blind optimism here—the almost willful ignorance that thinks unemployment will go away if we just don't think about it, or the health care crisis will solve itself if we just ignore it. That's not what I'm talking about. I'm talking about something more substantial. It's the hope of slaves sitting around a fire singing freedom songs; the hope of immigrants setting out for distant shores; the hope of a young naval lieutenant bravely patrolling the Mekong Delta; the hope of a millworker's son who dares to defy the odds; the hope of a skinny kid with a funny name who believes that America has a place for him, too. Hope—Hope in the face of difficulty. Hope in the face of uncertainty. The audacity of hope! In the end, that is God's greatest gift to us, the bedrock of this nation. A belief in things not seen. A belief that there are better days ahead. (Obama 2004)

The story of Jewish resistance in Warsaw, Vilna, and Łódź teaches us something else about hope. First, while hope can inspire individuals and communities to do great things, sometimes it is not hope, but hopelessness, that leads to extraordinary feats. Second, hope can be difficult to let go, even under dangerous, life-threatening circumstance. This drive to survive explains why some people in the Jewish ghettos interpreted their surroundings through the lens of hope, not allowing themselves to believe the disturbing rumors about death camps and mass killings, even though those rumors ended up being true.

Łódź survivor Noah H. was one of many who spoke of hope in his testimony. When asked why he survived the Holocaust, he said that he did not know—a common response among survivors. However, his reflections centered on the concept of hope:

> I don't know how I survived because I was always considered, at home, the weakest. I was always . . . have to be looked after. And I don't know, it was . . . it wasn't my strength. Or maybe I . . . I am . . . I . . . I hope. I'm a hoper, you know . . . I hoped, you know, that I will survive. I don't know, I did everything in my mind. Physically, I couldn't do a thing because I wasn't . . . I didn't take risks. Because the people sometimes risked. They had a good meal, they had a . . . a extra portion, or they got beaten up. I didn't do that. I didn't risk. I didn't have any additional things. I was, ah . . . I was starving. I was living in hunger from the beginning of the war, I mean, from 1940, middle of 1940, 'til the end . . .
>
> *How did you deal . . . the time in the ghetto? How did you keep up your hope? . . . What helped . . . you to survive?*
>
> It's a nature. Still, up to this day, I always hope. If you will come and tell me something, this and this happened, I know I hope it will change. [clears throat] I . . . it's my nature. You know, I took it . . . took after my father. I . . . I'm always full of hope, you know, something will happen, something will come. If you . . . I got a refusal from someone, I hope that he may change his mind, something like that. You know, I give it as . . . give it to you as an example. I prayed for it, mind you, many times in my life. But, uh, that's how I am. And that . . . it could be only the hope because I don't know . . . I don't know how I survived.

Finally, Ann K., a survivor of the Vilna Ghetto, at the end of her testimony, had this exchange with her interviewer:

> *Is there any message that you would like to leave for your children, or your grandchildren, or other people who see this tape?*
>
> Well, I want to . . . the reason I did it is because I want people to know that it really happened, because a lot of people are denying that the Holocaust never existed, it never happened. And I want to leave a message to my children, that no matter what happens in life, you always have to have hope, and always feel that it's going to get better, never to lose your hope. Because I always felt that I have to survive. No matter how bad it is, I have to survive. And if you give up hope, you lose everything, you don't have nothing. This is all I have to say.

What are the broader lessons for the politics of hope? Should leaders convince their communities to keep hope alive during trying times? Or is it more strategic to mobilize by claiming that all hope is lost? The answer depends on the context, on the threats and opportunities present in the situation, and especially, on how people perceive them. Sustaining hope, as a forerunner of action, may make sense in the context of a democracy where (presumably) people have rights to assemble and dissent. Under extremely repressive conditions, however, dire forecasts and, ultimately, hopelessness, may be the only path to collective action.

Final Thoughts

Toward the end of his testimony, Vilna survivor Aron K., the chimney sweep who joined the FPO and then fought as a partisan in the forests, said that until the day of his interview, he and his wife, a fellow partisan and survivor, did not talk much about their experiences in the Holocaust:

> *So, then let me ask you . . . now at this time, why did you decide to make the tape? Why did you feel now that you could talk about it?*
> Okay. There are two reasons, and my first reason is a very selfish one. I would like at one time if my grandchildren will be interested, they should be able to put it on and see who their grandparents were, what they went through, if they'll be interested . . . That's my primary reason. My second reason is [pauses] people accusing the Jews that we went like sheep to the slaughter. And if somebody will look at it, at least they will see that not all Jews went . . . went to the slaughter. Those are the two reasons.

I began this book by discussing the myth of Jewish passivity, and my desire to ask a different question: not why didn't the Jews resist, but why they *did*. Hope, and honor, help explain why armed resistance emerged in some of the Nazi-created Jewish ghettos but not others. Hope and honor are also central to how, I believe, we should remember the Holocaust. Let us honor the memories of victims of the Holocaust and genocide everywhere and let us hope that states and publics will work together, both to halt genocides and prevent them from occurring again.

APPENDIX

Data Sources

Data sources on the Holocaust are vast and varied. My analysis draws on a variety of such sources, including both published and archival data in the form of letters, diaries, memoirs, and documents preserved from the ghettos of Warsaw, Vilna, and Łódź. I use English-language versions of these sources, many of which were translated from their original Polish, Yiddish, and/or Hebrew. These include thirteen diaries, sixteen memoirs, and six collections of newspapers and other documents; I located another diary in Hebrew (itself a translation from Polish), which I had translated into English. I also visited one physical archive, at the United States Holocaust Memorial Museum in Washington, D.C., where I collected roughly 375 pages of documents (mostly flyers and newsletters) in Polish and Yiddish, all from the Warsaw Ghetto. I had these documents partially translated into English but soon realized that making full use of these data was beyond my willingness to lean on families and friends with the language skills to translate them. I therefore draw on these particular documents only sparingly. However, some of these documents, including famous letters written by Warsaw Ghetto fighters, also appear in the English-language collections that I use. All translations were done by native Polish and Yiddish speakers.

The fact that some of these data even exist is remarkable. Diaries and other documents kept by Jews in the ghettos can be thought of as a form of resistance in and of themselves. Whereas some people kept diaries individually, there were also collective efforts to record Jews' experiences in the ghettos. The best known of these is the famous "Oneg Shabbat" (in Yiddish, *Oyneg Shabbes*) archive from the Warsaw Ghetto. This archive, which contains underground newspapers, letters, and diaries, as well as reports on Ghetto life, was organized by Emmanuel Ringelblum, a historian and Ghetto resident who perished in 1944. He named this effort "Oneg Shabbat," a code name intended to hide the true meaning of the efforts from the Nazi authorities ("Oneg Shabbat" literally means "the joy of the Sabbath" and typically refers to a festive gathering on a Friday night, during the Sabbath). The materials that Ringelblum and his colleagues collected were placed in containers such as milk cans and buried in several locations in the Ghetto; most (not all) survived the destruction of the Ghetto and were recovered after the war (see Gutman 1989).

I also use videotaped oral testimonies from Holocaust survivors. There are several well-known archives of such data; these include the Shoah Foundation at the University of Southern California (USC), the Fortunoff Archives at Yale University, and the archives at the United States Holocaust Memorial Museum. To maintain consistency across the testimonies, I chose a single archive: the USC Shoah Foundation (see Shenker 2015 for more on the differences between these three archives).

Founded by filmmaker Steven Spielberg, the Shoah Foundation archive contains nearly 52,000 videotaped oral testimonies given by Holocaust survivors and witnesses between 1994 and 1999. This impressive archive includes testimonies from a wide range of those who experienced the Holocaust, including Jews, homosexuals, Jehovah's Witnesses, and Roma and Sinti (Gypsy) survivors, as well as political prisoners, liberators, and liberation witnesses. However, I limit my focus to testimonies from Jewish survivors. Their testimonies consist of interviews that were conducted by trained interviewers. Though the interview questions varied, all the testimonies had a similar format, beginning with prewar life and then covering personal experiences during the war including time spent in ghettos and, if relevant, participation in resistance. Interviews were conducted in the survivors' homes in the language of their choice and lasted an average of two and a half hours.

Importantly for my purposes, the Shoah Foundations archive's extensive testimony catalog allows researchers to identify testimonies based on a number of characteristics (e.g., survivor's gender, age, ghetto of residence, and notable experiences during the Holocaust, such as participation in organized resistance activities). I used these features to select separate random samples (forty from each ghetto) from among all the English-language testimonies available from survivors from each ghetto (246 testimonies from Vilna, 756 from Warsaw, and 1294 from Łódź). My final sample size was 120. I then obtained audio files for each testimony (thanks to access graciously provided by the archive) and had them all transcribed professionally.

While I limited my testimony sample to English-language testimonies from survivors, I do not believe that doing so biased my overall findings. The oral testimonies obviously came from Holocaust survivors, but my use of these data do not necessarily introduce a "survivor bias." These testimonies were not my sole source of data; as previously noted, I used a variety of primary and secondary sources, including primary sources (e.g., diaries) produced by people who perished during the Holocaust. Collectively, these sources help me construct narratives of the ghettos, including important events (or non-events) in each ghetto that shaped individuals' understanding of their situation. Further, I do not believe that my use of English-language testimonies led to any systematic bias. While the testimonies are in English, that is not the survivors' first language. In fact, many peppered their testimonies with words and phrases in Yiddish and Polish, which they usually also translated into English. More importantly, as noted, all interviews in the archive were conducted in the language of the survivor's choice. This was the same strategy used by David Boder, who recorded testimonies of Holocaust survivors in Displaced Persons camps in 1946 (see Rosen 2010). Although the survivors in my sample presumably chose English for their testimonies because it is a language with which they felt comfortable, it is still possible that they could not fully express themselves using a language that they did not grow up speaking. While I cannot rule out this particular limitation of my data, my interest lies in understanding the differences between ghettos, not individuals. In other words, what is important is that these testimonies were given by survivors of the ghettos of Warsaw, Vilna, and Łódź, and can help illustrate how people in those ghettos reached decisions about resistance. To the extent that the testimony data are biased, that bias should be constant across my cases, and should not affect my overall findings.

There is also the issue of whether there are any systematic differences between survivors who chose to give their testimony in English and those who opted for any other language. I regret that I cannot address this issue fully. However, it is notable that a majority of the testimonies of Jewish survivors from Warsaw, Vilna, and Łódź were given in English (54.7 percent of Warsaw survivor interviews, 53.6 percent of Vilna survivor interviews, and 62.9 percent of Łódź survivor interviews). Overall, a near-majority (24,028 out of 48,361, or 49.7 percent) of Jewish survivor testimonies in the archive were conducted in English. Further, my sample includes a range of English-speaking survivors: testimonies were collected in the United States, Canada, and Israel, as well as England, Australia, and South Africa. A group this broad may help improve the representativeness of my sample.

A particular strength of my testimony data is that they include information from both resisters and non-resisters. Given my interest in resistance, and my assumption that a simple random sample of testimonies would not yield very many testimonies from individuals who participated in resistance, I wanted to be sure that I obtained testimonies from both resisters and non-resisters. The archive's testimony catalog contained information about each survivor's participation in resistance activities, which allowed me to select stratified random samples from among the survivors of each ghetto, based on participation in resistance. Thus, my total sample of 120 survivors—forty from each ghetto—was expected to have twenty resisters and twenty non-resisters in each. Yet while my sampling process was intended to produce equal numbers of testimonies from resisters and non-resisters, it did not turn out that way. For instance, when reading the survivors' testimonies, I found some that were categorized as "resister" in the catalog participated in resistance activities later in the war, but not while they were living in either Warsaw, Vilna, or Łódź. Because such information could only be known after reviewing the complete testimony transcript, it was unfeasible to go back to the entire collection of testimonies to select and transcribe a new sample. My final sample therefore does not have equal numbers of testimonies from resisters and non-resisters. Table A.1 describes the characteristics of the sample of testimonies.

Beyond the particulars of my sample, it is worth noting that oral testimony data have weaknesses as well as strengths. Unfortunately, oral testimonies are not always accurate with respect to dates, times, and numbers. However, I do not use these data to provide definitive accounts of the history of each ghetto. Many of the events and historical figures described in these accounts are easily verified or corrected with published secondary sources. Further, in the tradition of comparative-historical sociology, my goal is to use all my primary and secondary sources to compare my cases, with an aim toward identifying patterns that can help explain why collective, armed resistance happened in one ghetto but not the others. As comparative-historical sociologists Elisabeth Clemens and Martin Hughes (2002: 201) note, in order to do such work social movement researchers "must discover evidence originally collected by others and make that evidence speak to core theoretical questions." In addition, as Shenker (2015: 11) explains, oral Holocaust testimonies "can be revealing even when they are not completely accurate in terms of historical content; they can still shed light on the ways in which witnesses perceive themselves and their labor through their stories" (see also Aleksiun 2014). Moreover, while testimonies given decades after the Holocaust may suffer from inaccuracies in historical detail due to individuals' problems with recall, they are beneficial in that they represent voices of those who could not, or would not, speak of their experiences in the more immediate aftermath of the war (Lentin 2000). (For more on the nature of videotaped oral Holocaust testimony and their limitations, see Langer 1991 and Shenker 2015; see also Sutton 2018 on the use of videotaped testimony to study survivors of state repression during the 1970s and 1980s in Argentina).

One final benefit of using oral testimony data is that they, like all primary sources, have the potential to reveal previously unknown details about life in the ghettos of Warsaw, Vilna, and Łódź. While some of the individuals and events they describe are well known, others are less so. I also assume, but cannot confirm, that for at least some of the individuals quoted in this book, this is the first time that their words appear in published research on the Holocaust. If that is the case, I am pleased to honor and memorialize these survivors by telling their stories.

Table A.1 Sample Characteristics of Survivor Testimonies (frequencies in parentheses)

	Warsaw	Vilna	Łódź
Survivor's age at start of war[a]			
Born after war started	2.5% (1)	2.6% (1)	0% (0)
0–6	10% (4)	2.6% (1)	2.5% (1)
7–12	25% (10)	17.9% (7)	17.5% (7)
13–16	22.5% (9)	33.3% (13)	30% (12)
17–21	30% (12)	35.9% (14)	35% (14)
22–30	10% (4)	5.2% (2)	15% (6)
31 and older	0% (0)	2.6% (1)	0% (0)
Gender			
Man	52.5% (21)	55% (22)	67.5% (27)
Woman	47.5% (19)	45% (18)	32.5% (13)
Religiosity before war[b]			
Religious	27.5% (11)	17.5% (7)	40% (16)
Traditional	42.5% (17)	60% (24)	47.5% (19)
Assimilated	20% (8)	10% (4)	10% (4)
Not mentioned in testimony	10% (4)	12.5% (5)	2.5% (1)
Participation in ghetto resistance and/or partisans			
Yes	22.5% (9)	45% (18)	20% (8)
No	77.5% (31)	55% (22)	80% (32)
Total (N = 120)	100% (40)	100% (40)	100% (40)

[a] Birth date was not included for one Vilna survivor, so those frequencies total to 39.

[b] "Religious" survivors described themselves as such. These were typically people from rabbinic and/ or Chassidic families. "Traditional" is a term used in many testimonies to describe people who were observant but not rabbis or ultra-religious. Individuals not raised observing the Jewish Sabbath, holidays, dietary laws, or rituals are "assimilated," a term also used in many testimonies.

Notes

Chapter 1

1. A near replica of this sculpture is located at Yad Vashem, Israel's national Holocaust memorial. The piece in Warsaw was constructed in part with labrodite stone from Sweden, originally purchased by the Germans for Hitler himself, who had intended to use it in post-war victory monuments (Young 1989: 83).
2. The Ghetto, and the city of Warsaw as a whole, were destroyed during World War II; as much as 85 percent of the buildings were razed (Richie 2013: 627). Because entire streets had to be rebuilt in the post-war reconstruction, some streets do not line up exactly with their pre-war locations.
3. Memorials to Mordechai Anielewicz are found throughout Europe and Israel. For instance, a kibbutz in Israel, Yad Mordechai, bears his name, and the POLIN Museum's address in Warsaw is 6 Mordechaja Anielewicza Street.
4. https://www.holocaustremembrance.com/, accessed October 2, 2021.
5. Twenty states—Arizona, Arkansas, California, Colorado, Connecticut, Delaware, Florida, Illinois, Indiana, Kentucky, Maine (effective 2023), Michigan, New Hampshire, New Jersey, New York, Oregon, Rhode Island, Texas, Virginia, and Wisconsin—mandate Holocaust education in public schools. (https://www.ushmm. org/teach/fundamentals/where-holocaust-education-is-required-in-the-us, accessed October 2, 2021)
6. A notable exception is the movie *Defiance*, starring Daniel Craig and Liev Schreiber as two of the Bielski brothers, Jewish men who created an armed unit of Jews that both engaged in resistance and housed and protected Jewish survivors in the forests of Belarus during World War II. The movie is based on a 1993 book by the same title, authored by sociologist and Holocaust survivor Nechama Tec.
7. For a discussion of the origins of this phrase, which predate the Holocaust, see Middleton-Kaplan 2014.
8. For an alternative view of Anne Frank that sees her diary as a form of resistance, see Brenner 1997. For more on children's diaries as a form of resistance during the Holocaust, see Dwork 2014.
9. See Ezra 2007; Middleton-Kaplan 2014; Popper 2010.
10. Quoted in Ezra 2007: 147.
11. See, e.g., Ainsztein 1979; Arad 1982; Arens 2011; Bauer 1989; Corni 2002; Epstein 2008; Finkel 2015; Grubsztein 1971; Gutman 1982, 1989, 1994; Henry 2014; Krakowski 1984; Levin 1985; Marrus 1989; Suhl 1968; Syrkin 1948; Tec 1993, 2013.
12. Other works have also provided myriad examples of ways in which Jews resisted, both individually and collectively (see Bauer 1989; Finkel 2017; Henry 2014; Grubsztein

1971; Marrus 1989). As just one example, Jewish men in the ghettos adopted a habit of going hatless, even during the cold Eastern European winters, as a means of quietly resisting against the rule that obligated all Jewish men to tip their caps to German soldiers (Gutman 1994). For more on varied treatments of resistance in general, see Hollander and Einwohner 2004; Scott 1985, 1990.

13. See Gamson and Meyer 1996; Jenkins 1983; Jenkins and Perrow 1977; McAdam 1982; McCarthy and Zald 1977; Morris 1984; Meyer 1990; Meyer and Minkoff 2004; Meyer and Staggenborg 1996; Tilly 1978.

14. See Blee 1991, 2002; Cunningham 2013; Futrell and Simi 2004; McVeigh 1999, 2009; Simi and Futrell 2010; Van Dyke and Soule 2002.

15. See Alimi 2007a, 2007b, 2009; Almeida 2003; Goodwin 2001; Kurzman 1996; Schock 2004; Shriver, Adams and Longo 2015.

16. See Braun 2016, 2019; Einwohner 2003; Einwohner and Maher 2011; Finkel 2015, 2017; Fox and Nyseth Brehm 2018; Gross 1994; Luft 2015a; Maher 2010; Soyer 2014. Other social scientists have explored additional aspects of the Holocaust, such as survival, gender differences in Holocaust experiences, the experiences of children, including hidden children and children of survivors, and collective memory. For such work, see Berger 2011; Jacobs 2004; Kopstein, Subotić, and Welch 2022; Levy and Sznaider 2006; Ofer and Weitzman 1998; Olick 2007, 2016; Stein 2014; Tec 2003; Vromen 2012; Wolf 2007; Wolf and Gerson 2007.

17. See Finkel (2017) for an analysis that takes a similar approach by comparing the ghettos of Minsk, Kraków, and Białystok. Comparative-historical sociology is characterized by "the use of systematic comparison and the analysis of processes over time to explain large-scale outcomes such as revolutions, political regimes, and welfare states" (Mahoney 2004: 81). On case selection and the use of comparison in comparative-historical sociology, see Bonnell 1980; Mahoney and Rueschmeyer 2003; Skocpol 1984; Skocpol and Somers 1980; Tilly 1989.

18. https://www.ushmm.org/wlc/en/article.php?ModuleId=10005059, accessed October 2, 2021. Shapiro, Rosenfeld, and Bloomfield (2012) state that there were 1,100 Nazi-created Jewish ghettos.

19. Hilberg 1979: 174.

20. The Lithuanian name for this city is Vilnius; the city is also known variously as Wilna (in German), Wilno (in Polish), Vilne (in Yiddish) and Vilna (in Russian and Hebrew) (see Shneidman 2002: xi). I use the name Vilna because it appears most often in the primary and secondary sources on which I draw.

21. Gutman 1982: xvi.

22. Harshav 2002.

23. Gutman 2006; Horwitz 2008.

24. See Hilberg 1979.

25. Gans (2002) refers to this distinction as one between "natural space" and "social space."

26. http://college.usc.edu/vhi/, accessed May 19, 2010.

27. Following the archive's recommended citation format, my bibliography lists the first and last name of each survivor whose testimony I quote. However, in the text, when

quoting testimonies I use the survivor's first name and last initial. When quoting other, published sources, I use complete first and last names. I follow this format so that the reader can tell at a glance whether I am citing an oral testimony from the archive or a published source. One survivor whose testimony appears in my sample of 120 also published her memoirs. I quote her from both sources, but for consistency in presentation, I use her first name and last initial in the text.

28. See Einwohner 2011. For more on the ethics of qualitative research beyond the IRB review, see the special issue of *Qualitative Sociology* on this topic, edited by Kathleen M. Blee and Ashley Currier. For more on the politics and ethics of naming respondents in social science research, see Guenther 2009; Weston 1991: 9; Whittier 2009: 19.

29. See Bauer 2001; Gerson 2007; King 2012; Melson 1992; Rosenbaum 2001.

30. For other examples of comparative studies of genocide by social scientists, see Fein 1979, 1993; Melson 1992; Nyseth Brehm 2017.

Chapter 2

1. See, e.g., Alimi's (2009) work on the Palestinian Intifada, Goodwin's (1997) analysis of the Huk rebellion, White and Fraser's (2000) work on the Irish Republican movement, and Viterna's (2013) study of women in guerrilla movements in El Salvador.

2. See Bracey 2016; Goodwin and Jasper 1999; Goodwin, Jasper, and Polletta 2001; Johnston and Klandermans 1995; McAdam, McCarthy, and Zald 1996.

3. Amenta and Zylan 1991; Cress and Snow 1996; Jenkins and Eckert 1986; Jenkins, Jacobs, and Agnone 2003; Kitschelt 1986; McCammon et al. 2001; McCarthy and Wolfson 1996; Meyer and Minkoff 2004; Meyer and Staggenborg 1996; Minkoff 1995; Reese et al. 2005; although see Meyer 2004 for a review of studies that have failed to find evidence of the role of political opportunity in movement emergence.

4. Alimi 2009; Kurzman 1996.

5. Finkel (2017) also seeks to understand decisions about Jewish resistance during the Holocaust. However, while we both study Jewish resistance as social scientists and seek to understand variation in resistance, we use different cases and focus on different outcomes and explanatory mechanisms. Notably, I focus on armed resistance only, whereas he looks at a range of responses. In addition, his study examines potential resisters' organizational capacity and the development of skills for resistance, while I focus on broader assessments of threat among resisters as well as non-resisters. Our inquiries are therefore complementary rather than contradictory.

6. Genocide is characterized by mass, sustained killings of non-combatants because of their membership in some group (e.g., as defined by race, ethnicity, or religion) (Owens, Su, and Snow 2013: 71; see also Luft 2015b). The term was coined by Raphael Lemkin in 1944 and was adopted by the United Nations in 1948, when genocide was decreed an international crime (Fein 1979: 3; United States Holocaust

Memorial Museum https://www.ushmm.org/wlc/en/article.php?ModuleId=10007 043, accessed September 20, 2017).

7. In his comparison of resistance in the ghettos of Minsk, Kraków, and Białystok, Finkel (2015) draws a distinction between selective and indiscriminate repression, and argues that resisters subject to selective repression at time t-1 are more likely to be able to plan for and successfully stage sustained resistance at time t. However, his focus is different from mine, and his conclusions are not necessarily inconsistent with my argument. Notably, Finkel's inquiry focuses on sustained armed resistance beyond initial emergence, while I am engaging with theories that seek to explain emergence. Second, he draws an analytically important distinction between selective repression and indiscriminate repression. He focuses on how potential resisters who are exposed to selective repression can learn from it and develop the "resister's toolkit" needed for sustained resistance during later periods of indiscriminate repression, a context in which it is difficult for new, aspiring resisters to mobilize the resources needed for sustained resistance. While his analysis shows that mobilization is possible under extremely repressive conditions, he still locates himself on the curve at which increasing repression leads to increased chances of action. He acknowledges (2015: 342) that decision-making, and potential for collective action, changes when repression becomes indiscriminate, and threats are immediate and lethal.

8. A separate, but related, literature uses the concept of frame resonance to examine the extent to which activists' messages resonate with broader cultural discourses as a way of understanding movement success (Ferree 2003; McCammon 2009).

9. As I explain in more detail in Chapter 4, shots were fired in the Vilna Ghetto during a brief skirmish between Jewish fighters and Nazi forces. However, Jewish fighters decided to leave the ghetto and carry out their resistance in the surrounding forests.

Chapter 3

1. See Polonsky (1998). Gutman (1982: 61) notes that the Nazis "were careful to call the ghetto the 'Jewish quarter,' in order to create the impression that it resembled the German and Polish quarters of the city, and they forbade others to use the term 'ghetto.'"

2. In the early years of the Ghetto, Jews were allowed to leave its confines temporarily, for work purposes; such movement required an official pass. Later, Jews found outside the Ghetto were subject to imprisonment and, eventually, death (Gutman 1982, 1994; Sloan 1958).

3. At various points in time, and as the Ghetto area continually changed, its borders were sometimes marked simply with barbed wire (Engelking and Leociak 2009).

4. In June 1941, official food rations for Warsaw Poles amounted to 699 calories per day; for Jews in the ghetto, they were 184 calories per day. In contrast, rations for Germans in Warsaw were 2,613 calories per day (Gutman 1990: 97).

5. Gutman (1994: 203) writes that while official German reports did not indicate that anyone anticipated resistance, one SS commander did bring a larger contingent of

troops than in earlier deportations from the ghetto; however, Gutman suggests even that commander did not expect the extent of armed resistance he encountered.

6. The ŻOB had some 2000 Molotov cocktails (Gutman 1982: 366).

7. Marek Edelman survived both the Uprising and World War II and went on to have a long career as an eminent cardiologist in Poland. (http://www.nytimes.com/2009/10/03/world/europe/03edelman.html; accessed February 10, 2018).

8. Szwajger writes that this merry-go-round was the inspiration for Polish Nobel Laureate Czesław Miłosz's poem, "Campo Dei Fiori."

9. Kurzman (1993: 31) writes that there were 800 fighters in the ŻOB; Gutman (1994: 204) estimates 750 fighters in total, 500 ŻOB and 250 ŻZW, while Freilich and Dean (2012: 459) report that there were 800 in both. Borzykowski (1976: 46) describes twenty-two different units in the ŻOB but does not note the overall number of fighters.

10. The English spelling of Yiddish, Polish, and Hebrew names can vary. Both Wilner and Vilner are correct spellings of this activist's surname; similarly, both Arieh and Aryeh are correct spellings of his first name.

11. Stroop's final report on the Ghetto's destruction, titled "The Jewish Residential District of Warsaw Is No More," was bound formally with an "elegant cover" and a "heading executed in artistic Gothic lettering"; several copies were made, including one that was found by American troops at Stroop's villa in Wiesbaden at the end of the war (Gutman 1982: 364–365).

12. Zivia Lubetkin, Tuvia Borzykowski, and others survived a harrowing escape through the city sewers, coming up through a manhole in the street on the Aryan side of the Ghetto; there, they were met by other resistance fighters and taken to relative safety (see Borzykowski 1976; Lubetkin 1981; Rotem 1994; Szwajger 1990).

13. (https://www.ushmm.org/wlc/en/article.php?ModuleId=10005069; accessed March 9, 2018).

14. Freilich and Dean 2012: 456.

15. Emmanuel Ringelblum (1900–1944) was a seasoned community activist as well as an accomplished historian. As a staff member of the Joint Distribution Committee (JDC) in Warsaw, a philanthropic organization founded by American Jews, he helped set up soup kitchens and organized other relief efforts in the aftermath of the German invasion in 1939. Around that same time he began keeping detailed notes in observation of daily life, and soon recruited other citizen-historians to keep similar notes and write reports about the Ghetto. While Ringelblum survived the Warsaw Ghetto, he was murdered on March 7, 1944, along with his wife, son, and thirty-eight other individuals, when their hiding place was discovered by Nazi forces (Sloan 1958).

16. Engelking and Leociak (2009: 102–106) devote an entire Appendix to minute accounts of changes in the Ghetto borders, street by street, between October 12 and November 22, 1940.

17. Szpilman's memoirs, published as a book titled *The Pianist*, were made into a feature film; actor Adrien Brody's portrayal of Szpilman won the Academy Award for Best Actor in 2003 (https://www.oscars.org/oscars/ceremonies/2003; accessed December 28, 2017).

18. Some Ghetto residents found smuggling to be quite lucrative. Smugglers who catered to the interests of relatively wealthy residents (i.e., those who had been well off before the war and who managed to hold on to their valuables) grew wealthy themselves by bringing liquor and gourmet foods into the Ghetto and selling them at black market prices (Donat 1978; Gutman 1982).

19. The poem "The Little Smuggler" ("*Mały Szmugler*") memorializes the child smugglers in the Warsaw Ghetto. Its author, Henryka Łazowertówna, was a resident of the Warsaw Ghetto and is believed to have perished in Treblinka. Excerpts from the poem are inscribed on a memorial to child victims of the Holocaust in Warsaw, in the Jewish cemetery (Engelking and Leociak 2009; Heberer 2011).

20. "Frankenstein" was notorious in the Ghetto and is mentioned in many memoirs and secondary sources. Rena Z. also talked about him in her testimony: "There was a German who called Frankenstein, he never had a cup of coffee til he killed five Jews every morning."

21. Hilberg, Staron, and Kermisz 1999; Freilich and Dean 2012: 456. German authorities also pressured the *Judenrat* to provide Jewish women for a brothel serving German soldiers, but the *Judenrat* refused (Brownmiller 1986; Person 2015, fn 27).

22. Y. L. Peretz (1852–1915) was a central figure in Yiddish literature. "*Bontshe Shvayg*" ("Bontshe the Silent"), one of his best-known short stories, is a tale of a man who suffers silently throughout a difficult life and continues to act meekly, even when welcomed into Heaven after his death. Written in 1894, the story can be interpreted as a disparaging comment on passivity in the face of injustice. Describing Peretz's work in general, Katz writes, "Peretz demands justice, and requires that people demand justice; for the world—and for themselves" (1991: x).

23. Founded during World War I, this organization was originally known as the Joint Distribution Committee of American Funds for the Relief of Jewish War Sufferers (Zuckerman 1993: 43, fn 15).

24. See Person 2015 for a discussion of women's jobs as waitresses in ghetto cafés and the ways in which many of these employees were sexually exploited.

25. Owning and operating radios was illegal, for Jews as well as Poles (Gutman 1982: 31).

26. See Gutman 1982: 202–206; Hilberg et al. 1999.

27. According to Lubetkin (1981: 71), 1000 youth joined HeHalutz in Warsaw; further, Dror ("Freedom," one organization that was part of HeHalutz) ran cultural activities and underground schools for youth, which were important not only for movement organizing but also for youth education, since the German authorities closed schools in the Ghetto.

28. See Zuckerman 1993: 148–158 for a detailed discussion of when and how various key activists in the Warsaw Ghetto first heard about the massacres at Ponar.

29. This quote refers to the news of the "grave digger from Chelmno," which Yitzhak, Zivia, and their fellow activists received in early January 1942. According to Zuckerman (1993: 157–158), the "gravedigger" was Yakov Groyanowski, from the village of Izbicza in Eastern Poland, sixty-five kilometers southeast of Lublin. He was taken, with other Jews from his town, to an abandoned castle near Chelmno in December 1941. There, they were assured by a German official that they would be

relocated to labor camps, but instead were placed in hermetically sealed trucks and killed with the trucks' exhaust fumes. Yakov was selected to work as a gravedigger, who dug pits and buried the bodies in a nearby woods. He escaped after several weeks and made it to Warsaw, where he shared his story.

30. See Zuckerman 1993: 159. "Dror" is Hebrew and "Frayhayt" is Yiddish; both words translate to "Freedom." The organization united with another movement, HeHalutz HaTzair ("The Young Pioneer") and was also known as Frayhayt/HeHalutz HaTzair (Zuckerman 1993: 27). It was part of the broader HeHalutz movement.

31. The Bund was a Socialist organization committed to the struggles of the Jewish worker in Poland. Given its primary focus on class struggles, it initially chose not to participate in a unified Jewish resistance effort, preferring that each movement operate independently (see Gutman 1982: 168–169; Zuckerman 1993: 171–175).

32. Lubetkin (1981: 111–112). Stronger ties to the Polish Underground gave the ŻZW access to more arms; in contrast, the ŻOB had to rely more on homemade explosives (Kurzman 1993).

33. Kermish 1986: 597, fn4; see also Ainsztein 1979: 68.

34. See Einwohner 2006 and Reger et al. 2008 for more on identity work in social movements.

35. Gutman 1982: 257; Zuckerman 1993: 254; see also Gutman 1982, ch. 8 for more on the Polish response to the mass killings of Jews in general. Kurzman (1993) also suggests that the AK and Polish government-in-exile in London were hesitant to help Jews for fear of losing support among anti-Semitic Poles.

36. Tuvia Borzykowski says that the ŻOB had ten pistols at the start of the January revolt (1976: 29); this figure is corroborated by Yitzhak Zuckerman (1993: 278).

37. Szerynski survived the assassination attempt but committed suicide in January 1943, during the *aktion* that prompted the January Uprising (Zuckerman 1993: 202, fn 59).

38. Zuckerman 1993: 203; see also Ainsztein 1979; Gutman 1982; Lubetkin 1981.

39. Israel Fürst (Yisrael First), the head of the Economic Department in the *Judenrat* and the official who served as the official courier between the *Judenrat* and the Gestapo, was assassinated by a member of Dror-HeHalutz (part of the ŻOB) on November 28, 1942 (Gutman 1982: 303; Zuckerman 1993: 247).

40. Ephroim Malamud was the Treasurer of the *Judenrat* (Hilberg et al. 1999: 216 fn 77).

41. While a very small proportion of the Ghetto community actually joined the two fighting organizations greater numbers participated in both active and passive resistance efforts, including "wildcat" groups who took up arms and fought on their own as well as numerous individuals who built bunkers and went into hiding (see Gutman 1982: 350–354).

42. Shmuel ("Arthur") Zygielbojm, a Bundist and early member of the *Judenrat* who was sent out of the Ghetto by the Bund to join the Polish Government-in-Exile in London as the Bund representative to the government, is one example of an activist who chose suicide as a form of resistance. He took his own life on May 12, 1943, after hearing that his wife and son perished in the Warsaw Ghetto Uprising. He was informed of their deaths by Jan Karski, a Polish Catholic who snuck into the Warsaw Ghetto and also attempted to spread the word about the Jewish genocide. Zygielbojm intended his

suicide as an act of protest against the lack of attention to the Jewish plight in Europe (Gutman 1982).

43. Members of the ŻOB did try to save others' lives, such as by obtaining forged identification papers and safe houses on the Aryan side for Jewish children (Meed 1979). However, the fighters did not plan to save their own lives. In fact, unlike other Jews in the Ghetto who had survived the Great Deportation, the ŻOB did not build its own bunker, but planned to fight to the death instead (Kurzman 1993: 45). As ŻOB fighter Simha "Kazik" Rotem explained in his memoirs, for the ŻOB to build a bunker would have been "against its purpose" (1994: 38).

44. See Cochavi 1995.

Chapter 4

1. Initially, Vilna Jews under Nazi occupation were required to wear white arm bands, either with yellow stars or with yellow circles with the letter "J" in the center. As of August 2, 1941, Jews were required to sew yellow stars in the front and back of their clothing, so that they could be identified from the front as well as the back (Arad 1982: 56, 94–95).

2. Abba Kovner survived the Holocaust and World War II and made his way to Israel, where he became a nationally recognized poet and literary figure (https://www.nytimes.com/1987/09/27/obituaries/abba-kovner-israeli-poet-dies.html, accessed November 2, 2018).

3. The FPO had access to a radio (which was expressly illegal under Nazi control); it was through radio broadcasts that they learned about the Warsaw Ghetto Uprising (Porat 2010: 91).

4. After taking control of the city, Germans briefly set up a joint German-Lithuanian administration in Vilna. Arad (1982: 46–50) argues that while this structure allowed Lithuanians to participate in the persecution of Jews from the outset, Lithuanians were more interested in persecuting Poles, owing to poor relations between Poles and Lithuanians stemming from centuries-long disputes over Vilna between the two countries. Germans soon put an end to these anti-Polish measures and by July 8 had dissolved the joint command, proceeding with focused attacks on Jewish communities in Vilna and throughout the newly occupied Soviet territories.

5. Irena Adamowicz completed many harrowing journeys between the major ghettos in Nazi-occupied Eastern Europe, serving as a liaison and sharing crucial pieces of information between the ghettos (Corni 2002; Gutman 1982). Jadwiga Dudziec assisted Jews by providing shelter, employment, and false documents. While Adamowicz survived the war, there is some confusion as to how Dudziec died. Porat (2010: 45) reports that she was captured by the Gestapo in August 1944, while Arad (1982: 188, fn 28) writes she was killed during an aerial bombardment in Vilna in July 1944. Both were named Righteous Gentiles by Yad Vashem, Israel's national Holocaust Memorial

and Museum (https://www.yadvashem.org/righteous.html, accessed November 7, 2018).

6. The Mother Superior developed such strong ties with Abba Kovner that she actually wanted to go to with him and the other Jews, believing that "God is now in the ghetto," but her attempt was thwarted when the guards refused to let her in (Porat 2010: 50–51). Anna Borkowska was named a Righteous Gentile by Yad Vashem, Israel's national Holocaust Museum, in 1984 (http://db.yadvashem.org/righteous/righteousName.html?language=en&itemId=4014050, accessed September 11, 2018).

7. Mordechai Tenenbaum-Tamaroff (1916–1943) was one of the leaders of armed resistance efforts in the Białystok Ghetto. He is believed to have committed suicide during the Białystok Ghetto Uprising when he was surrounded by German soldiers (Arad 1982: 234, fn 30; Zuckerman 1993: 33, fn 24).

8. This number is in line with Harshav's (2002: xliii) estimate of the size of the Vilna population at the start of the war, in September 1939. There were 57,000–60,000 Jews in Vilna as of the summer of 1941, the beginning of the German occupation of Vilna (Arad 1982: 215; Rojowska and Dean 2012: 1149).

9. One of the *aktionen* in the Ghetto was held on October 1, 1941, which was Yom Kippur, or the Day of Atonement (Arad 1982: 136).

10. Tosia Altman (1919–1943) played an important role as a courier, spreading information between the different ghettos and smuggling arms into the Warsaw Ghetto. As a fighter during the Uprising, she survived the poison gas attack at Miła 18 on May 8, 1943, and she was able to flee the Warsaw Ghetto through the sewers, but was later badly injured in a fire at a celluloid factory where she and other activists were hiding. She was then captured by the Gestapo and died on May 26, 1943 (Batalion 2021; Gutman 1982; Zuckerman 1993: 395–396).

11. Arad (1982: 239) calls these "quintets."

12. Among the services that it provided for the community, the hospital assisted pregnant women, who were at great risk during the time due to the Nazi edict that forbade Jews from having children. At the hospital, some women had abortions; the hospital also delivered babies, hid them, and falsified their birth certificates to show birth dates before the edict was passed (Arad 1982: 316; see also Tushnet 1972: 156).

13. It is not clear if Gens and his wife actually divorced or if that was just a rumor. Gens' wife and child lived near the Ghetto and survived the war (Shneidman 2002: 107–108; Tushnet 1972: 154).

14. Shneidman 2002: 106. For more on Gens, see Arad 1982: 125–126, fn 10; Porat 2010: 87; Tushnet 1972.

15. For the most part, the AK and AL did not support Jewish partisans, because they believed that Jews were all Communist or Communist sympathizers (Arad 1982: 249).

16. An estimated 81 percent of Lithuanian Jews who attempted to find and join partisan units in the forests perished during the war (Slepyan 2000: 6).

17. According to Moshe Shotan, Gens later used similarly derisive terms to refer to the FPO, calling them "cowards . . . writers, poets, dreamers . . . who imagined themselves to be . . . the main power and spirit in the ghetto" (quoted in Shneidman 2002: 128).

18. Abba Kovner later wrote, "The commander had the last word on every matter. We had faith in him and respected him. In no other important issue, and certainly not in a matter of life and death as this was, would the command come to a decision without him. It was out of the question" (quoted in Porat 2010: 125).

19. According to Shneidman (2002: 61–62), this woman was Wittenberg's mistress. Wittenberg's estranged wife was still alive at the time, and she and their son lived in the Ghetto.

20. It is not clear whether Wittenberg was murdered by the Gestapo, or if he took his own life; he requested cyanide from his comrades and met with Gens before turning himself in. It may be that he killed himself; it is also possible that Gens himself poisoned him, so that Wittenberg would not be tortured (Porat 2010: 125–128; Shneidman 2002: 64).

21. http://holocaustmusic.ort.org/places/ghettos/vilna/itsik-vitnberg/,   accessed September 17, 2018.

22. The FPO also participated in acts of sabotage outside the Ghetto. For example, Kovner himself created an amateur mine that other FPO members (including Vitka Kempner) smuggled out of the Ghetto and placed along railroad tracks, successfully derailing a German train (Porat 2010: 94–95).

Chapter 5

1. Hans Biebow (1902–1947) fled back to Bremen at the end of the war, but was caught and extradited to Łódź, where he was tried, convicted, and sentenced to death for war crimes (Horwitz 2008: 317–318).

2. Crago (2012: 81) states that between August 1 and August 29, 1944, more than 65,000 Jews were sent to Auschwitz, under the pretense that they were being relocated for labor; she also notes that 1000–1500 Jews, including 30–270 who managed to avoid deportations, stayed behind in Ghetto. An additional 5000 Gypsies (ethnic Roma and Sinti) who were also interned in a section of the Łódź Ghetto known as the "Gypsy camp" had been sent to Chelmno much earlier, in 1942 (Horwitz 2008).

3. Germany planned to use some of its newly occupied lands for resettlement for the *Volksdeutsche*, ethnic Germans who were living beyond Germany's borders. Łódź was not originally intended to be used in this manner but was later included, and was officially annexed to the Reich on November 8, 1939 (Horwitz 2008: 25; Miron 2009: 404).

4. For a list of Polish and German names for the streets in the Łódź Ghetto, see Dobroszycki 1984: 537–539.

5. Crago 2012: 77; Horwitz 2008: 53.

6. These numbers are reported in Crago 2012: 77; Miron 2009: 406; and Tushnet 1972: 15.

7. Crago 2012: 78. Trunk (2006: 15–16) offers a slightly different calculus, estimating that the Ghetto population was confined to a residential area that was 2.41 square kilometers, for a population density of 68,000 people per square kilometer. The average per room occupancy was 3.5, but in some cases, especially early in the life of the Ghetto, as many as twenty people were housed in a single room (2006: 16).

8. Disturbingly, there are charges that Rumkowski was a child molester (Eichengreen 2000; Horwitz 2008: 19–20).

9. See Horwitz 2008: 15 and Trunk 2006: 400. According to Tushnet (1972: 10) the title "Eldest of the Jews" reflected Nazis' belief that Jews were ruled by a secret council of elders; thus, the leader of the Jews had to be the "eldest."

10. Quoted in Sloan 1958: 47–48. Ringelblum's account was based on Rumkowski's visit to Warsaw in September 1940, before the Warsaw Ghetto was sealed, an occasion he used to brag to Jewish leaders in Warsaw about his own accomplishments in Łódź (see also Horwitz 2008: 126–127).

11. The *Chronicle of the Łódź Ghetto* was a daily bulletin created under the auspices of the Ghetto administration and containing news of events in the Ghetto as well as essays and other writings (see Dobroszycki 1984).

12. Rumkowski began performing weddings after September 1942, when Nazi officials abolished the rabbinate in the Ghetto. The *Chronicle of the Łódź Ghetto* contains an entry from October 28, 1942, describing the ceremony at which Rumkowski presided over the wedding of seven couples (Dobroszycki 1984: 277–279).

13. Trunk 2006: 207. Deaths from tuberculosis rose as well during this time, as tuberculosis was exacerbated and spread easily in the high-density, poorly nourished, immune-deficient population.

14. These numbers included Roma and Sinti, or Gypsy, victims who were deported to Łódź and briefly held in the "Gypsy Camp" before being sent to their deaths in Chelmno (Crago 2012: 80).

15. According to eyewitness accounts, Rumkowski was beaten to death in Auschwitz by crematorium workers before he ever got to the gas chambers. His assailants were Jews whose deportations he had facilitated (Adelson 1996: 51 fn).

16. Remarkably, one survivor, Josef Z., was able to use that through street to briefly communicate with his family. After being jailed for attempted food smuggling, he was placed on a bus and taken to a work camp. From the bus, he was able to throw a rock with a message on it into the Ghetto, thereby letting his family know he was alive.

17. Jurek Becker's (1996) novel *Jacob the Liar*, which was made into a 1999 film starring Robin Williams, also explores this theme.

18. Dawid Sierakowiak was also a member of this Communist cell. His diary mentions Niutek by name. However, Dawid eventually fell out of favor with the group, partially because he signed a holiday card for Rumkowski (which students in the Ghetto were encouraged to do) while his comrades did not (Adelson 1996).

19. Beno is an example of a Łódź Ghetto resident who was coded as a resister in the Shoah Foundation testimony archive; he clearly participated in resistance, but not as a member of a Jewish organization dedicated to armed resistance in the Ghetto.

Chapter 6

1. https://www.inyourpocket.com/warsaw/marek-edelman-mural_152827v,   accessed June 23, 2019.
2. Other well-known ghettos where Jews staged armed resistance include the Białystok and Częstochowa ghettos (see Corni 2002; Finkel 2017; Grossman 1987).
3. While the Amistad rebels did eventually return to their homeland, it was only after a long odyssey. During the revolt, two other crewmembers went overboard to escape, and the Spaniards were wounded and then placed in chains. However, with little sailing experience, the enslaved people were eventually forced to release the Spaniards, one of whom had been a merchant sea captain and knew how to sail the ship. Due to a combination of the Spaniards' trickery (by which they sailed east during the day and west at night) and a severe shortage of water on board, requiring that the ship make landfall earlier than planned, the ship ended up on the Long Island Sound where it was intercepted by the U.S. Navy, which suspected it was a pirate vessel. The U.S. forces released the Spaniards, who told the Americans about the revolt, and arrested the surviving enslaved people. After a long period of imprisonment in a New Haven, Connecticut jail and several well-publicized trials, including a ruling by the U.S. Supreme Court, the surviving rebels were released in March 1841 and eventually returned to Africa (Rediker 2013).
4. Because Jewish holidays follow a lunar calendar, their dates do not always coincide with the Gregorian, solar calendar used in most parts of the world.

References

Aaron, Sol. 1995. "Interview 803." *Visual History Archive*, USC Shoah Foundation. Accessed 25 February 2009.

Adelson, Alan, ed. 1996. *The Diary of Dawid Sierakowiak: Five Notebooks from the Łódź Ghetto*. Turowski, New York, and Oxford: Oxford University Press.

Adelson, Alan, and Robert Lapides, eds. 1989. *Łódź Ghetto: Inside a Community Under Siege*. New York: Viking.

Ainsztein, Reuben. 1979. *The Warsaw Ghetto Revolt*. New York: Holocaust Library.

Akselrod, Benjamin. 1996. "Interview 10188." *Visual History Archive*, USC Shoah Foundation. Accessed 25 February 2009.

Aleksiun, Natalia. 2014. "Survivor Testimonies and Historical Objectivity: Polish Historiography since *Neighbors*." *Holocaust Studies: A Journal of Culture and History* 20(1–2): 157–178.

Alimi, Eitan Y. 2007a. "The Dialectic of Opportunities and Threats and Temporality of Contention: Evidence from the Occupied Territories." *International Political Science Review* 28(1): 101–123.

Alimi, Eitan Y. 2007b. *Israeli Politics and the First Palestinian Intifada*. New York: Routledge.

Alimi, Eitan Y. 2009. "Mobilizing Under the Gun: Theorizing Political Opportunity Structure in a Highly Repressive Setting." *Mobilization* 14(2): 219–237.

Almeida, Paul D. 2003. "Opportunity Organizations and Threat-Induced Contention: Protest Waves in Authoritarian Settings." *American Journal of Sociology* 109(2): 345–400.

Almeida, Paul D. 2018. "The Role of Threat in Collective Action." Pp. 43–62 in *The Wiley-Blackwell Companion to Social Movements*, 2nd ed., edited by D. A. Snow, S. Soule, H. Kriesi, and H. J. McCammon. Oxford: Wiley-Blackwell.

Altman, Morris. 1995. "Interview 524." *Visual History Archive*, USC Shoah Foundation. Accessed 25 February 2009.

Amenta, Edwin, and Yvonne Zylan. 1991. "It Happened Here: Political Opportunity, the New Institutionalism, and the Townsend Movement." *American Sociological Review* 56(2): 250–265.

Andrews, Kenneth T. 2002. "Movement-Countermovement Dynamics and the Emergence of New Institutions: The Case of 'White Flight' Schools in Mississippi." *Social Forces* 80(3): 911–936.

Andrews, Kenneth T., and Charles Seguin. 2015. "Group Threat and Policy Change: The Spatial Dynamics of Prohibition Politics, 1890–1919." *American Journal of Sociology* 121(2): 475–510.

Anti-Defamation League. 2019. Audit of Antisemitic Incidents, 2019. Retrieved December 29, 2020 (https://www.adl.org/audit2019).

Arad, Yitzhak. 1982. *Ghetto in Flames*. New York: Holocaust Library.

Arendt, Hannah. 1963. *Eichmann in Jerusalem: A Report on the Banality of Evil*. New York: Viking Press.

Arens, Moshe. 2011. *Flags Over the Warsaw Ghetto*. Jerusalem and New York: Gefen Publishing House.

Aurbach, Berysz. 1996. "Interview 16241." *Visual History Archive*, USC Shoah Foundation. Accessed 25 February 2009.

Azab, Marian, and Wayne A. Santoro. 2017. "Rethinking Fear and Protest: Racialized Repression of Arab Americans and the Mobilization Benefits of Being Afraid." *Mobilization* 22(4): 473–491.

Barkan, Steven E. 1984. "Legal Control of the Southern Civil Rights Movement." *American Sociological Review* 49(4): 552–565.

Batalion, Judy. 2021. *The Light of Days: The Untold Story of Women Resistance Fighters in Hitler's Ghettos*. New York: HarperCollins Publishers.

Bauer, Yehuda. 1989. "Forms of Jewish Resistance During the Holocaust." Pp. 34–48 in *The Nazi Holocaust*, Vol. 7, *Jewish Resistance to the Holocaust*, edited by M. R. Marrus. Westport, CT: Meckler Corporation.

Bauer, Yehuda. 2001. *Rethinking the Holocaust*. New Haven: Yale University Press.

Bauman, Janina. 1986. *Winter in the Morning: A Young Girl's Life in the Warsaw Ghetto and Beyond, 1939–1945*. New York: The Free Press.

Becker, Jurek. 1996. *Jacob the Liar*. Translated by L. Vennewitz. New York: Arcade Publishing.

Bell, Joyce M. 2016. "Introduction to the Special Issue on Black Movements." *Sociological Focus* 49(1): 1–10.

Benford, Robert D. 1993. "'You Could Be the Hundredth Monkey': Collective Action Frames and Vocabularies of Motive within the Nuclear Disarmament Movement." *The Sociological Quarterly* 34(2): 195–216.

Beras, Pearl. 1996. "Interview 14393." *Visual History Archive*, USC Shoah Foundation. Accessed 25 February 2009.

Berger, Ronald J. 2011. *Surviving the Holocaust: A Life Course Perspective*. New York: Routledge.

Bergstrand, Kelly. 2014. "The Mobilizing Power of Grievances: Applying Loss Aversion and Omission Bias to Social Movements." *Mobilization* 19(2): 123–142.

Bettelheim, Bruno. 1960. "The Ignored Lesson of Anne Frank." *Harper's Magazine* (November): 45–50.

Biebers, Casimir. 1996. "Interview 12311." *Visual History Archive*, USC Shoah Foundation. Accessed 25 February 2009.

Bilski, Victor. 1997. "Interview 25400." *Visual History Archive*, USC Shoah Foundation. Accessed 25 February 2009.

Bimka, Eva. 1998. "Interview 43829." *Visual History Archive*, USC Shoah Foundation. Accessed 25 February 2009.

Blee, Kathleen M. 1991. *Women of the Klan*. Berkeley: University of California Press.

Blee, Kathleen M. 2002. *Inside Organized Racism: Women in the Hate Movement*. Berkeley: University of California Press.

Blee, Kathleen M. 2012. *Democracy in the Making: How Activist Groups Form*. New York and Oxford: Oxford University Press.

Bonnell, Victoria E. 1980. "The Uses of Theory, Concepts and Comparison in Historical Sociology." *Comparative Studies in Society and History* 22(2): 156–173.

Borzykowski, Tuvia. 1976. *Between Tumbling Walls*. Beit Lohamei Hagettaot and Hakibbutz Hameuchad Publishing House.

Bracey, Glenn E., II. 2016. "Black Movements Need Black Theorizing: Exposing Implicit Whiteness in Political Process Theory." *Sociological Focus* 49(1): 11–27.

Braun, Robert. 2016. "Religious Minorities and Resistance to Genocide: The Collective Rescue of Jews in the Netherlands during the Holocaust." *American Political Science Review* 110(1): 127–147.

Braun, Robert. 2019. *Protectors of Pluralism: Religious Minorities and the Rescue of Jews in the Low Countries during the Holocaust.* New York and Cambridge: Cambridge University Press.

Brenner, Rachel Feldhay. 1997. *Writing as Resistance: Four Women Confront the Holocaust.* University Park, PA: Pennsylvania State University Press.

Broidis, David. 1995. "Interview 9783." *Visual History Archive*, USC Shoah Foundation. Accessed 25 February 2009.

Brown, Gusta. 1995. "Interview 3538." *Visual History Archive*, USC Shoah Foundation. Accessed 25 February 2009.

Brownmiller, Susan. 1986. *Against Our Will: Men, Women, and Rape.* London, UK: Pelican Books.

Calhoun, Craig. 1994. *Neither Gods nor Emperors: Students and the Struggle for Democracy in China.* Berkeley: University of California Press.

Cerulo, Karen A. 2006. *Never Saw it Coming: Cultural Challenges to Envisioning the Worst.* Chicago: University of Chicago Press.

Cerulo, Karen A. 2014. "To Life: Optimism Bias and Technological Ties in the Face of the Worst." *Sociological Forum* 29(3): 743–748.

Choi-Fitzpatrick, Austin. 2017. *What Slaveholders Think: How Contemporary Perpetrators Rationalize What They Do.* New York: Columbia University Press.

Clarke, Lee. 2006. *Worst Cases: Terror and Catastrophe in the Popular Imagination.* Chicago, IL: University of Chicago Press.

Clemens, Elisabeth S., and Martin D. Hughes. 2002. "Recovering Past Protest: Historical Research on Social Movements." Pp. 201–230 in *Methods of Social Movement Research*, edited by B. Klandermans and S. Staggenborg. Minneapolis: University of Minnesota Press.

Cochavi, Yehoyakim. 1995. "The Motif of 'Honor' in the Call to Rebellion in the Ghetto." Pp. 245–254 in *Zionist Youth Movements During the Shoah*, edited by A. Cohen and Y. Cochavi. Translated by T. Gorelick. New York: Peter Lang.

Cohen, Rich. 2000. *The Avengers: A Jewish War Story.* New York: Alfred A. Knopf.

Corni, Gustavo. 2002. *Hitler's Ghettos: Voices from a Beleaguered Society, 1939–1944.* London: Arnold.

Crago, Laura. 2012. "Łódź." Pp. 75–82 in *The United States Holocaust Memorial Museum Encyclopedia of Camps and Ghettos 1933–1945*, Vol. II, edited by G. P. Megargee (General Editor) and M. Dean (Volume Editor) Bloomington, IN: Indiana University Press.

Cress, Daniel M., and David A. Snow. 1996. "Mobilization at the Margins: Resources, Benefactors, and the Viability of Homeless Social Movement Organizations." *American Sociological Review* 61(6): 1089–1109.

Cripps, Lucie. 1995. "Interview 2292." *Visual History Archive*, USC Shoah Foundation. Accessed 25 February 2009.

Cunningham, David. 2013. *Klansville, USA.* Oxford: Oxford University Press.

Cymber, Morris. 1995. "Interview 1651." *Visual History Archive*, USC Shoah Foundation. Accessed 25 February 2009.

Davenport, Christian. 2014. *How Social Movements Die*. Cambridge: Cambridge University Press.

Deane, Wolf. 1996. "Interview 19959." *Visual History Archive*, USC Shoah Foundation. Accessed 25 February 2009.

Dlugi, Anna. 1997. "Interview 31554." *Visual History Archive*, USC Shoah Foundation. Accessed 25 February 2009.

Dobroszycki, Lucjan, ed. 1984. *The Chronicle of the Łódź Ghetto, 1941–1944*. New Haven and London: Yale University Press.

Dodson, Kyle. 2016. "Economic Threat and Protest Behavior in Comparative Perspective." *Sociological Perspectives* 59(4): 873–891.

Donat, Alexander. 1978. *The Holocaust Kingdom: A Memoir*. New York: Holocaust Library.

Druskin, Bernard. 1996. "Interview 15942." *Visual History Archive*, USC Shoah Foundation. Accessed 25 February 2009.

Dugan, Kimberly B. 2004. "Strategy and 'Spin': Opposing Movement Frames in an Anti-Gay Voter Initiative." *Sociological Focus* 37(3): 213–233.

Duneier, Mitchell. 2016. *Ghetto: The Invention of a Place, the History of an Idea*. New York: Farar, Straus and Giroux.

Dwork, Debórah. 2014. "Raising their Voices: Children's Resistance through Diary Writing and Song." Pp. 279–299 in *Jewish Resistance Against the Nazis*, edited by P. Henry. Washington, DC: The Catholic University of America Press.

Earl, Jennifer. 2003. "Tanks, Tear Gas and Taxes: Toward a Theory of Movement Repression." *Sociological Theory* 21(1): 44–68.

Eichengreen, Lucille, and Rebecca Camhi Fromer. 2000. *Rumkowski and the Orphans of Łódź*. San Francisco: Mercury House.

Einwohner, Rachel L. 2003. "Opportunity, Honor, and Action in the Warsaw Ghetto Uprising of 1943." *American Journal of Sociology* 109(3): 650–675.

Einwohner, Rachel L. 2006. "Identity Work and Collective Action in a Repressive Context: Jewish Resistance on the 'Aryan Side' of the Warsaw Ghetto." *Social Problems* 53(1): 38–56.

Einwohner, Rachel L. 2007. "Leadership, Authority, and Collective Action: Jewish Resistance in the Ghettos of Warsaw and Vilna." *American Behaviorial Scientist* 50(10): 1306–1326.

Einwohner, Rachel L. 2009. "The Need to Know: Cultured Ignorance and Jewish Resistance in the Ghettos of Warsaw, Vilna, and Łódź." *The Sociological Quarterly* 50(3): 407–430.

Einwohner, Rachel L. 2011. "Ethical Considerations on the Use of Archived Testimonies in Holocaust Research: Beyond the IRB Exemption." *Qualitative Sociology* 34(3): 415–430.

Einwohner, Rachel L., and Thomas V. Maher. 2011. "Threat Assessments and Collective-Action Emergence: Death Camp and Ghetto Resistance during the Holocaust." *Mobilization* 16(2): 127–146.

Eisinger, Peter K. 1973. "The Conditions of Protest Behavior in American Cities." *American Political Science Review* 67(1): 11–28.

Engelking, Barbara. 2001. *Holocaust and Memory*. London: Leicester University Press.

Engelking, Barbara, and Jacek Leociak. 2009. *The Warsaw Ghetto: A Guide to the Perished City*. New Haven: Yale University Press.

Epstein, Barbara. 2008. *The Minsk Ghetto, 1941–1943: Jewish Resistance and Soviet Internationalism*. Berkeley: University of California Press.

Ezra, Michael. 2007. "The Eichmann Polemics: Hannah Arendt and Her Critics." *Dissent* Summer 2007: 155–156.

FBI. 2019. UCR Hate Crime Statistics—Incidents and Offenses. Retrieved December 29, 2020 (https://ucr.fbi.gov/hate-crime/2019/topic-pages/incidents-and-offenses).

Fein, Helen. 1979. *Accounting for Genocide.* New York: Free Press.

Fein, Helen. 1993. *Genocide: A Sociological Perspective.* London: Sage.Feinsilver, Malka. 1997. "Interview 36232." *Visual History Archive*, USC Shoah Foundation. Accessed 25 February 2009.

Fernandez, Luis A. 2008. *Policing Dissent: Social Control and the Anti-Globalization Movement.* New Brunswick, NJ and London: Rutgers University Press.

Ferree, Myra Marx. 2003. "Resonance and Radicalism: Feminist Framing in the Abortion Debates of the United States and Germany." *American Journal of Sociology* 109(2): 304–344.

Finkel, Evgeny. 2015. "The Phoenix Effect of State Repression: Jewish Resistance during the Holocaust." *American Political Science Review* 109(2): 339–353.

Finkel, Evgeny. 2017. *Ordinary Jews: Choice and Survival during the Holocaust.* Princeton: Princeton University Press.

Firestone, Adek. 1996. "Interview 7454." *Visual History Archive*, USC Shoah Foundation. Accessed 25 February 2009.

Fisher, Dana R. 2019. *American Resistance: From the Women's March to the Blue Wave.* New York: Columbia University Press.

Fox, Nicole, and Hollie Nyseth Brehm. 2018. "'I Decided to Save Them': Factors that Shaped Participation in Rescue Efforts during Genocide in Rwanda." *Social Forces* 96(4): 1625–1648.

Freilich, Miri, and Martin Dean. 2012. "Warsaw." Pp. 456–460 in *The United States Holocaust Memorial Museum Encyclopedia of Camps and Ghettos 1933–1945*, Vol. II, edited by G. P. Megargee (General Editor) and M. Dean (Volume Editor). Bloomington, IN: Indiana University Press.

Fremont, Theodore. 1997. "Interview 34385." *Visual History Archive*, USC Shoah Foundation. Accessed February 25, 2009.

Friedländer, Saul. 2007. *The Years of Extermination: Nazi Germany and the Jews, 1939–1945.* New York: HarperCollins Publishers.

Futrell, Robert, and Pete Simi. 2004. "Free Spaces, Collective Identity, and the Persistence of U.S. White Power Activism." *Social Problems* 51(1): 16–42.

Gamson, William A. 1992. *Talking Politics.* New York: Cambridge University Press.

Gamson, William A., and David S. Meyer. 1996. "Framing Political Opportunity." Pp. 275–290 in Comparative Perspectives on Social Movements, edited by D. McAdam, J. D. McCarthy, and M. N. Zald. Cambridge: Cambridge University Press.

Gans, Herbert J. 2002. "The Sociology of Space: A Use-Centered View." *City & Community* 1(4): 329–339.

Gaventa, John D. 1982. *Power and Powerlessness.* Urbana and Chicago, IL: University of Illinois Press.

Geneslaw, Dora. 1996. "Interview 12090." *Visual History Archive*, USC Shoah Foundation. Accessed 25 February 2009.

Gerson, Judith. 2007. "'In Cuba I was a German Shepherd': Questions of Comparison and Generalizability in Holocaust Memoirs." Pp. 115–133 in *Sociology Confronts the Holocaust: Memories and Identities in Jewish Diasporas*, edited by J. M. Gerson and D. L. Wolf. Durham, NC: Duke University Press.

Gerson, Judith M., and Diane L. Wolf, eds. 2007. *Sociology Confronts the Holocaust: Memories and Identities in Jewish Diasporas.* Durham, NC: Duke University Press.

Gieryn, Thomas F. 2000. "A Space for Place in Sociology." *Annual Review of Sociology* 26: 463–496.

Glass, Nathan. 1995. "Interview 2925." *Visual History Archive*, USC Shoah Foundation. Accessed 25 February 2009.

Glatstein, Mordecai. 1998. "Interview 46579." *Visual History Archive*, USC Shoah Foundation. Accessed 25 February 2009.

Goldman, Claire. 1996. "Interview 21227." *Visual History Archive*, USC Shoah Foundation. Accessed 25 February 2009.

Goldstone, Jack A. 1991. *Revolution and Rebellion in the Early Modern World.* Berkeley: University of California Press.

Goldstone, Jack A., and Charles Tilly. 2001. "Threat (And Opportunity): Popular Action and State Response in the Dynamics of Contentious Action." Pp. 179–194 in Silence and Voice in the Study of Contentious Politics, edited by R. R. Aminzade, J. A. Goldstone, D. McAdam, E. J. Perry, W. H. Sewell, Jr., S. Tarrow, and C. Tilly. Cambridge: Cambridge University Press.

Goldstone, Jack A., and Bert Useem. 1999. "Prison Riots as Microrevolutions: An Extension of State-centered Theories of Revolution." *American Journal of Sociology* 104: 985–1029.

Goodwin, Jeff. 1997. "The Libidinal Constitution of a High-Risk Social Movement: Affectual Ties and Solidarity in the Huk Rebellion, 1946–1954." *American Sociological Review* 62(1): 53–69.

Goodwin, Jeff. 2001. *No Other Way Out: States and Revolutionary Movements, 1945–1991.* Cambridge: Cambridge University Press.

Goodwin, Jeff, and James M. Jasper. 1999. "Caught in a Winding, Snarling Vine: The Structural Bias of Political Process Theory." *Sociological Forum* 14(1): 27–54.

Goodwin, Jeff, James M. Jasper, and Francesca Polletta, eds. 2001. *Passionate Politics.* Chicago: The University of Chicago Press.

Gould, Deborah. 2001. "Rock the Boat, Don't Rock the Boat, Baby: Ambivalence and the Emergence of Militant AIDS Activism." Pp. 135–157 in *Passionate Politics*, edited by J. Goodwin, J. M. Jasper, and F. Polletta. Chicago: University of Chicago Press.

Gould, Roger V. 1995. *Insurgent Identities: Class, Community, and Protest in Paris from 1848 to the Commune.* Chicago: University of Chicago Press.

Gross, Jan Tomasz. 1979. *Polish Society under German Occupation: The Generalgouvernement, 1939–1944.* Princeton, NJ: Princeton University Press.

Gross, Michael L. 1994. "Jewish Rescue in Holland and France during the Second World War: Moral Cognition and Collective Action." *Social Forces* 73(2): 463–496.

Grossman, Chaika. 1987. *The Underground Army: Fighters of the Bialystok Ghetto.* New York: Holocaust Library.

Grubsztein, Meir, ed. 1971. *Jewish Resistance During the Holocaust: Proceedings of the Conference on Manifestations of Jewish Resistance.* Jerusalem: Yad Vashem.

Guenther, Katja M. 2009. "The Politics of Names: Rethinking the Methodological and Ethical Significance of Naming People, Organizations, and Places." *Qualitative Research* 9(4): 411–424.

Gurr, Ted. 1970. *Why Men Rebel.* Princeton: Princeton University Press.

Gutman, Israel. 1982. *The Jews of Warsaw, 1939–1943*. Bloomington: Indiana University Press.

Gutman, Israel. 1989. "The Genesis of the Resistance in the Warsaw Ghetto." Pp. 118–159 in *The Nazi Holocaust: Historical Documents on the Destruction of European Jews*, edited by M. R. Marrus. Westport, CT: Meckler.

Gutman, Israel. 1990. "The Victimization of the Poles." Pp. 96–100 in *A Mosaic of Victims: Non-Jews Persecuted and Murdered by the Nazis*, edited by M. Berenbaum. New York: New York University Press.

Gutman, Israel. 1994. *Resistance: The Warsaw Ghetto Uprising*. Boston: Houghton Mifflin Company.

Gutman, Israel. 2006. "Introduction: The Distinctiveness of the Łódź Ghetto." Pp. xxix–lvii in *Łódź Ghetto*, by Isaiah Trunk. Bloomington and Indianapolis: Indiana University Press.

Harshav, Benjamin. 2002. "Introduction." Pp. xxi–lii in *The Last Days of the Jerusalem of Lithuania*, by Herman Kruk. New Haven and London: Yale University Press.

Heberer, Patricia. 2011. *Children during the Holocaust*. Lanham, MD: AltaMira Press (in association with the United States Holocaust Memorial Museum).

Helmer, Beno. 1995. "Interview 3810." *Visual History Archive*, USC Shoah Foundation. Accessed 25 February 2009.

Henry, Patrick, ed. 2014. *Jewish Resistance against the Nazis*. Washington, DC: The Catholic University of America Press.

Herbst, Noah. 1997. "Interview 26800." *Visual History Archive*, USC Shoah Foundation. Accessed 25 February 2009.

Hersh, Simon. 1995. "Interview 1711." *Visual History Archive*, USC Shoah Foundation. Accessed 25 February 2009.

Hilberg, Raul. 1979. *The Destruction of the European Jews*. New York: Harper Colophon Books.

Hilberg, Raul, Stanislaw Staron, and Josef Kermisz, eds. 1999. *The Warsaw Diary of Adam Czerniakow: Prelude to Doom*. Chicago: Elephant Paperbacks.

Hollander, Jocelyn A., and Rachel L. Einwohner. 2004. "Conceptualizing Resistance." *Sociological Forum* 19(4): 533–554.

Horn, Charles. 1997. "Interview 25181." *Visual History Archive*, USC Shoah Foundation. Accessed 25 February 2009.

Horowitz, Mira. 1995. "Interview 6842." *Visual History Archive*, USC Shoah Foundation. Accessed 25 February 2009.

Horwitz, Gordon J. 2008. *Ghettostadt: Łódź and the Making of a Nazi City*. Cambridge, MA: The Belknap Press of Harvard University Press.

Inwald, Irene. 1995. "Interview 3466." *Visual History Archive*, USC Shoah Foundation. Accessed 25 February 2009.

Israelski, Pola. 1995. "Interview 5498." *Visual History Archive*, USC Shoah Foundation. Accessed 25 February 2009.

Jacobs, Janet L. 2004. "Women, Genocide, and Memory: The Ethics of Feminist Ethnography in Holocaust Research." *Gender & Society* 18(2): 223–238.

Jasper, James M. 1997. *The Art of Moral Protest*. Chicago: University of Chicago Press.

Jasper, James M., and Jane D. Poulsen. 1995. "Recruiting Strangers and Friends: Moral Shocks and Social Networks in Animal Rights and Anti-Nuclear Protests." *Social Problems* 42(4): 493–512.

Jenkins, J. Craig. 1983. "Resource Mobilization Theory and the Study of Social Movements." *Annual Review of Sociology* 9: 527–553.

Jenkins, J. Craig, and Craig M. Eckert. 1986. "Channeling Black Insurgency: Elite Patronage and Professional Social Movement Organizations in the Development of the Black Movement." *American Sociological Review* 51(6): 812–829.

Jenkins, J. Craig, David Jacobs, and Jon Agnone. 2003. "Political Opportunities and African-American Protest, 1948–1997." *American Journal of Sociology* 109(2): 277–303.

Jenkins, J. Craig, and Charles Perrow. 1977. "Insurgency of the Powerless: Farm Worker Movements, 1946–1972." *American Sociological Review* 42(2): 249–268.

Johnson, Erik W., and Scott Frickel. 2011. "Ecological Threat and the Founding of U.S. National Environmental Movement Organizations, 1962–1998." *Social Problems* 58(3): 305–329.

Johnston, Hank, and Bert Klandermans, eds. 1995. *Social Movements and Culture*. Minneapolis: University of Minnesota Press.

Kadivar, Mohammad Ali. 2013. "Alliances and Perception Profiles in the Iranian Reform Movement, 1997 to 2005." *American Sociological Review* 78(6): 1063–1086.

Kagan, Aron. 1996. "Interview 10926." *Visual History Archive*, USC Shoah Foundation. Accessed 25 February 2009.

Kahn-Cullors, Patrisse, and asha bandele. 2018. *When They Call You a Terrorist: A Black Lives Matter Memoir*. New York: St. Martin's Press.

Kahneman, Daniel, and Amos Tversky. 1979. "Prospect Theory: An Analysis of Decision under Risk." *Econometrica* 47(2): 263–292.

Kaplan, Ida. 1996. "Interview 22515." *Visual History Archive*, USC Shoah Foundation. Accessed 25 February 2009.

Katsh, Abraham I., trans. 1999. *Scroll of Agony: The Warsaw Diary of Chaim A. Kaplan*. Bloomington: Indiana University Press.

Kelly-Thompson, Kaitlin. 2020. "There Is Power in a Plaza: Social Movements, Democracy and Spatial Politics." Unpublished Ph.D. dissertation, Purdue University.

Kendi, Ibram X. 2019. *How to be an Anti-Racist*. New York: One World.

Kermish, Joseph, ed. 1986. *To Live with Honor and Die with Honor: Selected Documents from the Warsaw Ghetto Underground Archives "O.S." [Oneg Shabbath]*. Jerusalem: Yad Vashem.

Khawaja, Marwan. 1993. "Repression and Popular Collective Action: Evidence from the West Bank." *Sociological Forum* 8(1): 47–71.

King, Charles. 2012. "Can There Be a Political Science of the Holocaust?" *Perspectives on Politics* 10(2): 323–341.

Kitschelt, Herbert P. 1986. "Political Opportunity Structures and Political Protest: Anti-Nuclear Movements in Four Democracies." *British Journal of Political Science* 16(1): 57–85.

Klajman, Jack, with Ed Klajman. 2000. *Out of the Ghetto*. London: Vallentine Mitchell.

Klor, Boris. 1995. "Interview 10135." *Visual History Archive*, USC Shoah Foundation. Accessed 25 February 2009.

Klug, Ann. 1997. "Interview 23709." *Visual History Archive*, USC Shoah Foundation. Accessed 25 February 2009.

Kopstein, Jeffrey, Jelena Subotić, and Susan Welch, eds. 2022. *Politics, Violence, Memory: The New Social Science of the Holocaust*. Ithaca, NY: Cornell University Press.

Kornhauser, William. 1959. *The Politics of Mass Society*. New York: Free Press.

Krakowski, Shmuel. 1984. *The War of the Doomed: Jewish Armed Resistance in Poland, 1942–1944*. New York: Holmes and Meier.

Krall, Hanna. 1986. *Shielding the Flame: An Intimate Conversation With Dr. Marek Edelman, the Last Surviving Leader of the Warsaw Ghetto Uprising*. New York: Henry Holt and Co.

Kruk, Herman. 2002. *The Last Days of the Jerusalem of Lithuania*. New Haven: Yale University Press.

Kurzman, Charles. 1996. "Structural Opportunity and Perceived Opportunity in Social Movement Theory: The Iranian Revolution of 1979." *American Sociological Review* 61(1): 153–170.

Kurzman, Dan. 1993. *The Bravest Battle: The Twenty-eight Days of the Warsaw Ghetto Uprising*. New York: Da Capo Press, Inc.

Landau, Aron. 1995. "Interview 10497." *Visual History Archive*, USC Shoah Foundation. Accessed 25 February 2009.

Lang, Berel. 2014. "Why Didn't they Resist *More*?" Pp. 27–39 in *Jewish Resistance Against the Nazis*, edited by P. Henry. Washington, DC: The Catholic University of America Press.

Langer, Lawrence L. 1991. *Holocaust Testimonies: The Ruins of Memory*. New Haven: Yale University Press.

Lederman, Abraham. 1996. "Interview 22054." *Visual History Archive*, USC Shoah Foundation. Accessed 25 February 2009.

Lentin, Ronit. 2000. "'Expected to Live': Women Shoah Survivors' Testimonials of Silence." *Women's Studies International Forum* 23(6): 689–700.

Lesser, Larry. 1996. "Interview 23459." *Visual History Archive*, USC Shoah Foundation. Accessed 25 February 2009.

Levin, Dov. 1985. *Fighting Back: Lithuanian Jewry's Armed Resistance to the Nazis, 1941–1945*. New York, NY: Holmes and Meier.

Levine, Allan Gerald. 2009. *Fugitives of the Forest: The Heroic Story of Jewish Resistance and Survival during the Second World War*. Guilford, CT: Lyons Press.

Levy, Daniel, and Natan Sznaider. 2006. *The Holocaust and Memory in the Global Age*. Philadelphia, PA: Temple University Press.

Lewandowski, Boleslaw. 1995. "Interview 2932." *Visual History Archive*, USC Shoah Foundation. Accessed 25 February 2009.

Liber, Sol. 1994. "Interview 58." *Visual History Archive*, USC Shoah Foundation. Accessed 25 February 2009.

Lichbach, Mark I. 1987. "Deterrence or Escalation? The Puzzle of Aggregate Studies of Repression and Dissent." *Journal of Conflict Resolution* 31(2): 266–297.

Lisker, Henry. 1997. "Interview 33654." *Visual History Archive*, USC Shoah Foundation. Accessed 25 February 2009.

Loren, Rubin. 1995. "Interview 2840." *Visual History Archive*, USC Shoah Foundation. Accessed 25 February 2009.

Loveman, Mara. 1998. "High-Risk Collective Action: Defending Human Rights in Chile, Uruguay, and Argentina." *American Journal of Sociology* 104(2): 477–525.

Lubetkin, Zivia. 1981. *In the Days of Destruction and Revolt*. Beit Lohamei Haghetaot (Ghetto Fighters' House).

Luft, Aliza. 2015a. "Toward a Dynamic Theory of Action at the Micro Level of Genocide: Killing, Desistance, and Saving in 1994 Rwanda." *Sociological Theory* 33(2): 148–172.

Luft, Aliza. 2015b. "Genocide as Contentious Politics." *Sociology Compass* 9(10): 897–909.

Lurie, Zofja. 1995. "Interview 6451." *Visual History Archive*, USC Shoah Foundation. Accessed 25 February 2009.

Maher, Thomas V. 2010. "Threat, Resistance, and Collective Action: The Cases of Sobibór, Treblinka, and Auschwitz." *American Sociological Review* 75(2): 252–272.

Mahoney, James. 2004. "Comparative-Historical Methodology." *Annual Review of Sociology* 30: 81–101.

Mahoney, James, and Dieter Rueschemeyer, eds. 2003. *Comparative Historical Analysis in the Social Sciences*. Cambridge, UK: Cambridge University Press.

Maisner, Abraham. 1995. "Interview 2474." *Visual History Archive*, USC Shoah Foundation. Accessed 25 February 2009.

Mandil, Lucia. 1996. "Interview 17517." *Visual History Archive*, USC Shoah Foundation. Accessed 25 February 2009.

Manko, Miriam. 1997. "Interview 28070." *Visual History Archive*, USC Shoah Foundation. Accessed 25 February 2009.

Mapen, Murray. 1995. "Interview 5278." *Visual History Archive*, USC Shoah Foundation. Accessed 25 February 2009.

Marrus, Michael R., ed. 1989. *The Nazi Holocaust*, Vol. 7: *Jewish Resistance to the Holocaust*. Westport, CT: Meckler Corporation.

Martin, Isaac William. 2013. *Rich People's Movements: Grassroots Campaigns to Untax the One Percent*. New York: Oxford University Press.

McAdam, Doug. 1982. *Political Process and the Development of Black Insurgency*. Chicago: University of Chicago Press.

McAdam, Doug. 1986. "Recruitment to High-Risk Activism: The Case of Freedom Summer." *American Journal of Sociology* 92(1): 64–90.

McAdam, Doug, John D. McCarthy, and Mayer N. Zald, eds. 1996. *Comparative Perspectives on Social Movements*. Cambridge: Cambridge University Press.

McCammon, Holly J. 2009. "Beyond Frame Resonance: The Argumentative Structure and Persuasive Capacity of Twentieth-Century U.S. Women's Jury-Rights Frames." *Mobilization* 14(1): 45–64.

McCammon, Holly. 2012. *The US Women's Jury Movements and Strategic Adaptation: A More Just Verdict*. Cambridge: Cambridge University Press.

McCammon, Holly J., and Karen E. Campbell. 2002. "Allies on the Road to Victory: Coalition Formation between the Suffragists and the Woman's Christian Temperance Union." *Mobilization* 7(3): 231–251.

McCammon, Holly J., Karen E. Campbell, Ellen M. Granberg, and Christine Mowery. 2001. "How Movements Win: Gendered Opportunity Structures and the State Women's Suffrage Movements, 1866–1919." *American Sociological Review* 66(1): 49–70.

McCarthy, John D., and Mark Wolfson. 1996. "Resource Mobilization by Local Social Movement Organizations: Agency, Strategy, and Organization in the Movement against Drinking and Driving." *American Sociological Review* 61(6): 1070–1088.

McCarthy, John D., and Mayer N. Zald. 1977. "Resource Mobilization and Social Movements: A Partial Theory." *American Journal of Sociology* 82(6): 1212–1241.

McKane, Rachel G., and Holly J. McCammon. 2018. "Why We March: The Role of Grievances, Threats, and Movement Organizational Resources in the 2017 Women's Marches." *Mobilization* 23(4): 401–424.

McVeigh, Rory. 1999. "Structural Incentives for Conservative Mobilization: Power Devaluation and the Rise of the Ku Klux Klan, 1915–1925." *Social Forces* 77(4):1461–1496.

McVeigh, Rory. 2009. *The Rise of the Ku Klux Klan: Right-Wing Movements and National Politics.* Minneapolis: University of Minnesota Press.

McVeigh, Rory, and Kevin Estep. 2019. *The Politics of Losing: Trump, the Klan, and the Mainstreaming of Resentment.* New York: Columbia University Press.

Meczyk, Riva. 1996. "Interview 13510." *Visual History Archive*, USC Shoah Foundation. Accessed 25 February 2009.

Meed, Vladka (Feigele Peltel Miedzyrzecki). 1979. *On Both Sides of the Wall: Memoirs from the Warsaw Ghetto.* New York: Holocaust Library.

Meed, Vladka. 1996. "Interview 15197." *Visual History Archive*, USC Shoah Foundation. Accessed 25 February 2009.

Melson, Robert F. 1992. *Revolution and Genocide: On the Origins of the Armenian Genocide and the Holocaust.* Chicago: University of Chicago Press.

Menkin, Michael. 1996. "Interview 18904." *Visual History Archive*, USC Shoah Foundation. Accessed 25 February 2009.

Metzger, Esther. 1997. "Interview 31492." *Visual History Archive*, USC Shoah Foundation. Accessed 25 February 2009.

Meyer, David S. 1990. *A Winter of Discontent: The Nuclear Freeze and American Politics.* New York: Praeger.

Meyer, David S. 2002. "Opportunities and Identities: Bridge-Building in the Study of Social Movements." Pp. 3–21 in Social Movements: Identity, Culture, and the State, edited by D. S. Meyer, N. Whittier, and B. Robnett. Oxford: Oxford University Press.

Meyer, David S. 2004. "Protest and Political Opportunities." *Annual Review of Sociology* 30: 125–145.

Meyer, David S., and Debra Minkoff. 2004. "Conceptualizing Political Opportunity." *Social Forces* 82(4): 1457–1492.

Meyer, David S., and Suzanne Staggenborg. 1996. "Movements, Countermovements, and the Structure of Political Opportunity." *American Journal of Sociology* 101(6): 1628–1660.

Middleton-Kaplan, Richard. 2014. "The Myth of Jewish Passivity." Pp. 3–26 in *Jewish Resistance Against the Nazis*, edited by P. Henry. Washington, DC: The Catholic University of America Press.

Milchberg, Irving. 1998. "Interview 42881." *Visual History Archive*, USC Shoah Foundation. Accessed 25 February 2009.

Mill, John Stuart. 1986 [1974]. *A System of Logic.* Charlottesville, VA: Lincoln-Rembrandt.

Miller, Byron A. 2000. *Geography and Social Movements: Comparing Antinuclear Activism in the Boston Area.* Minneapolis: University of Minnesota Press.

Minkoff, Debra C. 1995. "Interorganizational Influences on the Founding of African American Organizations, 1955–1985." *Sociological Forum* 10(1): 51–79.

Miron, Guy, ed. 2009. *The Yad Vashem Encyclopedia of the Ghettos during the Holocaust,* Vol. 1. Jerusalem, Israel: Yad Vashem, The Holocaust Martyrs' and Heroes' Remembrance Authority.

Mitchley, Halina. 1998. "Interview 40467." *Visual History Archive*, USC Shoah Foundation. Accessed 25 February 2009.

Morris, Aldon D. 1981. "Black Southern Student Sit-in Movement: An Analysis of Internal Organization." *American Sociological Review* 46(6): 744–767.

Morris, Aldon D. 1984. *The Origins of the Civil Rights Movement.* New York: The Free Press.

Moskowitz, Rose. 1996. "Interview 18818." *Visual History Archive*, USC Shoah Foundation. Accessed 25 February 2009.

Moss, Dana M. 2014. "Repression, Response, and Contained Escalation under 'Liberalized' Authoritarianism in Jordan." *Mobilization* 19(3) 261–286.

Muller, Edward N. 1985. "Income Inequality, Regime Repressiveness, and Political Violence." *American Sociological Review* 50(1): 47–61.

Neuhouser, Kevin. 1998. "'If I Had Abandoned My Children': Community Mobilization and Commitment to the Identity of Mother in Northeast Brazil." *Social Forces* 77(1): 331–358.

Neyman, Paula. 1995. "Interview 4788." *Visual History Archive*, USC Shoah Foundation. Accessed 25 February 2009.

Nivin, Sam. 1995. "Interview 5563." *Visual History Archive*, USC Shoah Foundation, Accessed 25 February 2009.

Noakes, John A. 2000. "Official Frames in Social Movement Theory: The FBI, HUAC, and the Communist Threat in Hollywood." *The Sociological Quarterly* 41(4): 657–680.

Nyseth Brehm, Hollie. 2017. "Re-examining Risk Factors of Genocide." *Journal of Genocide Research* 19(1): 61–87.

Obama, Barack. 2004. Keynote Address 2004 Democratic National Convention, July 27. Retrieved February 27, 2020 (http://obamaspeeches.com/002-Keynote-Address-at-the-2004-Democratic-National-Convention-Obama-Speech.htm).

Ofer, Dalia, and Lenore J. Weitzman, eds. 1998. *Women in the Holocaust.* New Haven and London: Yale University Press.

Olick, Jeffrey K. 2007. *The Politics of Regret: On Collective Memory and Historical Responsibility.* New York: Routledge.

Olick, Jeffrey K. 2016. *The Sins of the Fathers.* Chicago: University of Chicago Press.

Olson, Mancur. 1965. *The Logic of Collective Action.* Cambridge, MA: Harvard University Press.

Owens, Peter B., David Cunningham, and Geoff Ward. 2015. "Threat, Competition, and Mobilizing Structures: Motivational and Organizational Contingencies of the Civil Rights-Era Ku Klux Klan." *Social Problems* 62(4): 572–604.

Owens, Peter B., Yang Su, and David A. Snow. 2013. "Social Scientific Inquiry into Genocide and Mass Killing." *Annual Review of Sociology* 39: 69–84.

Park, Soon Seok. 2019. "Threat, Memory, and Framing: The Development of South Korea's Democracy Movement, 1979–1987." Unpublished Ph.D. dissertation, Purdue University.

Pelta, Samuel. 1996. "Interview 19525." *Visual History Archive*, USC Shoah Foundation. Accessed 25 February 2009.

Person, Katarzyna. 2015. "Sexual Violence during the Holocaust: The Case of Forced Prostitution in the Warsaw Ghetto." *Shofar: An Interdisciplinary Journal of Jewish Studies* 33(2): 103–116.

Polonsky, Antony. 1988. "Introduction." Pp. 1–54 in *A Cup of Tears: A Diary of the Warsaw Ghetto,* by Abraham Lewin. Oxford, UK: Basil Blackwell.

Popper, Nathaniel. 2010. "A Conscious Pariah." *The Nation*, March 31. Retrieved June 17, 2016 (http://www.thenation.com/article/conscious-pariah/).

Porat, Dina. 2010. *The Fall of a Sparrow: The Life and Times of Abba Kovner,* edited and translated by E. Yuval. Palo Alto, CA: Stanford University Press.

Prieto, Greg. 2018. *Immigrants under Threat: Risk and Resistance in Deportation Nation.* New York: New York University Press.

Rediker, Marcus. 2013. *The Amistad Rebellion.* New York: Penguin Books.

Reese, Ellen, Vincent Giedraitis, and Eric Vega. 2005. "Mobilization and Threat: Campaigns against Welfare Privatization in Four Cities." *Sociological Focus* 38(4): 287–309.

Reger, Jo. 2018. "Academic Opportunity Structures and the Creation of Campus Activism." *Social Movement Studies* 17(5): 558–573.

Reger, Jo, Daniel J. Myers, and Rachel L. Einwohner, eds. 2008. *Identity Work in Social Movements.* Minneapolis: University of Minnesota Press.

Reynolds-Stenson, Heidi. 2022. *Cultures of Resistance: Collective Action and Rationality in the Anti-Terror Age.* New Brunswick, NJ: Rutgers University Press.

Richie, Alexandra. 2013. *Warsaw 1944.* Hammersmith, London: William Collins.

Robbins, David. 1995. "Interview 3436." *Visual History Archive*, USC Shoah Foundation. Accessed 25 February 2009.

Robbins, Gabriel. 1995. "Interview 10326." *Visual History Archive*, USC Shoah Foundation. Accessed 25 February 2009.

Rojowska, Elżbieta, and Martin Dean. 2012. "Wilno." Pp. 1148–1151 in *The United States Holocaust Memorial Museum Encyclopedia of Camps and Ghettos 1933–1945*, Vol. II, edited by G. P. Megargee (General Editor) and M. Dean (Volume Editor). Bloomington, IN: Indiana University Press.

Roscigno, Vincent J., and William F. Danaher. 2001. "Media and Mobilization: The Case of Radio and Southern Textile Worker Insurgency, 1929 to 1934." *American Sociological Review* 66(1): 21–48.

Rosen, Alan. 2010. *The Wonder of Their Voices: The 1946 Holocaust Interviews of David Boder.* Oxford: Oxford University Press.

Rosenbaum, Alan S., ed. 2001. *Is The Holocaust Unique?* 2nd ed. Boulder, CO: Westview Press.

Rosenberg, Halina. 1995. "Interview 999." *Visual History Archive*, USC Shoah Foundation. Accessed 25 February 2009.

Rosenberg, Sol. 1996. "Interview 10098." *Visual History Archive*, USC Shoah Foundation. Accessed 25 February 2009.

Rosenfarb, Henry. 1995. "Interview 5541." *Visual History Archive*, USC Shoah Foundation. Accessed 25 February 2009.

Rubinstein, Elsa. 1996. "Interview 10766." *Visual History Archive*, USC Shoah Foundation. Accessed 25 February 2009.

Rudashevski, Yitskhok. 1973. *The Diary of the Vilna Ghetto.* Beit Lochamei Hagetaot: Ghetto Fighters' House and Hakibbutz Hameuchad Publishing House.

Rupp, Leila J., and Verta Taylor. 1987. *Survival in the Doldrums: The American Women's Rights Movement, 1945 to the 1960s.* New York: Oxford University Press.

Safferman, Eva. 1996. "Interview 18932." *Visual History Archive*, USC Shoah Foundation. Accessed 25 February 2009.

Schibuk, Zula. 1997. "Interview 37065." *Visual History Archive*, USC Shoah Foundation. Accessed 25 February 2009.

Schley, David. 1994. "Interview 681." *Visual History Archive*, USC Shoah Foundation. Accessed 25 February 2009.

Schmulewicz, Zalman. 1997. "Interview 36399." *Visual History Archive*, USC Shoah Foundation. Accessed 25 February 2009.

Schock, Kurt. 2004. *Unarmed Insurrections: People Power Movements in Nondemocracies.* Minneapolis: University of Minnesota Press.

Schoenberner, Gerhard. 2004. *The Yellow Star: The Persecution of the Jews in Europe, 1933–1945.* New York: Fordham University Press.

Schwartz, Michael. 1976. *Radical Protest and Social Structure: The Southern Farmer's Alliance and Cotton Tenancy, 1880–1890*. Chicago: University of Chicago Press.

Scott, James C. 1985. *Weapons of the Weak: Everyday Forms of Peasant Resistance*. New Haven, CT: Yale University Press.

Scott, James C. 1990. *Domination and the Arts of Resistance*. New Haven: Yale University Press.

Sewell, William Jr. 1996. "Three Temporalities: Toward an Eventful Sociology." Pp. 245–280 in *The Historic Turn in the Human Sciences*, edited by T. J. McDonald. Ann Arbor: University of Michigan Press.

Shainfarber, George. 1998. "Interview 42600." *Visual History Archive*, USC Shoah Foundation. Accessed 25 February 2009.

Shapiro, Paul A., Alvin H. Rosenfeld, and Sara J. Bloomfield. 2012. "Preface." P. xxv in *The United States Holocaust Memorial Museum Encyclopedia of Camps and Ghettos 1933–1945*, Vol. II, edited by G. P. Megargee and M. Dean. Bloomington: Indiana University Press.

Shenker, Noah. 2015. *Reframing Holocaust Testimony*. Bloomington: Indiana University Press.

Sheppet, Maurice. 1998. "Interview 44767." *Visual History Archive*, USC Shoah Foundation. Accessed 25 February 2009.

Sheres, Ted. 1996. "Interview 8826." *Visual History Archive*, USC Shoah Foundation. Accessed 25 February 2009.

Shneidman, N. N. 2002. *The Three Tragic Heroes of the Vilnius Ghetto*. Oakville, ON: Mosaic Press.

Shriver, Thomas E., Alison E. Adams, and Stefano B. Longo. 2015. "Environmental Threats and Political Opportunities: Citizen Activism in the North Bohemian Coal Basin." *Social Forces* 94(2): 699–722.

Simi, Pete, and Robert Futrell. 2010. *American Swastika: Inside the White Power Movement's Hidden Spaces of Hate*. Lanham, MD: Rowman & Littlefield.

Simmons, Erica S. 2016. *Meaningful Resistance: Market Reforms and the Roots of Social Protest in Latin America*. New York: Cambridge University Press.

Skocpol, Theda. 1979. *States and Social Revolutions*. Cambridge: Cambridge University Press.

Skocpol, Theda, ed. 1984. *Vision and Method in Historical Sociology*. Cambridge: Cambridge University Press.

Skocpol, Theda, and Margaret Somers. 1980. "The Uses of Comparative History in Macrosocial Inquiry." *Comparative Studies in Society and History* 22(2): 174–197.

Skuy, Sima. 1995. "Interview 5727." *Visual History Archive*, USC Shoah Foundation. Accessed 25 February 2009.

Slepyan, Kenneth. 2000. "The Soviet Partisan Movement and the Holocaust." *Holocaust & Genocide Studies* 14(1): 1–27.

Slepyan, Kenneth. 2006. *Stalin's Guerrillas: Soviet Partisans in World War II*. Lawrence, KS: University Press of Kansas.

Sloan, Jacob, ed. and trans. 1958. *Notes From the Warsaw Ghetto: The Journal of Emmanuel Ringleblum*. New York: McGraw-Hill Book Company, Inc.

Smolar, Abraham. 1997. "Interview 25818." *Visual History Archive*, USC Shoah Foundation. Accessed 25 February 2009.

Snow, David A., and Robert Benford. 1988. "Ideology, Frame Resonance, and Participant Mobilization." Pp. 197–218 in *From Structure to Action: Comparing Social Movement*

Research Across Cultures, edited by B. Klandermans, H. Kriesi, and S. Tarrow. Greenwich, CT: JAI Press.

Snow, David A., E. Burke Rochford Jr., Steven K. Worden, and Robert D. Benford. 1986. "Frame Alignment Processes, Micromobilization, and Movement Participation." *American Sociological Review* 51(4): 464–481.

Snyder, David. 1976. "Theoretical and Methodological Problems in the Analysis of Governmental Coercion and Collective Violence." *Journal of Political and Military Sociology* 4(2): 277–293.

Soyer, Michaela. 2014. "We Knew Our Time Had Come": The Dynamics of Threat and Microsocial Ties in Three Polish Ghettos Under Nazi Oppression." *Mobilization* 19(1): 47–66.

Spiegel, Jack. 1996. "Interview 15071." *Visual History Archive*, USC Shoah Foundation. Accessed 25 February 2009.

Staggenborg, Suzanne. 1986. "Coalition Work in the Pro-Choice Movement: Organizational and Environmental Opportunities and Obstacles." *Social Problems* 33(5): 374–390.

Staggenborg, Suzanne. 1991. *The Pro-Choice Movement: Organization and Activism in the Abortion Conflict*. New York: Oxford University Press.

Staggenborg, Suzanne. 1993. "Critical Events and the Mobilization of the Pro-Choice Movement." *Research in Political Sociology* 6: 319–345.

Stein, Arlene. 2014. *Reluctant Witnesses: Survivors, Their Children, and the Rise of Holocaust Consciousness*. New York: Oxford University Press.

Steiner, Joseph. 1995. "Interview 682." *Visual History Archive*, USC Shoah Foundation. Accessed 25 February 2009.

Stephens, Xenia. 1997. "Interview 33842." *Visual History Archive*, USC Shoah Foundation. Accessed 25 February 2009.

Stryker, Robin. 1996. "Beyond History versus Theory: Strategic Narrative and Sociological Explanation." *Sociological Methods & Research* 24(3): 304–352.

Suhl, Yuri, ed. 1968. *They Fought Back*. New York: Paperback Library, Inc.

Sutton, Barbara. 2018. *Surviving State Terror: Women's Testimonies of Repression and Resistance in Argentina*. New York: NYU Press.

Syrkin, Marie. 1948. *Blessed is the Match: The Story of Jewish Resistance*. New York: Alfred A. Knopf.

Szereszewska, Helena. 1997. *Memoirs from Occupied Warsaw, 1940–1945*. London: Vallentine Mitchell.

Szpigiel, Harry. 1996. "Interview 15648." *Visual History Archive*, USC Shoah Foundation. Accessed 25 February 2009.

Szwajger, Adina Blady. 1990. *I Remember Nothing More: The Warsaw Children's Hospital and the Jewish Resistance*. New York: Pantheon Books.

Tarrow, Sidney G. 1983. "Struggling to Reform: Social Protest and Policy Response During Cycles of Protest." Western Societies Paper No. 15, Center for International Studies. Ithaca, NY.

Tarrow, Sidney. 1989. *Democracy and Disorder: Protest and Politics in Italy, 1965–1975*. Oxford: Clarendon.

Tarrow, Sidney. 1998. *Power in Movement*. 2nd ed. Cambridge: Cambridge University Press.

Taub, Paula. 1996. "Interview 20049." *Visual History Archive*, USC Shoah Foundation. Accessed 25 February 2009.

Taylor, Verta A. 1989. "Social Movement Continuity: The Women's Movement in Abeyance." *American Sociological Review* 54(5): 761–775.

Tec, Nechama. 1993. *Defiance: The Bielski Partisans.* New York: Oxford University Press.

Tec, Nechama. 2003. *Resilience and Courage: Men, Women, and the Holocaust.* New Haven, CT: Yale University Press.

Tec, Nechama. 2013. *Resistance: Jews and Christians who Defied the Nazi Terror.* Oxford: Oxford University Press.

Tec, Nechama. 2014. "Jewish Resistance: Facts, Omissions, and Distortions." Pp. 40–70 in *Jewish Resistance Against the Nazis*, edited by P. Henry. Washington, DC: The Catholic University of America Press.

Tester, Griff M. 2004. "Resources, Identity, and the Role of Threat: The Case of AIDS Mobilization, 1981–1986." *Research in Political Sociology* 13: 47–75.

Tilly, Charles. 1978. *From Mobilization to Revolution.* New York: McGraw-Hill.

Tilly, Charles. 1989. *Big Structures, Large Processes, Huge Comparisons.* New York: Russell Sage Foundation.

Tilly, Charles. 2000. "Spaces of Contention." *Mobilization* 5(2): 135–159.

Trakinski, Simon. 1995. "Interview 612." *Visual History Archive,* USC Shoah Foundation. Accessed 25 February 2009.

Trakinski, William. 1995. "Interview 2050." *Visual History Archive,* USC Shoah Foundation. Accessed 25 February 2009.

Trunk, Isaiah. 1981. "Note: Why Was There No Armed Resistance against the Nazis in the Łódź Ghetto?" *Jewish Social Studies* 43(3/4): 329–334.

Trunk, Isaiah. 2006. *Łódź Ghetto.* Bloomington and Indianapolis: Indiana University Press.

Turek, Kristine. 1996. "Interview 13721." *Visual History Archive,* USC Shoah Foundation. Accessed 25 February 2009.

Turner, Ralph H., and Lewis M. Killian. 1957. *Collective Behavior.* Englewood Cliffs, NJ: Prentice-Hall.

Tushnet, Leonard. 1972. *The Pavement of Hell.* New York: St. Martin's Press.

Tversky, Amos, and Daniel Kahneman. 1981. "The Framing of Decisions and the Psychology of Choice." *Science* 211(30 January): 453–458.

Unger, Michal. 2002. "The Łódź Ghetto." Pp. 19–29 in *In Those Terrible Days: Writings from the Łódź Ghetto* by Josef Zelkowicz. Jerusalem: Yad Vashem.

Useem, Bert. 1985. "Disorganization and the New Mexico Prison Riot of 1980." *American Sociological Review* 50(5): 677–688.

Van Dyke, Nella. 2003. "Crossing Movement Boundaries: Factors that Facilitate Coalition Protest by American College Students, 1930–1990." *Social Problems* 50(2): 226–250.

Van Dyke, Nella, and Sarah A. Soule. 2002. "Structural Social Change and the Mobilizing Effect of Threat: Explaining Levels of Patriot and Militia Organizing in the United States." *Social Problems* 49(4): 497–520.

Viterna, Jocelyn. 2013. *Women in War: The Micro-Processes of Mobilization in El Salvador.* Oxford: Oxford University Press.

Volk, Michael. 1998. "Interview 47814." *Visual History Archive,* USC Shoah Foundation. Accessed 25 February 2009.

Vromen, Suzanne. 2012. *Hidden Children of the Holocaust: Belgian Nuns and their Daring Rescue of Young Jews from the Nazis.* New York: Oxford University Press. Wagner, Sima. 1995. "Interview 9508." *Visual History Archive,* USC Shoah Foundation. Accessed 25 February 2009.

Waltman, Toby. 1996. "Interview 16215." *Visual History Archive*, USC Shoah Foundation. Accessed 25 February 2009.

Wdowinski, David. 1985. *And We Are Not Saved*. New York: Philosophical Library.

Weinstein, Leon. 1995. "Interview 2962." *Visual History Archive*, USC Shoah Foundation. Accessed 25 February 2009.

Weston, Kath. 1991. *Families We Choose*. New York: Columbia University Press.

White, Robert W., and Michael R. Fraser. 2000. "Personal and Collective Identities and Long-Term Social Movement Activism: Republican Sinn Féin." Pp. 324–46 in *Self, Identity, and Social Movements*, edited by S. Stryker, T. J. Owens, and R. W. White. Minneapolis: University of Minnesota Press.

Whittier, Nancy. 2009. *The Politics of Child Sexual Abuse: Emotion, Social Movements, and the State*. Oxford: Oxford University Press.

Wiesel, Elie. 1995. "Why So Little Resistance?" Pp. 262–263 in *Can It Happen Again? Chronicles of the Holocaust*, edited by R. K. Chartock and J. Spencer. New York: Black Dog & Leventhal.

Wlodarczyk, Anna, Nekane Basabe, Darío Páez, and Larraitz Zumeta. 2017. "Hope and Anger as Mediators between Collective Action Frames and Participation in Collective Mobilization: The Case of 15-M." *Journal of Social and Political Psychology* 5(1): 200–223.

Wolf, Diane L. 2007. *Beyond Anne Frank: Hidden Children and Postwar Families in Holland*. Berkeley: University of California Press.

Wood, Elisabeth Jean. 2001. "The Emotional Benefits of Insurgency in El Salvador." Pp. 267–281 in *Passionate Politics*, edited by J. Goodwin, J. M. Jasper, and F. Polletta. Chicago: The University of Chicago Press.

Yancey-Bragg, N'dea. 2021. "'Stop Killing Us': Attacks on Asian Americans Highlight Rise in Hate Incidents Amid COVID-19." *USA Today*, February 11. Retrieved February 12, 2021 (https://www.usatoday.com/story/news/nation/2021/02/12/asian-hate-incidents-covid-19-lunar-new-year/4447037001/).

Young, James E. 1989. "The Biography of a Memorial Icon: Nathan Rapoport's Warsaw Ghetto Monument." *Representations* 26: 69–106.

Zabielak, Rena. 1996. "Interview 12029." *Visual History Archive*, USC Shoah Foundation. Accessed 25 February 2009.

Zeleznikow, Abram. 1997. "Interview 27584." *Visual History Archive*, USC Shoah Foundation. Accessed 25 February 2009.

Zelkowicz, Josef. 2002. *In Those Terrible Days: Writings from the Łódź Ghetto*. Jerusalem: Yad Vashem.

Zeller, Helen. 1996. "Interview 22423." *Visual History Archive*, USC Shoah Foundation. Accessed 25 February 2009.

Zhao, Dingxin. 2009. "Organization and Place in the Anti-US Chinese Student Protests after the 1999 Belgrade Embassy Bombing." *Mobilization* 14(1): 107–129.

Zyskind, Josef. 1998. "Interview 48887." *Visual History Archive*, USC Shoah Foundation. Accessed 25 February 2009.

Zuckerman, Yitzhak ("Antek"). 1993. *A Surplus of Memory: Chronicle of the Warsaw Ghetto Uprising*. Translated by B. Harshav. Berkeley: University of California Press.

Zyskind, Josef. 1998. "Interview 48887." *Visual History Archive*, USC Shoah Foundation. Accessed 25 February 2009.

Index

Printed in the USA/Agawam, MA
April 27, 2022

792273.015